Vanilla Pop

Sweet Sounds from
Frankie Avalon to ABBA

JOSEPH LANZA

CHICAGO
REVIEW
PRESS

An A Cappella Book

Library of Congress Cataloging-in-Publication Data
Lanza, Joseph
    Vanilla pop : sweet sounds from Frankie Avalon to ABBA / Joseph Lanza.—1st ed.
        p. cm.
    Includes bibliographical references (p. 205), discography (p. 211), and index.
    ISBN 1-55652-543-5
    1. Popular music—History and criticism. I. Title.
    ML3470.L36 2004
    782.42164—dc22
                                                                    2004013367

Cover and interior design: Rattray Design
Cover photo: FoodPix

Published by Chicago Review Press, Incorporated
814 North Franklin Street
Chicago, Illinois 60610
ISBN 1-55652-543-5
Printed in the United States of America
5 4 3 2 1

Ingredients

Acknowledgments

My warmest thanks to the following recording artists, engineers, and producers for their interviews for this book and other projects:

Frankie Avalon, Charles Blackwell, Russell Faith, Ethel Gabriel, Snuff Garrett, Bobb Goldsteinn, John Gummoe, Frank Hunter, Brian Hyland, Claudine Longet, Johnny Mann, Bob Marcucci, Mitch Miller, Bob Morgan, Stu Phillips, Peter Udell—and a singular thank-you to Bobby Vee for his good thoughts and moral support.

Thanks to my editor, Yuval Taylor, for believing in the idea. Also special thanks to: John Beecher, Brian Chidester, Irwin Chusid, Dawn Eden, Jack Fetterman, Josh Glenn/*Hermenaut*, Robert Heide, Robert Hull, Matthias Künnecke, Jim Meehan, Domenic Priore, Roy Quady, John Repsch, *Roctober*, John Strausbaugh/*NY Press*, Universal Music Germany, and Lothar Winkler.

Introduction

I Hear the Great White Milk Shake

Meet Wayne Willoughby, age twenty-four, a restless individual who, like many other disaffected young adults, has chosen to pacify his problems by withdrawing from the world and into a set of headphones. He joins many of his ilk as he ambles in solitude along city streets, suburban thoroughfares, and mall concourses—his face registering a distant, stoic expression as private soundscapes flood his daydreams.

In the past, Mr. Willoughby was content to settle for a socially sanctioned regimen of metal, grunge, indie rock, trip-hop, electronica, and even smatterings of Lilith Fair folk. But on an otherwise godless, ordinary day, something snapped. An auditory epiphany changed his life as he stood in line to purchase a tube of toothpaste at his local Duane Reade drugstore. Try as he might to concentrate on the bass-heavy dance track thumping from his headset, he could not ignore the sweet signals that beamed from the on-premise music system's ceiling speakers.

The song was the Cascades' 1963 recording of "Rhythm of the Rain." Thanks to the store's proprietor, who was benevolent enough to provide customers with a program of Top 40 "oldies," Wayne discovered an angelic message whose blend of honey-coated crooning, creamy choral harmonies, rippling guitar, and tongue-tingling chimes affected him as no sound ever had before. Knowing that Duane Reade played its programmed music on a rotation system, he made a point of coming back to the store at approximately the same time of day, and he was often prescient in his ability to predict when "Rhythm of the Rain" would once again glisten over the product aisles.

One day, an older friend who was more attuned to pop music archaeology came along with him on the excursion. After confirming the song's identity, the friend graciously lent him a copy of it from his own record collection. Wayne played it over and over again. Compared to his usual musical diet, this was

Romantic and sweet—
Glistening and squeaky-clean—
Soft and effervescent—
Smooth and refreshing!

"Rhythm of the Rain" had all the sparkly qualities that had fallen out of fashion but that Wayne Willoughby now craved. The song's effect on him was initially indescribable, but the key ingredient of his sensation became clear once he looked up the Cascades in the *All-Music Guide* and encountered this savory sentence:

The Cascades were pure vanilla ice cream in their harmony approach; so much so that when they were recording their hit, "Rhythm of the Rain," at the Gold Star Studios, producer Phil Spector asked them if they were cutting a demo for Ricky Nelson!

This "vanilla ice cream" insight, provided by the late songwriter/guitarist and former Brownsville Station member Cub Koda, christened Wayne's quest along that rocky road to audio nirvana.

Ordinarily, Wayne's discovery would be just another example of someone expanding his or her musical horizons. But in this case, he has embarked upon a wondrous, if lonely, journey.

He has no idea that his surname conjures the dreamscape of a *Twilight Zone* episode called "A Stop at Willoughby." Here, a man addled by his domestic and office-drone lot in life takes his routine train commute home one day to discover the town of Willoughby—a parallel world from yesteryear where wistful tunes ring out from street corners and ice cream parlors.

This man who stopped at the town of Willoughby was appreciably older than Wayne. A somewhat wizened dreamer, he was likely in his forties. But "Rhythm of the Rain" struck Wayne with such a visceral impact that he experienced contrary emotions. He was recharged with a sense of wonder that had been missing from him since boyhood, but he also experienced a melancholia expected of someone twice his age. Normality dictates that a young man of Wayne's years and sensibility, with the same frustrated ambitions and studied cynicism, would gravitate more toward heavier, nastier music before withering into a lump. But for Wayne, the Cascades' chiming tune, with its graceful lyrics and magnificently fey vocals, filled a vacuum.

Wayne Willoughby, like the *Twilight Zone* character, had at last found his neural getaway, albeit decades after "Rhythm of the Rain" made its Top 40 radio debut. For him, this love plaint ignited not some bout with nostalgia, but a joyful call to arms. His mission inspires the following impressionistic history of vanilla pop—a musical form that pervaded popular culture for decades, was abandoned for quite a while, and is only now enjoying its long-deserved rediscovery and formal classification.

Apprehending vanilla pop's sound involves renewing one's appreciation for the taste for vanilla itself. Vanilla, far from being the absence of flavor, has all along been the preeminent flavor. "Vanilla proved to be the perfect flavoring," Lee Edwards Benning wrote in her recipe book *Make Mine Vanilla*. "It was suave, smoothing out the harshness of other flavors, such as chocolate and eggs. It was neutralizing, taking the acidity out of lemons and limes. It was supportive, enhancing the richness of fellow ingredients, such as butter and sugar. It was versatile, providing all the flavor by itself or maximizing the flavors of other ingredients."

The only edible member of the orchid family, the vanilla bean was initially cultivated in Mexico, where the Aztecs used it to enhance their chocolate drinks. By the 1500s, once transported to Europe, Spain adopted it as a perfume and only later discovered its spellbinding effect on the tongue. The sensation spread through Europe. "Ah, you flavor everything," the eighteenth-century English essayist Sydney Smith complimented his daughter Lady Holland. "You are the vanilla of society." Zipping into the time machine, one can contrast Smith's encomium with that of the snooty character Frasier Crane (in the television show *Frasier*), who describes one of his fine wines as having the "brooding, almost dangerous presence of vanilla."

In the late 1700s, returning to the States after serving as an ambassador to France, Thomas Jefferson brought with him the beans; his countrymen and -women eventually turned into the world's most insatiable vanilla consumers. According to the Jefferson Papers at the Library of Congress, Jefferson handwrote the first known American ice cream recipe, with directions that called for "first putting in a stick of Vanilla" into an olio of cream, sugar, and egg yolks. From then on, vanilla has been America's First Flavor and has sated our palates with sweetness and subtlety. Citing a 2001 article by the International Dairy Foods Association entitled "Eating It Up: Ice Cream Sales and Usage Trends," Good Humor–Breyers states that vanilla continues to be America's number-one ice cream choice. Indeed, vanilla has become a school-book paragon of the virtues of American migration leading to assimilation: a once-foreign substance that entered and augmented the flavor, without destroying the essence, of a larger creamy mixture.

In recent years some ad campaigns, particularly those from the ice cream trade, have endeavored to rescue vanilla from its "plainness" stigma by lauding its quietly exotic properties. From their headquarters in Atlanta, those pioneering manufacturers of brown carbonated drinks have pitched their Vanilla Coke with the slogan "smooth and intriguing." "Vanilla is the essence of elegance and sophistication," say the marketers at Häagen-Dazs. "This perfect marriage of pure, sweet cream and imported vanilla creates a sweet scent of exotic spice and a distinctive taste that lingers on your tongue. How can something so simple be so profound?" Even the spirits industry has joined the flavor rave with a strain of Absolut vodka called Vanilia.

Beneath its seeming simplicity, vanilla is multifaceted. "Vanilla," according to the publication *Dairy Field,* "is the only flavor with the FDA's Federal Standard of Identity Regulations." It has "more than 250 identified components that contribute to its flavor" and "is also one of the most highly regulated ingredients in the food industry." International Flavors and Fragrances, a leading manufacturer of scent and taste sensations, considers all of these intricacies when claiming that vanilla "evokes memories of home and hearth, warmth and cuddling."

Yet, despite its rising gustatory stature, appreciation of vanilla as a form of pop music has lagged behind. This is a creepy inversion of values: the most loved choice on the ice cream menu has become, in many respects, a forbidden flavor—proscribed more by professional peer pressure than by any iron-clad taboos. For many, vanilla pop lacks "street cred," or authenticity. Yet the notion of "authentic" music is itself a manufactured illusion, overlaid by decades in which throaty Bob Dylanites and the denizens of bebop have altered the art of singing by doctoring vocals with a gravelly and bitter aftertaste.

Though the words *vanilla pop* can mean different sounds to different people, the mere mention of the genre today elicits arrogant grunts from those whose biases are steeped in jazz, R&B, rock, soul, bluegrass, country, and other ethnically and regionally "authentic" music. A song like "Rhythm of the Rain," when retained in its pure melodic state, is therefore liable to be considered "too bland" instead of delectable, "too safe" instead of mild-mannered, "too lightweight" instead of soft and soothing, or "too syrupy" instead of sweet-tempered. In short, vanilla pop lacks a sufficient amount of grit and "groove"—a "deficiency" that shall from here on, in this book, be deemed an asset.

The condemnation of being "too white" has also become an inescapable albatross. The music is certainly "white" in its adherence to what was once a Caucasian consensus on what constituted sweet and heavenly sounds. These people were, after all, the mainstream of American culture when recorded popular music reached its pinnacle in the postwar years and throughout the 1960s. But vanilla pop is not merely "white music"—an appellation that could just as easily apply to Appalachian bluegrass, Italian opera, French chansons, Celtic sea chanteys, Ukrainian peasant dances, German *oom-pa-pah*, Scandinavian folk songs, and heavy metal rock, as well as sundry forms of classical, baroque, and romantic concert music. Vanilla pop is more exact, connoting what a 1950s detergent ad once touted as "whiter than white," a phrase that (contrary to what some fashionable academes may deem as "racist") was meant for bedsheets, not Klan sheets.

Anti–vanilla pop sentiments also seem to be predicated on class warfare: the upper class romanticizing the ethos of the working class in order to gang up on the mores of the middle class. The Ray Conniff Singers and the Carpenters are neither *refined* enough to merit highbrow regard nor *gritty* enough for blue-collar heroism. Most middle-class kids growing up in the 1960s, however, likely had no problem supplementing their psychedelic record collections with a song or two by the Lettermen.

Vanilla has continued to be the most popular selection—the ingredient that cleanses the palate and, when applied acoustically, freshens the ear. Like the ice cream flavor, vanilla music has layers of complexities and nuances that trigger multisensory pleasures. Just as the vanilla bean predated modern medicine as a tool for healing and soothing, so does vanilla music call forth celestial choirs that, in days past, chimed in places of both worship and public commerce to spread spiritual, emotional, and physical well-being. As our hero,

Wayne Willoughby, discovered, modern-day music fans can similarly musically self-medicate by listening for:

- Extreme studio processing, with an emphasis on high-register vocals and sparkly acoustics, resulting in the secular equivalent of Christmas carols;
- A singing style that falls straight on the melody and is delivered in a clear, unadorned vocal line. Its lucid pronunciation rarely, if ever, sways into the raw inflections associated with blues, country, jazz, or harder rock;
- Songs structured on flowing melodies and smooth chord progressions, and simple vocal harmonies that do not overlap into the slithery syncopation usually associated with "jazz phrasing";
- Ethereal sound effects such as massed strings, celestas, chimes, guitars, and pianos, that provide either a creamy or a fizzy vanilla kick. The effect is all the more enhanced when processed through echo chambers or galvanized by double-tracking; and
- On the mood rating scale, an overall sound that falls in the categories of *sweet and earnest, happy or amiable, carefree or innocent,* and *melancholic or wistful.*

To achieve the qualities listed above, recording studios employ a factory of ready-made effects and influences from which to sculpt their audio glazes. Modernized and electronically tailored to provide solace during the other 364 days, the most lucent vanilla pop harmonies can sometimes suggest a holiday mood, albeit one that is embellished with discreet electric guitars, processed violins, and lyrics that rhapsodize about romantic love instead of salvation in an afterlife.

For most of the twentieth century, pop music fans enjoyed sweet and pretty songs without the slightest knowledge that they were indulging in a "guilty pleasure." The aesthetic assumptions that today make a tune "vanilla" were, yesterday, simply the hallmarks of a beautiful song. If a Doris Day record struck listeners as dulcet and delightful, they did not have a "critically correct" nag poking at the windmills of their minds to scold them about any deficiency in rawness or rhythm.

Vanilla vocals do offer a contrast to jazz vocals. Jazz singers tend to boast and strut around a tune, pecking at it like frenetic roosters one moment and slithering around it like mercenary snake charmers the next. Most current music criticism confuses vocal pyrotechnics with style and regards such singing as giving voice to a song's true "soul," but, from a vanilla viewpoint, jazz singing is a form of evasion—a set of mannerisms based on fear of the melody.

Recording artists, however, cannot always be counted on for vanilla consistency. Even Doris Day indulged in swing, and harmony groups such as the Association tried, albeit in vain, to project a more rocking edge. The art of vanilla pop is more a matter of special moments when singers, songwriters, musicians, and studio mavens coalesce into a heightened blend. Some artists are more attuned to the taste than others. The Doodletown Pipers and the Cowsills, Frankie Avalon and Pat Boone, the Four Preps and the Lettermen, Chad & Jeremy and Harpers Bizarre, the Association and the Johnny Mann Singers, the Sandpipers and the Carpenters, and, of course, Doris Day and ABBA have drifted more consistently into the Vanilla Zone than others.

A brief voyage along the Vanilla Straits can start with Doris Day's "*Que Sera, Sera* (Whatever Will Be, Will Be)" (1956) and Pat Boone's "Love Letters in the Sand" (1957). Captivating sights along the teen idol tundra include Frankie Avalon pining for his "Venus" (1959), Brian Hyland sighing over a lovelorn letter in "Sealed with a Kiss" (1962), Shelley Fabares cooing over her "Johnny Angel" (1962), and Bobby Vee plying his "Charms" (1963) over a pillow-soft orchestra. The darker clouds of the British Invasion lift when Chad & Jeremy harmonize ever so gallantly to "A Summer Song" (1964). Next on the tour are such clean-cut but rock-influenced chorales as the Cowsills and their mind-bending balladry on "The Rain, the Park, and Other Things" (1967). And, as the 1960s exhibits come to an end, the Sandpipers gently close the decade with "Come Saturday Morning" (1969).

The theme park travelogue then eases into the early 1970s and its Melancholy Mile. Tourist tears flow to the Carpenters' "For All We Know" (1971) and Bread's otherworldly "If" (1971). The vanilla sensorium starts to recede at this point, as pop purveyors such as the Jacksons and the Osmonds, along with Southern permutations on Charlie Daniels, inject gratuitous *oomphs* derived from both country and R&B. The atmosphere by the mid-1970s bubbles a bit more with the mannerly power pop of ABBA's "Knowing Me, Knowing You" and "Fernando" (1976), but by the time the ride enters the 1980s and the treble knobs get sabotaged, a threatening pall of synthesized thumps creeps into the soundscape. Fewer and farther between, the vanilla artists flash by like translucent sprites, leaving barely an afterimage. Standard-bearers such as singer-songwriter Tommy Page manage to turn down the rhythm machine at intervals to croon ballads including "A Shoulder to Cry On" (1991).

There are some artists, such as Connie Francis and Ricky Nelson, who float at the flavor's edge yet have had a marked influence on artists more firmly in the vanilla camp. They shall wander, however, in and out of the following discussion, which is slanted toward a particular aesthetic; the artists and songs have been carefully selected with all biases intact. In short, this is much like other books that purport to be "definitive" histories. Here is a good example: "First the deal-makers in fast food took the malt powder out and made the milk shake," Donald Clarke laments in *The Rise and Fall of Popular Music*, "then in the music business they took the soul out and made pop rock." Such a statement reflects ingrained musical prejudices. Just because they may fall more in line with the current cognoscenti, they are no less biased than this pro-milkshake appreciation for a pop music history in danger of being forgotten in another decade or two. In this regard, readers may feel at times like alien abductees trying to retrieve stolen memories. Like any excursion that attempts to shed some light on an increasingly obscured past, this trip backward is really a trip forward. So, with Wayne Willoughby's blessing, this book shall attempt to refocus the world's pop sensibility to the sounds, as well as to the visionary men and women, traversing the vanilla extreme.

1

White-Bread Rhapsodies

It's Shrill Rock 'n' Roll to Me

At the Fourteenth Annual Rock and Roll Hall of Fame Induction Dinner in 1999, Billy Joel gladly accepted his award but could not resist adding some sour notes. "I'm from Levittown, and this is not supposed to happen to people like me," he asserted at the podium. "I know I've been referred to as derivative. I'm derivative as hell. There wouldn't be any white people in here if they didn't let us derivative people in."

Joel's off-color remark could be laughed away as innocuous (and socially acceptable) race-baiting, but it also reveals the shibboleth of rock 'n' roll ideology: the assumption that black R&B is real and anything other (or "whiter") is less authentic. Through the years, audiences have been cajoled into making a choice: There was Little Richard, and then there was Pat Boone; Bo Diddley, and Bobby Vee. One form of music has been perceived as the true, earthy prototype of rock 'n' roll; the other, its fake or "white-bread" imitation.

Whenever anyone mentions "white-bread" music, eyebrows are likely to rise in self-righteous indignation. This is, after all, the music that the "squares" enjoyed as they played their Pat Boone versions of Little Richard songs in a *Leave It to Beaver* world. In contrast, the rebels (who would eventually molder and grow norms of their own) enlisted the likes of Howlin' Wolf and Jerry Lee Lewis to spray Middle America's picket fence with boogie-woogie graffiti.

As simplistic and general as this premise might seem, such anti–white-bread sentiments reflect a prevailing bias that meets with little to no dissent. For the most part, affluent whites themselves, with mixed motives coming across as alternately masochistic and patronizing, propagate this view. And no one could have been more self-effacing in this regard than Billy Joel that evening when Ray Charles stood before him as the award presenter. Face-to-face with the R&B legend, the "piano man" apparently lost his center of gravity and tried to regain balance by appealing to a collective sense of white guilt.

Considering the Rock and Roll Hall of Fame's musical politics, Billy Joel made his mea culpa in the right company. This is the organization that enshrines Elvis Costello yet ignores more mainstream rock 'n' roll pioneers such as Pat Boone and Connie Francis. The Hall of Fame appears to be fostered on the notion that the only way to feel "real" is to simulate a direct descent from the whole-grain "roots" music of New Orleans jazz, Mississippi Delta blues, Appalachian bluegrass, and gospel.

Years, decades, and perhaps even centuries have nourished an ethos promoting the raw over the refined and the sassy over the sentimental. One of the best examples comes from rock 'n' roll's famed composing team Jerry Leiber and Mike Stoller. Referring to Pat Boone and Elvis Presley, Stoller, a staunch R&B advocate, confessed to author Ted Fox: "We had strong feelings about what we thought was authentic; one of the things we felt was not authentic was a white singer singing the blues."

Such dark regard for white-bread music also reveals a tendency to fetishize "blackness" as an antidote to romanticism. Often, when critics complain about a song's "whiteness," the racial reference could be a mere conceptual shell for deeper qualms about sentimentalism, especially when it involves guys getting in touch with their proverbial "feminine side." One wonders if the many white R&B advocates are really trying to reinforce a sense of devil-may-care "manliness."

Leiber and Stoller fessed up to such an antiromantic bias with their misgivings for the 1960s Motown sound: "At first we thought it was white-bread," Leiber recalled. "We thought that Motown was Madison Avenue for black people. We said, 'Man, those are white teenage stories. What does that have to do with black culture?' We'd have discussions about that with some black music people from time to time. They'd say, 'What? Are you in love with the ghettos? Are you in love with that old regionalism? Things are changing, man. That's not the black image any longer.'"

This messy maw of racial and sexual politics goes back to America's pre-eminent songwriter, Stephen Foster. Poor Stephen Foster. To this day, the embarrassing legacy of "blackface" minstrel tunes besmirches his name, though he was at heart a romantic who wanted to linger in blissful repose and write parlor arias about beautiful dreamers and melancholy dreams. Momentary dictates of commerce and fashion impelled him to placate hoodlum tastes with rowdy tunes that milked racial caricatures and enabled white exoticists to apply burnt cork and indulge their bawdiest, darkest fantasies. What a pity that, out of Foster's two hundred or so compositions, about a miserable thirty were written in the "doo-dah" style patronizingly referred to as "Ethiopian songs."

Minstrel shows originated in America way back in the late 1700s and came from the Yankee north. History would record Edwin P. Christy as the minstrel circuit's most prominent blowhard. As the leader of the legendary Christy Minstrels, he was one of Foster's biggest patrons. Organized in 1842, and originating in the chilly wilds of Buffalo, New York, the Christy Minstrels were arguably the most successful of these traveling shows. As early as 1854, however, some music critics were already castigating minstrel songs for their lack of "authenticity." An anonymous writer for the *New York Musical Review* cited Christy's performances of more tenderhearted Foster fare such as "Old Folks at Home" and "My Own Kentucky Home" as examples of a "bleaching process."

The jolly and mischievous Foster who wrote "Oh, Susannah!," "Camptown Races," and "Ring De Banjo" would wither with time as he flowered into an unapologetically introspective man. In many ways, America can trace the consistent themes in its romantic ballads through the obsessions that informed Foster's personality. As historian H. Wiley Hitchcock put it, the vast majority of Foster's songs "lie wholly within the tradition of the British-American genteel airs that had arisen in the eighteenth century out of the musical needs and tastes of the growing middle class . . . the roots of this type of song are to be found not in the music of slaves, roustabouts, or frontiersmen, but in the stage songs of English ballad-opera composers or in the airs of British periodical publications like *The Monthly Melody*, or *Polite Entertainment for Ladies and Gentlemen*."

Foster's music came of age in the mid-nineteenth century, precisely the period that author Ann Douglas, in her snarling tome *The Feminization of*

American Culture, described as a time when "boys with weak health or indoor tastes, likely to be introspective and sensitive, stayed at home." As historian Nicholas Tawa points out, "The sweet singer gave a delicate and warm coloring to a carefully delineated melody, thereby arousing pleasant sensations in the listener. The chaste singer performed naturally and simply, eschewing unnecessary ornamentation and mannerisms that diverted the listener's attention from song and singer."

Even some of Foster's more sympathetic biographers fail to override their vanilla-hostile prejudices, tarring the "dulcem melodie" with adjectives like "mawkish," "saccharine," and "syrupy." On the subject of Foster's "Beautiful Dreamer," biographer John Tasker Howard lapses into a sugar attack when contemplating how "even this sentimentalizes in a bit more saccharine fashion than the best of the Foster songs. Its nine-eight, waltz-like rhythm does not have the dignity of 'Come Where My Love Lies Dreaming,' nor the melodic chastity of the earlier song. It smacks somewhat of the idiom of Irving Berlin." Mark Twain also alluded to minstrel songs as an alternative to sissy ballads: "The piano may do for love-sick girls who lace themselves to skeletons, and lunch on chalk, pickles, and slate pencils. But give me the banjo. . . . When you want *genuine* music—music that will come right home to you like a bad quarter . . . when you want all this, just smash your piano and invoke the glory-beaming banjo!"

Even the taste buds of such naysayers seem at times conflicted: refined flour ("white bread") is often interchanged with sugar ("syrupy") and chicken fat ("schmaltz") to describe songs and singers deemed too romantic, insufficiently cool, and, ultimately, insufficiently black. Charles Hamm, among the few historians to lend a sympathetic ear to "syrupy" tastes, comes to the rescue by citing an early-nineteenth-century critic's anonymous appreciation of composer Thomas Arne: "There was in Arne's compositions a natural ease and elegance, a flow of melody which stole upon the senses, and a fullness and variety in the harmony which satisfied, without surprising the auditor by any new, affected or extraneous modulation."

In other words, pretty songs, love songs, that seem so simple and are yet so craftily constructed, commanded an appeal *precisely* because they met a demand. Hamm discusses how much of this music resulted from an amalgam of tightly structured English song and the intimate and melodic Italian "bel canto." This contrast of strict form and sentimental singing (minus the heavy operatic excesses) informed such early Tin Pan Alley fare as "Sweet Adeline" but progressed to accommodate changing musical trends from ragtime to rock 'n' roll. No matter what was in vogue from one decade to the next, the "white-bread" tune served as America's musical fiber through most of the twentieth century. Its performers sang about love and romance with an élan fluctuating between starry-eyed optimism and wistful melancholy—all with tones that sifted out the chunks of attitude now so common to most jazz, country, blues, R&B, rock 'n' roll, and curious species of "world music."

The antiromantic mindset may seem like the desperate wails of overly apologetic liberals or terminal hipsters, but it betrays a reverse-Puritanism practiced (often unconsciously) by people of many political persuasions. Just as rock 'n' roll was the hobgoblin that threatened 1950s suburbia, the vanilla-soft sounds associated with Pat Boone are today's bogeyman—an interdiction as parochial, provincial, and ripe for rebellion as the one declared against rock 'n' roll in the days of Ozzie and Harriet.

Flash-forwarding to the present day, Billy Joel gets caught up in similar thematic qualms. He always seems at a queasy crossroads: aspiring to be a rowdy rock 'n' roller, yet garnering a reputation for what Ann Douglas (speaking in general terms) refers to as "feminine literary sentimentalism . . . saccharine greeting-card poetry, and the weakly soulful lyrics of certain popular singers."

Despite the post–Rolling Stones–era purists who contend that the music can be traced to discernible "roots," rock 'n' roll essentially functioned as a more aggressive and wily outgrowth of Tin Pan Alley. It was "derivative" from the start, with similar commercial interests and the same cross-pollination of cultural influences. Early rock 'n' roll was as much a cover medium for old standards as it was a forum for new songwriters. "Blueberry Hill" may now be most associated with Fats Domino, but it was originally a cowboy song performed by Gene Autry in the 1940 film *The Singing Hill,* and it was written by three Tin Pan Alley veterans named Al Lewis, Larry Stock, and Vincent Rose.

Through the years, some schools of thought have implied that a term like "vanilla pop" is redundant, since all "pop" music has undergone a "bleaching process" to please what was, at least at one time, the white middle-class majority. "The separate designation of pop and R&B bears explaining," Fredric Dannen opines in his book *Hit Men.* "Pop in the record industry is a euphemism for white; R&B means black." If this is the case, then the artists sounding the most vanilla took pop to its aesthetic perfection. If rock 'n' rollers could take a tune and submit it to a hardcore rhythmic treatment, the more vanilla artists could likewise help rock 'n' roll morph into smoother, softer, and sweeter variations.

Your Hit Parade and the "Lanolized" Sound

Your Hit Parade was a major source of this "derivative" mien. From its inception as a 1930s radio program, the show celebrated the week's most popular songs. Hitting television in the 1950s, it continued the tradition with visual counterparts to its stellar interpretations. Announcer Andre Baruch would explain how sheet music and phonograph record sales, as well as jukebox coin tallies, provided "an accurate, authentic tabulation of America's taste in popular music."

By the late 1950s, the cast of *Your Hit Parade* consisted of the high-pitched, immaculate blonde Dorothy Collins, the smooth and gentle baritone Russell Arms, the golden-throated Gisele MacKenzie (who had replaced June Valli), and Snooky Lanson, the affable clown of the pack, who sounded huskier and appeared more comfy in the novelty numbers. The group served as America's sanitarians of song during an increasingly dirty era. Schooled in the Perry Como and Doris Day modes, the *Your Hit Parade* singers had neither the facility for nor the intention of appearing "hip." Watching these broadcasts so many years since their original inception, one is amazed at the relative stiffness of their inflections, as well as their heroic refusal to conform to the seemingly "freer" strictures imposed by jazz and the blues.

A fine example is the April 16, 1955, telecast, in which Collins performed her interpretation of LaVern Baker's recording of "Tweedlee Dee." Collins made no attempt to copy the original singer's style, converting it instead into a pseudo–Swiss Alps revue. Her hair in golden braids, she peers from the window of a huge cuckoo clock as human figurines clad in lederhosen dance around her. Here, Collins uses her charm-school vocals to approximate not Baker but Georgia Gibbs, a Massachusetts-bred singer who became Pat Boone's female counterpart with her 1955 version of "Tweedlee Dee" and other R&B covers.

By the June 9, 1956, telecast, the traditionalist program could not get around the fact that Elvis Presley's "Heartbreak Hotel" was a sleeper. The job of performing it was dropped onto Gisele MacKenzie, who, dressed in Vampira garb, turned the song into a humorous horror show. MacKenzie removed any trappings of raunchiness in favor of comic camp—an approach that resulted in mannerisms not really all that variant from Presley's own ghoulish affectations. *Your Hit Parade*'s wholesome image harbored one flaw: its main sponsor was the American Tobacco Company. As chic and socially acceptable as smoking may have been back then, audiences were already aware of the cigarette's cloudy reputation. Many probably could not help but notice a contradiction between smokers' pollution and the clean larynxes of the program's cast. But the show's other prominent sponsor—Richard Hudnut—helped clear the air. Hudnut specialized in beauty products, particularly an "enriched crème shampoo" with a powdered egg formula fashioned to give hair a "wonderful sheen." The company that took pride in "lanolized" hair was a perfect match for the squeaky-clean singers, as well as the equally angelic background chorus of the Ray Charles Singers (no relation to the soul singer), who cast a bright and smooth finish to songs deemed otherwise too rough.

The Dean of Clean

Billy Joel, perhaps with childhood images of *Your Hit Parade* still haunting him, made a point of mentioning two stars as examples of "derivative" singing: Pat Boone and Frankie Avalon. The guy who wrote "Just the Way You Are" can talk all he wants about growing up in suburban Levittown and being inspired by soul singers on the radio, but most of his MOR repertoire owes a bigger debt to Boone and Avalon than to Chuck Berry or Gene Vincent.

Pat Boone came of age during this crucial phase of pop's lanolization process. As benevolent and wholesome as he presented himself, he was bound to offend a growing segment of America's intelligentsia. This was a time in the 1950s when Jack Kerouac wrote in his legendary beat novel *On the Road*: "At lilac evening I walked with every muscle aching among the lights of 27th and Welton in the Denver colored section, wishing I were a Negro, feeling that the best the white world had offered was not enough ecstasy for me, not enough life, joy, kicks, darkness, music, not enough night."

In 1957 Norman Mailer, with even more condescension, published an essay that celebrated what he called "a new breed of adventurers, urban adventurers, who drifted out at night looking for action with a black man's code to fit their facts. The hipster had absorbed the existentialist synapses of the Negro and for practical purposes could be considered a white Negro." Eschewing the

"The Dean of Clean" forged a middle ground between the crooners of yesteryear and postwar teen idols.

topic of race at least directly, Lawrence Ferlinghetti codified the issue to one of socioeconomic class by declaring "I am a social climber climbing downward" in his 1958 poem "Junkman's Obbligato."

Boone represented the antithesis of Ferlinghetti's "downward" spiral. He did not smoke, drink, swear, or engage in other major sins. Ice cream was, however, one mortal temptation he could barely resist. The inducement helped him get his first performance engagements when he was just a tyke. Like Doris Day, who used to serve her guests treats from a living room soda fountain as a Christian Science alternative to liquor, Boone embraced ice cream as a guilt-free sensual delight. Ice cream themes would pop in and out of his autobiographical books, interviews, and especially the vanilla imagery he evoked in his musical self-appraisals.

The November 30, 1990, issue of *Goldmine* magazine published Boone's letter to the editor, in which he judiciously used the term "vanilla" to describe his music and explain why he was never considered a Rock and Roll Hall of Fame nominee. "The 'purists,'" he wrote, "the folks who really like the down and dirty, real and raunchy, original R&B/R&R, are not likely to appreciate my records or the part they played in the whole evolution of music."

He preferred to croon ballads, but Boone had an impact on early rock 'n' roll that is much more indelible than the Rock and Roll Hall of Fame's testy tribunal would care to acknowledge. If one wanted to slip on a Casey Kasem hat and consider chart numbers, Boone made a clean sweep from the mid-1950s into the early 1960s. He appeared on the singles charts sixty times, six times at #1. As rock 'n' roll's "Golden Era" dawned, Boone proved second only to Elvis Presley in commercial prowess.

Boone's smooth and sweet singing was a seamless match to his clean-cut looks and lifestyle. Up until Boone, there were jazz singers, country singers, and, most important, ballad singers and crooners. But with the advent of rock 'n' roll, balladeers braved unprecedented challenges. Unlike country, blues, or R&B, which had their own ethnic enclaves, or jazz, which was, by its nature, given to lengthy improvisation, rock 'n' roll was a time-tested medium of two- or three-minute songs.

Others attempted, with varying success, to present rock 'n' roll with ballad-friendly personalities. In the 1956 movie *Don't Knock the Rock*, crooner Alan Dale portrayed Arnie Haines, a rock 'n' roll star who tries to change the ways of a stuffy old town that wants to ban the savage beat. Dale, a Brooklyn lad born Aldo Sigiamundi, arrived in the early 1950s as a baritone of the red-wine school of singing that Russ Columbo fostered back in the 1930s and Perry Como nurtured in the 1950s. The film even features a scene in which Dale's character rests on a beach with the movie's female protagonist, and, after lapsing into the kind of romantic ballad to which his throat was more accustomed, seems almost to mourn the changing times.

Still, Dale drank, smoked, greased his hair, and exhibited an urbane swagger. Pat Boone, however, was pious, incorruptible, and nicotine-free. He was born in Jacksonville, Florida, and claims descent from Daniel Boone. As might be expected, he also grew up singing in his church. His spiritual convictions no doubt informed his straight-ahead image, and his religiosity could go to extremes. He would not star in a Marilyn Monroe film, for instance, because he felt that kissing the leading lady would have real-life adulterous implications. He refused the title role in *The St. Bernard Story* for fear that portraying a Catholic would violate his Protestant convictions.

Boone was, after all, the man who outcleaned Perry Como by refusing to host a television show because its sponsor was the American Tobacco Company. The sparkly voiced Dorothy Collins apparently had no problem using her crystal clear pipes to hail the wonders of Lucky Strikes lung soot during the *Your Hit Parade* commercial breaks, but Boone would have none of it. The job instead went to Como. Apparently more at peace with auto exhausts, Pat went on to host ABC-TV's *The Pat Boone Chevy Showroom* in 1957.

Randy Wood of Dot Records was also corralling 1950s artists such as the Fontane Sisters (who often backed Boone's records) to perform R&B covers. Such covers, which often came out weeks, even days, after an original version was released, were churned out to capitalize on a song's potential for mainstream appeal. Most associate covers with white versions of black R&B tunes, but the practice extended to country music and even to other pop songs whose original singers were not as famous and, therefore, not as salable as the cover artist.

It was no surprise that Wood took an interest in Boone after witnessing his performances on *Arthur Godfrey's Talent Scouts* and *The Ted Mack Amateur Hour*. Before long, he had Boone doing a cover of the Charms' "Two Hearts, Two Kisses." "I'm imagining a Perry Como or Eddie Fisher sort of ballad, in three-quarter time," Boone recalled to music historian Joe Smith, "and Randy puts on this little R&B thing by the Charms. . . . I said, 'Randy, do you have that thing on the right speed?'"

"Two Hearts, Two Kisses" was cover fodder for several other artists at the time, including the Crew Cuts, Doris Day, and Frank Sinatra. But Boone's rendition stands out through the years as the most controversial one, even though it is essentially less vanilla than the others. At the risk of submitting Mr. Boone to double jeopardy, one could say that Boone's version was not vanilla enough. Its arranger, Billy Vaughn, an easy-listening instrumental star whose style varied from lushly inventive to monotonously minimal, could have sweetened it up with strings and celestial sound effects. Instead, the sparse instruments and Boone's comparatively harsh delivery made it relatively raw.

In later years, many white cover artists would make a self-effacing habit of stating how their versions of R&B tunes helped the original songs get more exposure, disregarding how much their own records were pop treasures in their own right. Current and tarnished rock 'n' roll re-history often villainizes the Crew Cuts, who recorded a sweetened version of the Chords' R&B song "Sh-Boom." Decades later, cult director John Waters likely had the Crew Cuts in mind when, in his movie *Cry-Baby*, he parodied a harmony group performing "Sh-Boom." The clean-cut balladeers were the movie's suburban scoundrels—the perfect foil for the slovenly antihero reprobates from the other side of the tracks.

From the musical viewpoint of those nurtured on vanilla, the Chords' version of "Sh-Boom," with its scat syllables, sultry saxophone, and deep-throated vocals, sounded coarse and unfinished. Lead singer John Perkins agreed with the rest of the group that the recording was, in his words, "pretty muddy sounding." Perkins and company believed they were cleaning up a sound that many R&B performers then and since would take pride in calling "down and dirty." The Crew Cuts' version of "Sh-Boom," which reached *Billboard*'s #1 spot by the summer of 1954, was subsequently dubbed by many as the first rock 'n' roll song to top the charts (and for nine consecutive weeks).

The Crew Cuts' talents extended beyond the cover realm: their first major single, "Crazy 'Bout Ya Baby," was self-penned. Their approach to rock 'n' roll was similar to that of bandleader Ray Anthony when his orchestra and chorus performed "Rock Around the Rock Pile" in the 1956 Frank Tashlin film *The Girl Can't Help It*. The rhythm was spirited and the instruments were in keeping with the swing generation's idea of "letting loose," but the vocals had more of an immaculate sparkle. When in unison, the Crew Cuts were distinctive precisely because they were singing rock 'n' roll like Yuletide carolers.

THE CREW-CUTS
HIPPODROME BUILDING, CLEVELAND, OHIO

Exclusive MERCURY RECORDING ARTISTS

Their merging of rock 'n' roll beats with big-band brass may make them seem less than vanilla, but the Crew Cuts were best known for their sweet, smooth, and twinkling harmonies.

Even something as sexually ruffling as "Do Me Good Baby" succumbed to their musical manicure. Their approach to R&B songs was to reinterpret rather than to imitate. (One can at times hear similar vanilla enrichments from the Jordanaires. Despite their white gospel origins, the quartet's background choruses sweetened the acidity of many an Elvis Presley record. Their smooth four-part finish to "Teddy Bear," for instance, could easily have been a Crew Cuts effort.)

Though slotted for more contoured rock 'n' roll, the Crew Cuts had such an innate talent for light and frothy harmonies that one senses their relief whenever Mercury, their record label, allowed them to veer from swinging rhythms toward sweeter tunes. The 1954 single "Twinkle Toes" and its B-side, a snow-white holiday soft-shoe number called "Dance, Mr. Snowman, Dance," are extreme examples. "Twinkle Toes," obviously intended as a kids' ditty and released in the fall of 1954 just in time for the pre-Christmas season, deserved a better commercial run. But, even with its somewhat risqué overtones, this fairy-light air about one of Santa's impish helpers was too much of a radical departure from what Crew Cuts fans had expected. Even then, insecure teenagers may have been too threatened by such unadulterated vanilla and, when peer pressure hijacked their souls, felt compelled to reject the song.

The Crew Cuts would eventually part ways with Mercury when the label's A&R executive Art Talmadge aggressively hinted that they should sound more like their fellow Canadians, the Diamonds—a group that made more dogged efforts to imitate actual R&B with tunes such as their cover of the Gladiolas' "Little Darlin'." Then, in 1957, they made one of their best recordings—a cover of the Sonny James country ballad "Young Love." Again, instead of copying the original version note per note, the group's baritone and arranger Rudi Maugeri put together a different arrangement, leading with a tenor on the opening verse before pouring on a cream-soda chorus. Unfortunately, Randy Wood of Dot Records, in his ongoing quest to find a singing idol to supplement Pat Boone, heard the group perform the song at the Los Angeles Cocoanut Grove. Not content to just applaud a good act when he heard it, Wood arranged for screen beauty Tab Hunter to release a rendition that upstaged both James and the Crew Cuts by topping the charts for several weeks in the early part of the year. Hunter's victory at the Crew Cuts' expense proved once again that the cover game was an equal-opportunity usurper.

According to Pat Boone, many DJs who would otherwise avoid R&B assumed that he was black. Only when he followed up with Fats Domino's "Ain't That a Shame" did listeners get to hear rock 'n' roll beats delivered with Boone's tempered fire and valedictorian diction. At the time, Boone was a student at Columbia University. In keeping with his collegiate pedigree, he initially wanted to change the song's name and lyrics to "Isn't That a Shame." Grammar aside, Boone was ill at ease when confronted with the song, feeling it contrary to his nature. To get through the ordeal, he summoned the musical influence of another inspiration: his soon-to-be father-in-law, Red Foley, the man to whom Boone himself refers as "the country Bing Crosby." When the time came to adapt his style to Domino's rock 'n' roll beat and slangy lyrics, Boone imagined singing it the way Foley would do it—warmly and smoothly.

Vanilla aficionados are nonetheless likely to get frustrated when hearing Boone's covers of "Ain't That a Shame" or Little Richard's "Tutti Frutti." Both records are, at least structurally, more bare-bones rock 'n' roll than detractors of the last few decades would have the world believe—as close to rock 'n' roll as it usually got back then. But Boone *did* make efforts to lighten the songs. Little Richard sang, "Boy, you don't know what she's doing to me," but Boone insisted on "Pretty Suzie is the girl for me." Sadly, the spoon-fed verdict regarding this Richard–Boone foil is that Boone had "diluted" the original. But to call Boone's version of this and other such songs "watered down" is to call the water glass half-empty. He did not water down so much as sweeten up, with a more genial alternative to Little Richard's earthier threat.

Boone subsequently reacted to the scorn heaped upon his cover versions with a mixture of defensiveness and veiled apology. He would later say that "if it hadn't been for my versions of those songs, along with Elvis and Nat Cole and others, Billy Joel probably wouldn't have known about them at all! I really resented his denigration when he mentioned my name in particular along with Frankie Avalon when he accepted his induction into the Hall of Fame."

"Regarding this thing about covers," Boone also told Joe Smith in *Off the Record*, "everybody was aware that the original artists were not going to get played on 90 percent of the radio stations in America. They were not going to play an R&B record by Chuck Berry, or Fats Domino, or Little Richard. In fact, the original artists hoped and prayed their records would get covered by someone who could get airplay because it meant their records were going to get even more recognition in their own field."

"My records of 'Two Hearts,' 'At My Front Door,' 'Ain't That a Shame,' 'Gee Whittakers,' 'Tutti Frutti,' 'Long Tall Sally,' or 'I'll Be Home' are vanilla compared to the originals," he later told *Roctober* magazine in 2000. "What people don't understand is, had they been truly authentic, they wouldn't have gotten played either. Because pop radio was not ready for the alien sound of authentic R&B. That's why R&B had their own stations, but 95 percent of American radio were pop stations."

"They couldn't understand the words," Boone also recalls. "The music didn't sound like it had been done slickly and professionally in a big studio, like Perry Como's or Vic Damone's." Someone like Jerry Lee Lewis may have gotten closed out of pop formats precisely because he was every bit as raw and as threatening as he wanted to be. Decades later, myopic historians can conveniently look upon this era of the 1950s as unfair, but how can one not sympathize with *Today Show* host Dave Garroway as he watched with horror while airing footage of Jerry Lee Lewis setting fire to his piano? The truly raw and raunchy rock 'n' roll artists wanted it both ways: to offend, and to gain the consumer confidence of the white, hyperwashed middle class who, after all, had more disposable income.

Boone would refer to himself as one of the early rock 'n' roll era's "mid-wives," but his ultimate place in rock 'n' roll history was as a liaison between the crooners of yesteryear and a new kind of balladeer who sounded as smooth as a Vic Damone but who retained a more youthful luster. Unlike Elvis, who slobbered a dirty drawl even when attempting pop lullabies like "Love Me Tender," Boone could render a melody with a bit of the airy, dreamy gloss that stars such as Frankie Avalon and Brian Hyland would soon perfect.

With the release of his first major lush theme, "Friendly Persuasion," Boone acquired a new charisma. Dimitri Tiomkin's elaborate and melodically stunning title song to the Gary Cooper movie about Quaker conscientious objectors got all dolled up with shimmering strings and lyrics that Boone rolled out as smoothly as a dollop of vanilla soft serve. It was also different from the standard love ditty in that it was an outright celebration of religious rapture. When Boone sings, "Thee pleasures me in a hundred ways," he has his sights set on his benevolent Maker.

While "Friendly Persuasion" established him as a teen incarnation of Vic Damone, Boone's most famous record, "Love Letters in the Sand," made him a supreme rock-a-balladeer. Crooner Gene Austin, as well as the Ted Black Orchestra, had already made the Nick Kenny song a standard by 1931, but Boone and Billy Vaughn were able to apply a slackened variation on the sock-hop tempo while keeping to the middle of the road. Even after he reached his "Love Letters" fame, however, Boone strove for something more billowy—an effect he achieved with greater success on the minimally arranged yet more highly angelic 1958 release "Gee, But It's Lonely." Phil Everly, of the Everly Brothers, wrote the woebegone ballad, a song about a young man left alone at the prom, and Boone's clear voice bravely balanced the emotion of the lyric against somber guitar chords and choral background before trailing off in a lonesome echo.

Of his many albums, Boone came into his own with *The Touch of Your Lips*, a collection of ballads with gossamer arrangements by Gordon Jenkins. The title tune and renditions of chestnuts such as "My Romance" and "Long Ago and Far Away" show off his desire to convey a mellow, clean-living intimacy. The songs are of a more traditional Tin Pan Alley tincture, but the naked innocence in his voice bespeaks a crooner who made his mark in the era of the teenager. Jenkins's sweeping romanticism was a perfect complement to Boone's airy tones.

Boone's relevance as the flipside of Elvis was not lost on one of Tin Pan Alley's most prized specimens. Irving Berlin, whose heart usually wavered to sentimental melodies and waltzes, snarled when Elvis transmogrified "White Christmas" into a hip-swiveling anthem. But Berlin loved Boone. When Dot Records released the 1958 album *Pat Boone Sings Irving Berlin*, the composer's words on the back cover declared, "Pat Boone sings these ballads the way I like to hear them sung."

A Dream Date for Venus

To grasp the late-1950s appeal of Billy Joel's other whipping boy, Frankie Avalon, one may want to refer to the surreal moment in the 1958 film *Go, Johnny, Go!* when nattily dressed Alan Freed and Chuck Berry are sitting together in some nightclub, dreaming up how "Johnny Melody" (the teen idol whom they so far know only through anonymous records) would look. Freed, in his unmistakably grating voice, declares, "He's gotta be six feet tall, with blond, wavy hair, apple cheek complexion." (The mystery singer later turns out to be dark-haired, not so tall, and rather average-looking Jimmy Clanton, who, in real life, turned out the American Top 40 smash "Venus in Blue Jeans.")

No star of the time challenged Freed's Fallacy with greater success than Frankie Avalon. While the blond Eddie Cochran was all twitchy and dissonant, the dark-haired, olive-skinned Avalon was what the vanilla-hostile rock historian Nik Cohn sneeringly called "an exact reflection of what white American middle-class teenagers really liked and dreamed of." Unlike Paul Anka or Connie Francis, Avalon did not emote in front of the microphone in Judy Garland fashion. The reason Billy Joel felt compelled to include Avalon in his calumny is more difficult to understand. Far from being "derivative," Avalon introduced a new angle to the pop crooner who eschewed R&B covers for original songs, most of which his manager-producers wrote.

Avalon's rise as a vocalist was very similar to that of Bobby Vinton (who started as a sax player and became a singer by serendipity). A proud product of South Philadelphia, Avalon was born Francis Thomas Avallone on September 18, 1939. His first musical passion was the trumpet, which he started mastering as a child. Armed with a horn and lots of ambition, Avalon trumpeted with Rocco & His Saints, a local combo that also included drummer Robert Ridarelli, also known as Bobby Rydell.

Around this time, two enterprising gentlemen named Bob Marcucci and Peter De Angelis formed Chancellor Records and were scouting for rock 'n' roll singers. Frankie talked Marcucci and De Angelis into stopping by to watch him perform with the Saints at a South Philly club, assuming they would like the band's fair-haired lead vocalist Andy Martin. "Frankie said he had a guy in his group I'd like to hear," Marcucci says. "But the kid got up and sang, and we were about to leave. Then after Frankie went up and sang a couple of tunes, we told him, 'We want you!' He said, 'But I'm not a singer.' Of course, we disagreed."

By 1957 Avalon had already stirred up high-school hormones with his first screen appearance in the shake, rattle, and roll musical feature *Jamboree!* Though neither were avid rock 'n' roll fans, Marcucci and De Angelis anticipated teen-fever lucre when they wrote Avalon's first big hit, "De De Dinah." Avalon, suffering from a head cold, ended up singing it, at Marcucci's request and despite De Angelis's objection, while holding his nose. This ear-defying gimmick alone helped the record ascend to *Billboard*'s Top 10, securing Avalon a performance on *American Bandstand*. Avalon stuck to the naughty nasal approach on the follow-up single "Ginger Bread," a true precursor to the randy candy of the late 1960s "bubblegum."

More melodically inclined, Marcucci and De Angelis set their hearts on making Avalon a balladeer. Radio listeners finally got to hear Avalon's voice relaxed and unencumbered by horseplay with the release of "I'll Wait for You." Despite the obvious nod to Ricky Nelson's "Lonesome Town," Avalon exhibited his own creamy-on-the-melody finesse, all set against a "doo-wah" chorus, countrified guitar, and tantalizing echo. Many radio listeners, unaccustomed to hearing a voice so melodic yet so refreshingly untrained, felt invigorated as Avalon started his journey into melody with baby steps.

And then there was "Venus"! This most ethereal of Avalon recordings set a high standard for vanilla production values. Accompanied by orchestra, bells, chimes, a subtle calypso pace, and an otherworldly female chorus, Avalon sings out the Ed Marshall tune with an almost supernatural insight into the listeners' romantic dreams. His voice, though sometimes tentative, is smooth, viscerally pleasing, and exact on every note. The country succumbed to Avalon's spell as well when the record went to *Billboard*'s #1 spot for five consecutive weeks. The next #1 entry—the Marcucci–De Angelis composition "Why?"—has Avalon in a duet with a mysterious chanteuse, the gleaming instruments heightening the near-hypnotic nursery-rhyme cadences. Even an academe like Charles Hamm, reluctant to appreciate Avalon's adolescent style, could not help but acknowledge this particular record's "smooth, rich musical texture of soft, shimmering amplified guitars and a humming chorus."

Russell Faith, among Avalon's other leading songwriters, also had a knack for agile melodies and sprightly words that best suited the singer's personality on tunes like "Togetherness." Avalon's recording of Faith's "Voyage to the Bottom of the Sea" is the title theme to Irwin Allen's 1961 film, in which he also starred in the role of Lieutenant Danny Romano. The song is among his most accomplished recordings, capturing his clear voice with cascading strings, a flock of seagulls, and the lure of ghostly background sirens calling out from oblivion. "I thought it was a difficult song to get across with that title," Avalon admits. "But they made it work."

Avalon emerged as a new kind of teen dream who came across not as a self-preening delinquent clambering for attention, but as an affable boy-next-door who never resorted to affectation and who conveyed the ballads as if he were one among his listeners. Avalon was living proof that America's youth enjoyed a vibrant musical culture during that fertile transition between Elvis Presley's army induction and the British Invasion.

"Frankie was very vanilla," Marcucci continues. "His voice was like his appearance, cute and adorable. Back in our day, the groups would be doing ballads—like the Lettermen. Frankie was one among that first batch of young people. He had a sweet voice and the appearance of someone loving and warm, different from the kids around there. We always had a beautiful chorus. I'd say, 'Give it echo, more.' Glen Campbell was with us on the guitar during the sessions on the West Coast, along with Leon Russell. Al Caiola was also on the 'Venus' session."

Avalon looks back with pride on his romantic musical roots. "What Bob and Peter were trying to accomplish with me at that point was to make me more of a romantic singer, à la Frankie *Sinatra*. And I've always loved crooners like Perry Como. I remember one phrase in 'I'll Wait for You' when the band and the music cuts off, and I'm alone singing, 'I love you.' When I did this on stage, the audience was knocked out. Since then, most of my recognizable songs through all the years have been ballads."

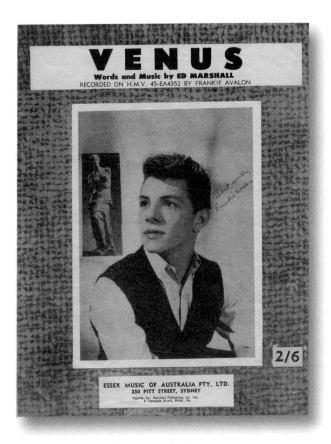

Frankie Avalon: the ultimate vanilla singer.

At times, Marcucci and De Angelis tried to fashion him as a more swaggering Vegas-style performer, such as on the songs "Swingin' on a Rainbow" and "Tuxedo Junction," but Avalon's talents seemed better focused on mellower material. This is evident in songs such as "Where Are You?," with its lush, weepy orchestra serenading "a rendezvous just meant for two." Though De Angelis orchestrated most of his songs, Avalon also worked with other notable arrangers. Don Costa & His Orchestra backed "A Miracle," with its dramatic buildup typical of other Teddy Randazzo compositions, and "You Are Mine," an early Marcucci–De Angelis collaboration that (according to Marcucci) Dick Clark employed to propose to his wife. The latter was also the title track from the exemplary 1962 album in which Avalon sings several romantic standards.

Avalon is forthright when assessing his place in pop history: "Some rock historians say that artists from my era were manufactured. But there had to be some kind of genuine charm with the music and lyrics. We are still doing this. Everybody could sing 'Venus.' Everyone knew it was #1. People drove in their cars to it. It told a very melodic and lyrical story. I still sing 'Venus' on stage, and when that introduction starts, I can feel that electricity with every audience. It's not just a throwaway song. Even if artists like myself never get credit from the industry itself, this music will always have meaning for people."

Today, the raunchy sounds that once terrorized the Lawrence Welk generation have become the norm. The original rebels have grown old; all those shakes, rattles, and stammers, once so shocking, have devolved into desperate and empty gestures. Anyone who wants to resist the humdrum and subvert the subversive would do well to start with Boone and Avalon—the guys who went against the whole grain of rock 'n' roll's manufactured badness by being just the way they are.

2

Twinkle and Shine!

The Mitch Miller Years

"Frustration, nostalgia, and love!" According to Rosemary Clooney, Mitch Miller once considered this threefold formula essential for a good pop song. Clooney should know, for she was among the vocalists whose fame followed the trail that the pop A&R man blazed at Columbia Records between 1950 and 1961.

With his accent on delicious vanilla ballads and snappy novelty tunes, Miller played a major role in shaping Top 40 sounds and attitudes during the postwar years. Critics have been divided about Mr. Miller's impact on the music scene. The complimentary Stephen Holden declared: "Miller had a gift for choosing pop novelties that stuck to the brain like chewing gum to the soles of your shoes." But James Miller, with sympathies apparently more attuned to rock, described Mitch Miller's music as "trifling, sweet, and airy songs smothered in the musical equivalent of whipped cream." Sweet and airy? In the best possible sense. Whipped cream? Delectably so. But trifling? That all depends on what one considers "serious" pop music.

Miller's goatee, slicked-back hair, and intense eyes (colleagues called him "the Beard") might easily have allowed him to pass for one of the Beats of his time. If anything, he was a counter-Beat who engineered songs that the great, washed masses populating Eisenhower's (as well as Stevenson's) America loved to hear. His efforts sound extremely high gloss or vaporous by today's dull and dense standards. He tended to buck trends like bebop and doo-wop by making most of his melodies instantly recognizable, his singers clear and precise, and his arrangements replete with unabashedly contrived effects and ear-licking hooks.

Even while keeping to the mainstream, Miller maintained a cheeky, sur-realistic streak. Enamored with echoes, whistles, celestas, and other tasty ear candy, he would go to excessive lengths for the right ambiance, whether through the cavernous Columbia studio stairwells or to a New York City church.

The Echo

Nineteen forty-seven was a banner year for otherworldly discoveries. American pilot Kenneth Arnold saw nine "flying saucers" approaching Mt. Rainier and jumpstarted the UFO craze; the military allegedly pickled some extra-terrestrial visitors in Roswell, New Mexico; and, last but not least, Mitch Miller invented what music industry mavens from then on would refer to as the "echo chamber."

Les Paul often gets the credit for tinkering with echo and "sound-on-sound" effects in his early days at Capitol Records, but Miller, while still a producer at Mercury, experimented with similar effects with notable success on songs by Vic Damone and Frankie Laine.

"My engineer Bob Fine and I invented echo," Miller recalls. "If you listen to those old records, everybody sounds like they're singing through wool. I went to Bob Fine when I was at Mercury and said, 'Put a halo around the voice. Can you do that?' So that it sounds like in the halls. And so he did. The reverberation chamber started out in the bathroom. You put a loudspeaker and a mike in the bathroom or hallway. You take the sound from the studio, which is all dry; then you pipe it through the loudspeaker in the bathroom. As it comes out, you take a touch of that sound through the microphone, add [it] to the original sound—and you get the reverberation. What you do is you add spices. Les Paul will give me credit. He's the nicest man."

By 1950 Miller moved over to lead the Columbia pop division, bringing the likes of Patti Page along with him. He also got a great deal of echo by using a studio, on 30th Street in New York City, that had been converted from a Greek church. He used echo for all sorts of musical purposes and styles, but he employed it best on ballads that stressed themes of wistful romance and lost hearts. Somehow, the singers just sounded all the lonelier when their voices bounced off the walls and radiated in sonic afterglow.

In more earthly terms, Mitch Miller and the various Columbia engineers made the recording studio sound as if it were inundated with Freon, creating a rarefied enclosure where the notes came out cool and clean. He was also adept at deploying what was, by the dawn of the 1950s, the new miracle of magnetic tape. In Miller's hands, the art of overdubbing begot masterworks that were alternately dreamy and quaintly bizarre.

Miller delighted in thinking up previously unheard-of musical amalgams and veering his singers in unpredictable directions. His output was vast and included many styles. He had a predilection for the unpredictable and unthinkable, such as having Burl Ives sing with a Dixieland band, pairing Dinah Shore's voice with bagpipes, or asking Tony Bennett to do cowboy tunes. "You must remember," Miller emphasizes, "we had to sell a person strictly by their sound. And if anyone had a distinctive sound, you detected different personality traits within that sound that they didn't even know were there. So that on every one of my records, after the first four bars you knew who the person was, nobody had to tell you."

Rock 'n' roll's rebellion has been lionized to no end, but credit is overdue for Miller's counter-rebellion. When it came to procuring new talent, he was less than friendly to the burgeoning rock 'n' roll and, when offered a chance to record Buddy Holly, passed. But the brash new sound probably inspired him to vie for the attention of younger audiences with songs that were often a catchy and sparkly alternative to the rock 'n' roll beat.

Mitch Miller's Cover Story

While Pat Boone transformed R&B, Miller and his cadre of arrangers and engineers were doing the musical equivalent of genetic reengineering. Whether he will ever admit it or not, Mitch Miller had a hand in white-bread song interpretation—be it adaptations of black R&B or white country and blue-grass. Oddly, Miller's take on the cover game is a bit surprising. "You'd have Pat Boone ripping off Little Richard," he retorts when confronted with the subject. "You could die laughing, it was white-bread—'hooty-tooty, hoody-hoody,' I mean, c'mon. Give me a break!" Odder yet, Doris Day (at Columbia) and Frank Sinatra (at Capital) also sported their own cover versions of

"Two Hearts, Two Kisses" around the time Boone released his. "If you think mine sounds vanilla," Boone would later tell *Goldmine*, "you ought to hear them."

Miller's whipped-cream country was another milestone in acoustic mischief. He morphed several Hank Williams songs from their gritty regionalism into a softer blend. Rosemary Clooney went to #1 in 1952 with "Half as Much" and Tony Bennett took a smooth crooner approach a year earlier on "Cold, Cold Heart." A few years later, Miller treated the bona fide country star Marty Robbins to a much more lacquered approach.

In 1957 Miller helped Robbins record one of pop history's greatest country crossovers, "A White Sport Coat (and a Pink Carnation)." He had previously persuaded newcomer Guy Mitchell to record a pop version of "Singin' the Blues," which Robbins had already recorded in Nashville. Now it was Robbins's turn to try and tap into a wider, less regional market. There was no way that any producer or engineer could extract vanilla from his voice, but Miller at least bypassed the Grand Ole Opry's grainy standards by having Ray Conniff come up with the essential sweeteners to liberate Robbins from the honky-tonk: lots of echo; a tidy melody; a chirpy choral section; and a tight, regulation-style rhythm replacing country shuffle.

Bob Morgan, who started working with Miller by reading his unsolicited mail before serving as a Columbia A&R assistant, remembers the others who helped develop the studio's high-gloss sound excursions. He was there when Johnny Mathis made his renowned recording of "Misty," and Morgan later brought in the talents of the Brothers Four, who intoned Miller-style echoes on "Greenfields."

"Ray Conniff was a big player," Morgan recalls, "but Al Ham [who would later become famous for his syndicated *Music of Your Life* radio program] also played a big role and didn't get much credit. Ham produced the Ray Conniff recordings. I witnessed Al sitting with Conniff, suggesting changes in arrangements. Al came out of New Haven and was a bass player with Artie Shaw. He had wonderful arranging and music skills when he went to Columbia's research department. By then, they were using 'limiters' to reduce dynamic range. Al Ham was instrumental in that slapback echo effect. He was adept technically and used that sound for Mitch Miller sing-alongs, the echo for Johnny Mathis's voice, and for Tony Bennett—that's why people thought Tony lisped."

The Singers' Svengali

Rosemary Clooney also identifies Miller as a "Svengali" for singers. Exacting, dictatorial, and perpetually energetic, he would make demands on his performers that seemed at times insane but in most cases yielded fruitful results. He induced several Sinatra temper tantrums by requesting too many novelty items, eventually prompting the blue-eyed blusterer to storm out of the studio. Tony Bennett was also known to have a snit or two when Miller would have him do those "cowboy" songs or take him even farther away from his Brooklyn roots on records like the Hawaiian-flavored "In the Middle of an Island." Frankie Laine, however, seemed more at ease when traversing Miller Time, wailing away on his Wild West ballads as the stratospheric echoes lifted him into less rugged geography.

All of the above-mentioned singers were essentially middle-of-the-road prima donnas intent on playing the personality card with every note. But others, such as Patti Page, demonstrated a more spirited willingness to come at least close to unadulterated vanilla pop. Page started out with a more countrified sass that belied her Oklahoma background, but Miller encouraged her sweet and motherly style, whose influence would permeate singers all the way down to Karen Carpenter. At Mercury, Miller and Page came out with the thirteen-week #1 sleeper "The Tennessee Waltz" in 1950, a multitracked, melancholic delicacy that led to follow-up successes including "Mockin' Bird Hill" in 1951, "I Went to Your Wedding" in 1952, and "The Doggie in the Window" in 1953. Miller included Page in his pioneer dubbing session back in 1949 by having her sing to herself on a country song called "Money, Marbles, and Chalk"—an effort he managed to put together in those pretape days by transferring one acetate onto another. Page was among the most popular vocalists of the 1950s; by the late 1960s, she would emerge as one of adult contemporary music's veteran voices with her mild-mannered, skillfully engineered versions of "Gentle on My Mind" and the undying 1965 theme "Hush, Hush, Sweet Charlotte."

One profound Miller coup involved convincing a certain young man to forsake jazz interpretation for a brilliant pop career. From the time he took his first singing lessons, John Royce Mathis preferred what his father called "sweet songs." He studied with an opera coach and continued to develop his voice, even while attending college in San Francisco, where he had cultivated another passion—field and track. Athletics almost eclipsed his crooner calling, but the untiring romantic forfeited a chance at the 1956 Olympics try-outs in order to pursue his muse.

Mathis's life took a significant turn when he met nightclub owner Helen Noga. A vigorous and pushy woman, Noga assumed the dual role of manager and surrogate mother. She soon introduced him to Columbia's jazz producer, George Avakian, who, after hearing him perform in a San Francisco club called Ann Dee's, signed Mathis up for his first recording sessions. But Avakian's intervention proved to be a mixed blessing. The self-titled 1957 debut album consisted of jazzed-down arrangements, with Mathis often lapsing into imitations of his favorite jazz divas.

When the ever-persistent Noga finally hooked him up with Miller, Mathis's career quandary soon ended. "On one tune," Miller recalls, "he sounded like Ella Fitzgerald; on another he sounded like Lena Horne. Lena said, 'He stole everything but my gown.' The whole company at the annual sales convention—everybody was so excited about this. And then—nothing happened. Even if it was playing, people didn't buy it. And he had a manager who owned the bar that he used to sing in. She came to me and pleaded, 'Why don't you take him on?' I said that with the kind of voice he had he's very special material, and it would take me time. Then she began to cry. So I got my songwriting friends together."

Scoffing at the previous album's smoky bar sound, Miller proceeded to vocally remold Mathis, literally standing over him to make sure his notes stuck firmly to the beat. "If they wanted a long phrase," he told Ted Fox, "I would show them what to do. I did this with Johnny Mathis a lot. He was a very fast learner. In fact, I would stay with Mathis in the studio, and when I wanted that special choirboy quality I'd have a signal. I'd shake my hand in a certain way and stay right with him while he was recording, and he'd soar."

Looking for a dreamy ballad, Miller consulted composer Bob Allen (who wrote hits for Miller's other protégés, the Four Lads). He chose Allen's "It's Not for Me to Say" and again employed the orchestral skills of Ray Conniff, who, into the mid-1950s, was a major easy-listening arranger and conductor. By the spring of 1957 the winning combination of Mathis's voice and Conniff's echo-redolent studio acoustics begot a Top 20 favorite. The team followed up with another Allen tune, "Chances Are," which became Mathis's first #1 hit.

Some performers might resent Miller's autocratic approach, but Mathis welcomed the new direction. The resulting—and revitalizing—difference in his style became an object lesson on the fundamental differences between jazz and pop singing. In place of slippery syncopation, Mathis adopted a tighter, less ruffled delivery that worked to optimum results on such celestial dream pieces as "Wonderful! Wonderful!"

"I Want to Hear Those Postcards in Your Voice"

Doris Day truly came into her own as a pop singer during Miller's Columbia tenure, but she'd already started adding vanilla embellishments to her songs when singing in some of those breezy Warner Brothers musicals of the late 1940s. Led by the studio's musical director, Ray Heindorf, with the lyrics of Sammy Cahn and Jule Styne's music, she recorded the lilting "It's Magic" for *Romance on the High Seas* in 1948. A year later she sounded bright and sentimental on the Harry Warren–Ralph Blane title song for *My Dream Is Yours*, as well as on the song "I'll String Along with You." In the follow-up musical *It's a Great Feeling*, Jack Carson stars opposite her, playing his usual affable ham and uttering to Doris the memorable line: "When you sing, I want to hear those postcards in your voice."

Day's big-screen musical manicure was a departure from her jazzier material, performed with Les Brown and His Band of Renown, which included tunes such as "Sentimental Journey." Even Brown recalls her as postcard sunshine in A. E. Hotchner's Doris Day biography: "Doris was very loyal to me, primarily, I think, because she liked the nature of my band. I ran a tight ship, no dope, no booze, no hard language. One reporter wrote that the X band played on booze, and the Y band played on dope, but Les Brown and His Band of Renown played on milk shakes. The label stuck, and we became known as the Milk Shake Band. And if ever there was a milk-shake girl, it was Doris!"

By the dawn of the 1950s, Miller's Columbia sound lab collaborated with Hollywood to perfect the Doris Day that the world has subsequently known and loved. Brightness and sweetness were waxed into both her audio and visual impressions. In movies such as *On Moonlight Bay* (1951) and *By the Light of the Silvery Moon* (1953), Warner Brothers cast her in an idyllic, but ever receding, nostalgic time zone. The period costumes were quaint, the tunes were generally sentimental, and, as Doris herself would admit, "I felt very real in the make-believe parts I had to play." Cast in the tomboy title role of the 1953 musical Western *Calamity Jane*, she played against type as Wild Bill Hickok's boisterous gal pal. But she stole the show with the effervescent and decidedly feminine "Secret Love"—a performance that earned the year's Best Song Oscar and a #1 pop chart position.

All the inspirational cheer going into those vocal postcards came with an unavoidable subtext. Doris Day, in all likelihood, experienced darker days than Ozzy Osbourne. Able to open her tear spigots at will, she earned the nickname "Miss Lachrymose" from her dolorous behavior while on the set of *Romance on the High Seas*. Her perky songs and image contrasted with the sometimes grisly details of her personal life, which included four marriages, abusive husbands, heart palpitations, emotional and financial insecurities, misgivings as a mother, squandered fortunes as a businesswoman, and an ultimately unsatisfying bout with Christian Science. Such dream decimators intensified when she and her son, Terry Melcher, brushed with the Manson family.

The fact that Day introduced the chirpy "*Que Sera, Sera* (Whatever Will Be, Will Be)" in an Alfred Hitchcock murder mystery underscores her contradictions. Hitchcock's 1956 remake of *The Man Who Knew Too Much* called for her to give a recital of the song to a rather snooty bunch of Brits—a climactic moment when her kidnapped son cries for help while hearing her voice through a wall. With open-ended lines such as "Will we have rainbows, day after day?" the song's literal message becomes supremely relevant for her character who, when singing it earlier in the film to her child, had anticipated more bliss than foul play. Audiences walking out of the film would never feel the same when "*Que Sera, Sera*" came on the radio. The tune also summarized Day's philosophy on life at the time, which revolved around rather fatalistic notions about preordination that she'd absorbed through Mary Baker Eddy's book *Science and Health with Key to the Scriptures*.

To emanate these aural sparkles, Day also worked with some of Columbia's greatest and most pillowy arrangers. She joined Percy Faith on "When I Fall in Love" (with the Norman Luboff Choir) and the heartfelt, crisply enunciated "I'll Never Stop Loving You" (from the film *Love Me or Leave Me*). Frank De Vol (who would go on to compose the famous theme for the television series *My Three Sons*) handled her arrangements on "*Que Sera, Sera*" and some of her other memorable Top 40 entries, including the sonically lacquered Best Vocal Performance Emmy Award winner "Everybody Loves a Lover" from 1958.

Though her vast output of records reflected different styles, and she did not consistently live up to her glossiest moments, it's the bright and shiny Doris Day who endures in the public's memory. "The guys who look at her

Though she started out as a brassier big-band singer with Les Brown, Doris Day eventually cultivated a more sugar-spun style that matched her image. Her ultimate vanilla record, "*Que Sera, Sera* (Whatever Will Be, Will Be)," was from the 1956 Alfred Hitchcock film *The Man Who Knew Too Much*. The song also came out at the same time this Lustre-Creme ad appeared. Like the shampoo, Day's singing—on this and many other Mitch Miller–era productions—evoked another of her movie titles: the 1959 comedy *Twinkle and Shine*.

on the screen and think she's the girl next door would love to ravage her but they wouldn't dare admit it," James Garner, Day's Hollywood costar, declared. "They're not going to mess up that vanilla ice cream cone, no way—but in the dark recesses of their minds, they want her."

Cozy Compact Choirs

In the 1950s the art of the tight four-part harmony started to quake before the improvisational demon of "doo-wop." Miller recorded the Four Lads, a quartet from north of the 49th Parallel that had met at St. Michael's Cathedral Choir School in their hometown of Toronto. As a vocal lineup, they conformed more to a strict four-part structure. Bernard Toorish was second tenor, Frank Busseri was the baritone, Connie Codarini supplied the bass, and James Arnold was the first tenor. While they later professed to having various musical influences from spirituals to lighter barbershop quartet fare, the Lads' choirboy chimes permeated their best work.

They went by various names, and had been all set to call themselves the Four Dukes when they appeared on *Arthur Godfrey's Talent Scouts*. But another group by that name threatened them with an order to cease and desist. While in New York, they appeared regularly at Le Ruban Bleu nightclub, where Julius Monk, the club's impresario, introduced them as "the quintessence of quartet" while advising them to adopt the Four Lads as their permanent moniker.

Meanwhile, the Lads' manager, Michael Stewart, who also handled the gospel group the Golden Gate Quartet, fashioned the Lads' clean-cut image. He saw to it that they sported plaid jackets, short hair, and bow ties. Spirituals were dropped from their Ruban Bleu repertoire in favor of pop ballads. In the summer of 1950, after Stewart had molded them into four cuddly crooners, Miller happened to catch their act, and he brought them into his fold. Among the Lads' first jobs was to provide the vocal background to Johnnie Ray's first two-sided smash hit, "Cry" and "The Little White Cloud That Cried." Though Ray would wring his hands, wave his arms, and even kneel as he whimpered through the dire straits of romantic rejection in song after song, the Lads' cooing helped to temper Ray's studio-confined nervous breakdowns.

Soon second tenor Toorish started writing vocal arrangements and songs pseudonymously. As the Lads began cutting their own singles, Miller pushed them toward novelty songs. Toorish adapted their 1952 release "The Mocking Bird" from Dvorak's New World Symphony. The Lads proceeded with an up-tempo version of Gershwin's "Somebody Loves Me," a giddy history lesson on "Istanbul (Not Constantinople)," and a madcap chantey with "Gilly Gilly Ossenfeffer, Katzenellen Bogen by the Sea," then frolicked along to Neal Hefti & His Orchestra on the South African tune "Skokiaan."

One would think that, with acts like Elvis sneaking in to steal the pop world's thunder, the Lads would have joined their fellow Torontonians the Crew Cuts on the rock 'n' roll bandwagon. Instead, they went in an entirely different direction. Many of their subsequent songs were more romantic, and their voices, mere studio playthings until then, became more relaxed as they drifted into their natural chorister mode. They made a major career shift with a tune that, while being far from rock 'n' roll, exuded enough youthful pluck to attract teenagers as well as adults. Again, composers Bob Allen and Al Stillman came through with "Moments to Remember."

On "Moments," the Lads worked with the lilting backdrop of Ray Ellis and His Orchestra as they pined, with lovelorn nostalgia, over lost hearts and haunted places. Along with soaring strings, evocative reverberation, and a ghostly female to reinforce the whimsy, "Moments to Remember" showed the Lads as a quartet that sang more like a choir—more in unison, without the assigned parts sliding into each other in the way that barbershoppers approximate a human harmonica. The song also cast some bittersweet brightness over the autumn of 1955. It would become one of the great post–World War II airs about adolescence and school angst—the kind of ballad that would inform other seasonal affective classics such as "See You in September" and "Sealed with a Kiss." By the 1960s, harmonists such as the Lettermen and the Vogues would also excel with their own "Moments to Remember."

Many other recordings performed with Ray Ellis's backing demonstrate how a four-man (or -woman) group could sound less like a churning and swooping barbershop quartet and more like a compact choir. "No, Not Much!"—the Lads' Stillman-Allen follow-up to "Moments"—was equally dedicated to a creamy commingling of vocal parts. Other Stillman-Allen entries, including "Who Needs You," "There's Only One of You," and "Enchanted Island," as well as the Lads' self-penned "My Little Angel," heightened the heavenly blend, boasting a tightly controlled yet emotionally convincing style that had an obvious influence on the Lettermen.

The crisp Canadian breeze that scooped the Four Lads southward also produced the Crew Cuts, another group that personified Canuck cleanliness and order. Like the Lads, the Crew Cuts came from a church choir background at Toronto's St. Michael's Cathedral Choir School.

While the Lads, as well as Ray Conniff's chorus, deserve proper credit for heralding the splendor of Columbia's air-conditioned chimes, Miller was using the same techniques for his own choral endeavors as early as 1950 with the release of "Tzena, Tzena, Tzena." Switching from Israeli folk songs to the antebellum south, Miller and His Orchestra and Chorus topped the charts in 1955 with a version of "The Yellow Rose of Texas." Here, with a jolly unison quality that would inform his later Sing-Along records, Miller subjected the Civil War campfire tune to some creative censorship, substituting a salute to the Lone Star State's "flowers" instead of its "high yaller" girls.

Three years later, Miller's series of Sing-Along albums became his prime focus. The series spanned four years, with twenty LPs (sixteen of which were on *Billboard*'s Top 10). The male chorale would be the force behind his much-remembered television show, which ran from 1961 to 1964. To put these albums together, he surveyed the musical tastes of groups such as the Boy Scouts and the Girl Scouts, along with various Kiwanis and Rotary clubs, asking what songs the people preferred. He proceeded to make what he called "a Chinese menu" of standards, with harmonies that were kept simple enough for listeners to vocalize along to the albums' printed lyrics.

Miller's stouthearted glee club forged on with a variety of time-honored songs for various occasions, while drum brushes, harmonica, and accordion usually adorned the echo chamber. Melodies such as "You Are My Sunshine," "By the Light of the Silvery Moon," "Till We Meet Again," and "That Old Gang of Mine" prompted long-ago and far-away thoughts, while the reverberant technology transmitting them suggested a modern enclosure sealed off from campfire impurities.

Inveterate jazz propagandist Tony Bennett rarely concurred with Miller about aesthetics or repertoire, but in his autobiography, *The Good Life*, he hails Miller as "perhaps the single most influential producer in the history of recording." Producer Sam Phillips once claimed that rock 'n' roll is "ugly and honest," but Miller sought a style that was pretty and honestly artificial. With the right balance of frustration, nostalgia, and love, he whipped his musical cream into shape and enjoyed his just desserts (even if he turned down Buddy Holly).

3

Bobby Tomorrow

obert Thomas Velline was just fifteen when the weight of popular
mythology fell on his shoulders. Like hundreds of other fans, he
had tickets to see Buddy Holly at the Winter Dance Party in Fargo,
North Dakota, on the night of February 3, 1959. But when he and his brother
Bill heard on the radio of the plane crash that took the lives of Holly, the Big
Bopper, and Richie Valens, Velline got a sinking feeling.

Velline and his brother had formed a rock 'n' roll band, and the two
answered a radio announcer's request for local fill-ins to replace the casualties.
The celebrated Dion (still crooning with the Belmonts) showed up, and
Holly's lead guitarist, Tommy Allsup, arrived as well (a miracle of good fortune, as he had originally been scheduled to be on the doomed flight). But
these performers were too grief-stricken to comfort the audience of weepy
teenagers. When his time came to take the stage, Velline—soon known to the
world as Bobby Vee—stood agape as the band started performing.

"The Winter Dance Party was just an emotional train wreck," Vee recalls.
"People were having out-of-body experiences. Tommy Allsup was onstage
with glossed-over eyes. Dion was unable to communicate. Here we were—
these little Fargo guys coming to the stage to volunteer our services. The radio
stations had no idea who we were and didn't audition us. My life changed that
night when the curtain opened up. I was the kid. I got up onstage. I knew I
had to sing when they introduced us. I thought I was going to die. When the

band started playing, I started hearing sounds coming out of my mouth and was surprised."

By early 1960, Holly's dimpled successor was making his mark. As Vee regaled audiences onstage and on vinyl, however, some hard-core Holly enthusiasts had less kindly sentiments about the cuddly all-American. "The Holly fans were in two camps," Vee confirms in his reserved and courteous manner. "Among the Generals, the guys really into him, there was resentment. I sensed that." John Beecher, who headed England's first official Buddy Holly Appreciation Society in the early 1960s, is more terse: "Bobby is a sweet man, but at the time, most of us were irritated. He was being hailed as the next Holly, but he sounded a little too hiccuppy and too pretend."

The term "hiccuppy" was likely not a pejorative tag among many of Vee's fans. Most of them adored the way he whipped even more buoyancy into Holly's "go-lightly" finesse. To appreciate Vee's nice-guy allure, one need only consider the man whose shoes he filled. Holly himself resisted getting lumped in with the typical teenage hellion. For those who preferred their music and image raw and gritty, he was at times a bit of a nuisance. He tended to wear foppish clothes, and his vocal leaps made him seem a bit fey. Even with his Texas accent, he hinted at a dandy's pedigree whenever he played what his bone-brained rivals regarded as "sissy" paeans to romantic love. Yes, he recorded too many songs with a harder edge to be classified as purely vanilla, but Holly helped to liberate rock 'n' roll from its earthy weight by playing the giddy swain on tunes such as "Everyday," especially with all those heavenly sound effects to laminate his lyrics.

Holly edged farther into what rock 'n' roll hardballers would consider taboo territory when he sang to pizzicato strings. Credit for that gravity-defying foray goes to arranger/conductor Dick Jacobs. In 1953, Jacobs made an impact on popular music when he became a recording manager at Decca subsidiary Coral Records. There, he helped to fine-tune acts such as the McGuire Sisters and supplied variations on the pop instrumental. In 1956 Dick Jacobs and His Orchestra recorded an interpretation of Elmer Bernstein's themes to the Otto Preminger film *The Man with the Golden Arm* and made an acclaimed version of "Fascination" from *Love in the Afternoon*. Jacobs's greatest pop innovation bar none was the pairing of plucked strings to a plucky beat.

Levitating more toward the light, Buddy Holly relished the chance to add a full string orchestra to his next recording date. These were the historic sessions at New York City's Pythian Temple Studio that included Jacobs's glossy arrangements of "Raining in My Heart" and "True Love Ways." One of the songs Holly decided to perform was "It Doesn't Matter Anymore"—a gesture of good faith to its composer, Paul Anka. Though he had yet to finish the tune, Anka pleaded with Holly to add it to the session. Holly agreed, but Anka did not have the final version ready until about two hours before the session began, at which point Jacobs had to think of a quick fix to make up for the lost time. "We had violins on the date and I had no time to harmonize the violins or write intricate parts," Jacobs confessed to an interviewer, "so we wrote the violins all pizzicato. . . . That was the most unplanned thing I have ever written in my life."

Those recordings led many to speculate as to which direction Holly might have gone had gravity been less draconian. His career was fraught with so many different styles that rock purists hoped he would go one way, and easy-listening enthusiasts the other. For those who preferred the melodies sweet, Bobby Vee was Holly's saintly successor. Vee's first recordings were a little rough, particularly with his Holly impersonation on the self-penned Soma Records release "Suzie Baby." But Liberty Records producer Snuff Garrett, who was friends with Holly, had better plans for the singer.

Thomas Leslie Garrett, born 1939 in Dallas, Texas, entered the music world as a teenager and was about twenty years old when he became one of Hollywood's first pop producers. By 1961 he was Liberty's A&R head and in a position to help mold pop to the sound and image he saw fit. Thanks to Garrett, as well as to a retinue of fine engineers, arrangers, musicians, and songwriters, Bobby Vee was shaped into a musician who filled a void. "The key to my sound is Snuffy Garrett," Vee admits. "He said that's where the music is going and said Buddy Holly told him."

"When Buddy started recording with strings," Garrett remembers, "he would call me every night, play me the masters. They were the last things he did. I loved those. When I started producing records, I wanted to go into the direction where Buddy was going at the end. I made tunes for people to like. I wanted pretty lyrics on what I thought in those days were unrequited love songs, story songs. I loved them."

Between the times of the death of Holly and the British Invasion, adolescent pop was adrift in love ditties whose sexual references were either cutely couched or nonexistent. Teenagers had certainly been around before the first sock-hop generation forged a consumer niche, but during that unique period of the late 1950s and early 1960s, the postwar youth outranked yesteryear's bobby-soxers as voracious music lovers. They were ever ready to cash in their allowances for records that incited them to wax romantic over their current crushes. While hard-core rock 'n' rollers pushed their fans into the backseats of cars, Vee and other likeminded pop stars satisfied a yearning for either endless foreplay or an approach to romance as benign as those choice *Our Gang* moments when Alfalfa sings to Darla.

Garrett intuited all this and, while looking for just the right song to bring out Vee's good nature, sought inspiration from across the Pond. There, English sensation Adam Faith had appropriated Holly's pixie-dust plucking on a British tune called "What Do You Want?" John Barry, in his pre–film composer days, was Faith's arranger, and he incorporated pizzicato rock into a technique he called "stringbeat."

Recorded in March 1960, Vee's version of "What Do You Want?" retained such Holly affectations as the drawn-out "baaaabaay," but his own voice was now peeping out from the Holly legend. The record did not catch on as expected, but it offered an exemplary mating game between a rocking beat and the sweetening effect a simple phalanx of studio violins could achieve. Soon, with more gorgeous strings to bolster his tone, Vee emerged as a performer lucky enough to look the way he sounded. His bright tone and "bouncy-bouncy" delivery, accented at times with snippets of that "r"-hugging Fargo accent, made Vee come across on vinyl as every bit the charmer that Buddy Holly biographer Ellis Amburn describes as "smooth-skinned, bright-eyed, with a huge Mickey Rooney smile and perfect teeth."

That same year, Liberty released *Bobby Vee Sings Your Favorites*, a concept album of sorts that was intended to feature one side dedicated to 1950s rockers and the other to ballads. Vee and Garrett wanted to placate Hollyphiles by recording the rock side at Clovis, New Mexico, under the auspices of Holly's ex-producer, Norman Petty. Petty even penned a letter for inclusion on the back cover and was likely perplexed when Liberty failed to include the Tex-Mex–style tracks recorded in his studio on the final release.

Garrett's change of plan occurred once he and Vee returned to Hollywood to press the ballad side. On hand were the Johnny Mann Singers, a full string orchestra, and several members of Little Richard's rhythm section, who were waiting to amalgamate otherwise warring musical elements. Ernie Freeman, a blues and jazz practitioner from New Orleans, may have seemed the least likely choice as an arranger for a vanilla tune, but he had already succeeded in turning out confectionary masterpieces dominated by layers of violins, bells, harps, and an array of other radiant flavors.

"I was a Freeman freak," Garrett reflects, justifying his ultimate musical decision. "I asked Si Waronker at Liberty, and said there's one arranger I wanted to use. Felix Slatkin and he kind of smiled and said there are lots of greater arrangers. But I wanted Ernie. I put him under contract; we worked together for five or six years. I don't know a note from another, but I hired some of the best musicians in the world. I ran a totalitarian dictatorship—didn't deal with girlfriends, wives, boyfriends. I ran the ship going up or going down."

Garrett, betraying the sentimental scamp lurking beneath his mercenary persona, also turned the album into a collection of his own favorite oldies. The songlist included tributes to the Fleetwoods' "Mr. Blue," the McGuire Sisters' "Sincerely," and "Young Love," which Sonny James, Tab Hunter, and the Crew Cuts released simultaneously in 1957. One particular track, a version of Ivory Joe Turner's "Since I Met You Baby," employs a Pat Boone–style cover route. But Vee made no attempt to acknowledge the song's R&B origins with any pseudo-soulful obeisance. He instead opted to dramatize it as a Holly-inspired croon with shades of a country drawl that do not detract from a plain-speaking middle-American accent. The album's highlight is the final cut, a version of Holly's "Everyday" that comes alive with lush pizzicato and additional sweeps of string.

Sentimental tastes aside, Garrett had to run a business. With the goal of getting a song into the Top 10, both he and Vee settled upon the flip side of "Since I Met You Baby"—a dulcet version of an old R&B number called "Devil or Angel," which had been released by the Clovers in 1956. True credit goes to a prescient DJ at Pittsburgh's KQV, who turned the record over one day and soon ignited an airwave chain reaction. Along with Freeman's orchestra, the Johnny Mann Singers (six tightly harmonized voices, divided equally between male and female) fired the finishing glaze.

When the follow-up 1960 album, sensibly titled *Bobby Vee*, arrived, Vee was still finding what would become his comfortable niche in Garrett's sound gallery. Among the highlights of the album was a track he felt very ambivalent about recording, but, with Garrett's urging, made into an unprecedented challenge to the canons of "cool." It was a version of "One Last Kiss," the notorious theme song of the primping, prima donna rock 'n' roll idol Conrad Birdie in the musical *Bye, Bye Birdie*. The story, with its obvious references to the recently drafted Elvis Presley, revolves around the hoopla of Birdie's army induction and his highly publicized farewell concert in Sweet Apple, Iowa. Composers Charles Strouse and Lee Adams carefully crafted "One Last Kiss" with enough verbal simplicity and metronomic repetition to be the ultimate hip-swiveler parody.

Thinking back on the circumstances for its inclusion, Vee admits to being initially puzzled: "It was clear to me it wasn't a rock 'n' roll song. It was a follow-up to 'What Do You Want?' 'One Last Kiss' could have been written in the mid-fifties, in a Broadway musical. I grew more on that session. It was one of those mile markers for me. It took me in a different direction and held up with Snuffy's intentions. Looking back, it's one of the best records I made. I knew it was a satire. It was coming from a different place and was beautifully produced. But at the time, I wasn't happy with it."

Vee was quite comfortable with songs that were both blithely romantic and playful. His voice shared the natural glister of contemporaries such as Johnny Tillotson, who came from a country music background but, with Top 40 entries that included "Poetry in Motion," offered a reprieve from orally aggressive loutishness. Among the most appropriate Vee vehicles was his second album's opening track. Judging by the words alone, "Rubber Ball" (written by Gene Pitney under his mother's name, Ann Orlowski) is a celebration of happy masochism. But, thanks to the generous studio doctoring and Vee's knack for transmitting a kittenish gleam through the impersonal circuitry, the message came out sounding doe-eyed instead of demeaning.

"Rubber Ball" also turned out to be Vee's second gold record. This was Vee's entry into the art of double-tracked vocals—an extra kick that jibed with the sugar rushes of fluttering strings, a brisk snare drum, and cheery coaxing from Johnny Mann's female choristers. In essence, "Rubber Ball" was Bobby Vee's first major release to function as a benevolent audio drug—an impact that retains its power to this day.

"I call it melodic singing," Snuff Garrett contends, nurturing his soft side. "If you have a really good song, you want to present it in what you picture its best light. I would not have been really good at making garage records. I like pretty, unrequited love songs. Simple, wonderful songs are the name of the game. They are harder to come by than people think they are. Vanilla music is nice. I like vanilla. I like the smell. It's perfect for me."

Vee's prospects became even brighter when he commingled with a husband-and-wife team that was earning a reputation as the cream of Brill Building songwriters. Gerry Goffin and Carole King contributed several tracks

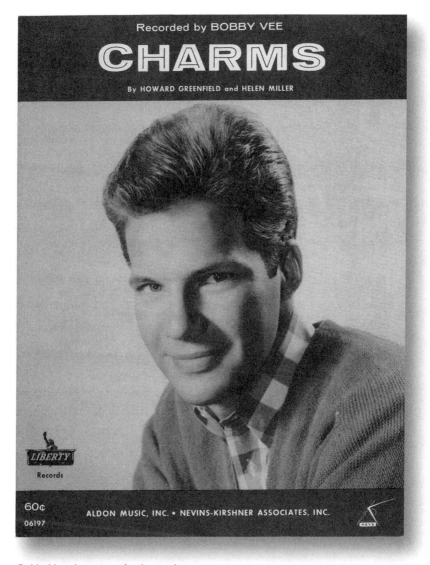

Bobby Vee: the voice of a dream date.

to Vee's next LPs, *Take Good Care of My Baby* and *A Bobby Vee Recording Session,* both of which were recorded at Hollywood's United Studio on Sunset Boulevard. The first album's title song, which was also the first Goffin-King single release to buttress the Vee mystique, marked (for those still keeping score) the singer's ascent to *Billboard*'s #1 spot.

Over forty years since its release, Vee provides an apt assessment of the record's ingredients: "If you break down 'Take Good Care of My Baby,' you hear these lush pizzicato strings that are quite simple; you hear a guitar going *chink-chink, chink.* You can break it down to four or five pieces. Ernie Freeman was a master of simplicity. Earl Palmer's drums were also important. On 'Run to Him,' they were almost nonexistent, but with a nice steady pulse—a slowed down, modified rockabilly beat unusual for a drummer from New Orleans, where much of the music was swing or shuffle. The backbeat wasn't a big snare drum, it was the hi-hat—two cymbals on a stand—very simple."

Vee's Goffin-King songbook became increasingly intricate and, at times, idiosyncratic. His interpretation of "Will You Love Me Tomorrow?" contrasted with the version that the Shirelles had previously belted out. Instead of moaning and sweating like an Elvis or a Roy Orbison, Vee donned vocal velvet gloves, opting for a mild-mannered, understated approach that called attention to the sobworthy lyrics. The song's theme is, after all, about an insecure lover who senses his heartthrob's waning interest. What better way to present it than through near-shivers?

A Bobby Vee Recording Session included, with Vee's avid approval, other Goffin-King treasures that included "Sharing You," "A Forever Kind of Love," and an especially florid ballad called "My Golden Chance." All three demonstrated Vee's affinity for nectarous tonal patterns, particularly when he dramatized stories about unfulfilled desire couched in deceptively euphoric song structures. "A lot of the old songs from the fifties and sixties," Vee once observed, "were sad songs done in a happy way."

In 1962 David Wolper and Lew Erwin produced a television documentary about Vee's life and career called *The Idol.* The designated song was initially "Teenage Idol," a forlorn ballad that a United Airlines pilot composed and that Ricky Nelson ended up appropriating, to international acclaim. Goffin and King came to the rescue. In the spirit of Paul Anka's "Lonely Boy," their song "The Idol" tells of a privileged emotional castaway, all alone despite the throngs of adoring fans that surround him.

As he continued to map Vee's orchestral strategies, Ernie Freeman also worked with Vic Dana, who briefly substituted for Gary Troxel in the Fleetwoods and became another dapper balladeer of the good-guy variety. Born Samuel Mendola Jr. in Buffalo, New York, Dana started out as a dancer, but he grew into a dark, handsome, and shy singer. Dana's appealing, reedy tenor fit well with Freeman's orchestral twinkle on songs such as "More (Theme from *Mondo Cane*)" and a pop rendition of the country ditty "I Love You Drops." His most poignant Freeman arrangement, however, was also responsible for his ascension to fame. "Little Altar Boy," a sad yet spiritually majestic number about the confessions of a world-weary sinner, would live on as a Christmas favorite years after its initial appearance in the autumn of 1964. Dana tended to cover songs tailored more toward adult audiences, such as "Red Roses for a Blue Lady"—a factor that lured him from his gravity-free teen appeal into the denser Wayne Newtonian physics associated with Vegas singers.

While Dana decorated Memory Lane with versions of Robert Maxwell's "Shangri-La" and Dick Glasser's "I Will," Vee continued to address teens and post-teens with his own songwriters' cornucopia. Along with the reliable supply of Goffin-King and Jerry Keller numbers, Barry De Vorzon, who would go on to become a major producer, contributed "The Opposite," which Vee describes as "a sort of reverse twist on the cause and effect of love." The team of Robert Feldman, Gerald Goldstein, and Richard Gottehrer contributed "A Letter from Betty" and a teasingly self-referential number about romantic frustration called "Bobby Tomorrow." Vee's career hit a few snags, particularly with the Jack Keller–Bill Buchanan teardropper "Please Don't Ask About Barbara," which Dick Clark, in the process of divorcing a wife also named Barbara, refused to allow on *American Bandstand*.

By 1963, when he released the LP *The Night Has a Thousand Eyes*, Vee had also added Burt Bacharach and Hal David to his family of tunesmiths. They had Vee specifically in mind when writing the pep rally "Be True to Yourself." As Bacharach played a hyperactive piano, Vee conformed to the composer's frenzied note fluctuations and successfully relayed the "follow your heart" dictum. The album's title song, however, was a Vee milestone. "The Night Has a Thousand Eyes" continues to be among the most original 1960s tunes. Starting out with a jaunty rhythm and pizzicato, it soon meanders into an exotic, snake-charming melody (perhaps as an oblique association of the song's title to the Arabian *1,001 Nights* tale). Among the song's composers is a Marilyn Garrett—a female alter ego in the world of "Snuffy" pseudonyms. "That's my credit," Garrett admits years later. "That was the second-highest selling single I ever had with Bobby—one of my two or three favorite records."

Vee immediately followed "Night" with the Howard Greenfield–Helen Miller composition "Charms"—undoubtedly the most vanilla of Vee's Top

40 recordings, and a repertoire standout. Starting out with sparkly chimes reminiscent of the misty music box that opened Buddy Holly's "Everyday," the melody soon alights onto a gentle backbeat until the strings enter by the second verse to carry Vee through to the end. Vee appreciates how the song is "a little unique even in my collection. When I go out and work, I do all the Top 10 records. It is the first song on the list of requests; the second is 'Please Don't Ask About Barbara.' Both songs dropped off the edge because they weren't in the top of the charts. As time marches on, people don't care much about numbers and chart positions (if they remember them at all). What they care about is how the music affected them personally."

Like many recording artists who continued into 1964, Vee was pressured to adapt to Beatlemania. He and Garrett came up with an album called *The New Sound from England*, an attempt to acquire the Mersey beat. A paradox looms in this regard. Spoon-fed rock history states that the Beatles rescued America from the likes of Bobby Vee, yet the Fab Four themselves, especially Paul McCartney, adored Vee's songs. "In the early sixties, I met the Beatles," Vee remembers. "They used to do my songs in Germany, like 'Sharing You,' 'Take Good Care of My Baby,' and "More than I Can Say." They had "Devil or Angel" and "Take Good Care of My Baby" on their demo for EMI. Paul McCartney was enamored with the Brill Building stuff. That was Songwriting 101."

As the 1960s advanced, Vee fell on leaner times. He rebounded a bit with "Come Back When You Grow Up" and the hippy-dippy inflected "Beautiful People," but another side of his life surfaced during the "Summer of Love" in *C'mon Let's Live a Little*—an otherwise forgettable Paramount feature from 1967. In it, Vee played a hillbilly guitarist who saves a girl (Jackie DeShannon) from a car crash and, through his gallantry, wins admission to college. With no trace of smarm, Vee comes across as the gentle and shy guy everyone would expect, even as somewhat uncomfortable with both the camera and the heavy-handed anti-hippie script. But in those moments when he performs, strumming his guitar and staring into space like a tenderhearted misfit, he is the righteous "square" forced to cross paths with a troublemaking campus radical. "You look like a boy without problems," Jackie DeShannon's character tells him at one point in the film. "You're not bugged with this crazy, mixed-up world."

Vee, even in his saddest songs, carried a sonic bounce—in contrast to Bobby Vinton, who based his musical persona mostly on themes about

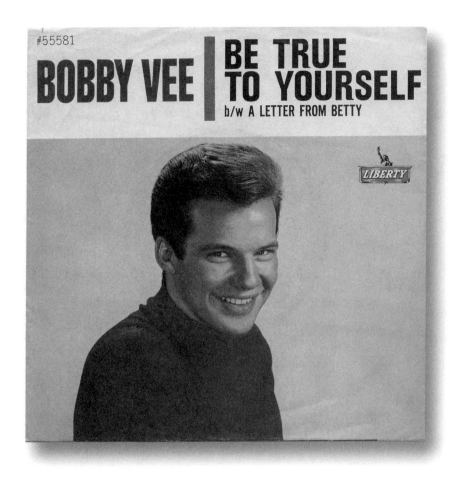

lovelorn solitude. Vinton was the vanilla cream to Vee's vanilla fizz. Though he once modestly described his style as a hybrid of Johnny Mathis and Hank Williams, his singing bears neither Mathis's pampered virtuosity nor Williams's rootsy twang. Even when the Beatles came along and attempted to change many of pop music's rules, Vinton never swayed to fashion's whim.

In an earlier incarnation, Vinton attempted to bring big-band music to Kennedy-era teenagers. He had impressive credentials: a degree in music composition from Duquesne University and knowledge of several instruments. Still, his aspirations to be what he described as "the Lawrence Welk of the younger set" were misbegotten. Desperate to try something new, he offered his singerly ambitions to some of the Epic Records' executives, who thought

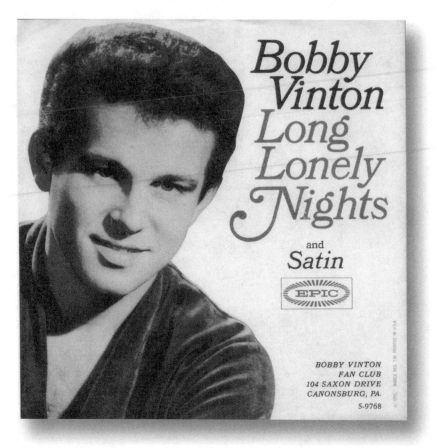

Pop's Lonely Knight.

he was crazy. Undeterred, he rifled through a pile of discarded demos to find a dainty doily of a tune called "Roses Are Red (My Love)." He recorded his own demo and played it for the same cadre of skeptics, who responded with surprised delight. "Roses," with its weepy piano, schoolbook metaphors, and aerated vocal lines, went to #1 by mid-1962.

Producer Bob Morgan, who ascended from his duties at Columbia Records to help set up Epic's ground floor, remembers the "Roses" sessions. "We did two different recordings with arranger Bill Ramal, who was sort of a rock and roll arranger for Johnny & the Hurricanes. Our first approach was kind of that, but Bobby and I didn't care for it. That's when we decided to get Robert Mersey, who went with a country-pop approach."

Vinton continued with his Top 40 roster—satin pillows imbued with melodies of love that could simultaneously calm and heighten pangs of unfulfilled desire. He thrived on a fan base that yearned as much for emotional sustenance as the vulnerable date bait he personified from song to song. On "Let's Kiss and Make Up," "Rain Rain Go Away," and the gloom-inducing Burt Bacharach–Hal David composition "Blue on Blue," he converted near nursery rhymes into believable hymns for the abandoned.

"Bobby had the pathos with the voice," Bob Morgan says. "He had the cry in his voice, he sounded lonely. You get a sense he wasn't a winner; he was looking over his shoulder. He wasn't the aggressor; he was there to be cuddled. He could kiss the girls but wasn't sexually threatening. The songs we did, 'Blue on Blue,' 'Blue Velvet,' 'There! I've Said It Again'—we really knew we had something back then with that particular thing. Vinton felt those songs. It was very honest."

Vinton's songs had moody streaks. No record better demonstrates this than "Mr. Lonely," which he cowrote while serving in the army at Fort Dix. The poignant piano returns, along with a horn section that suggests a variation on "Taps." The lyrics tell of a misty-eyed soldier who languishes through romantic rejection's battlefield. The handwringer's roll call continued with "Coming Home Solder," "Long Lonely Nights," "Satin Pillows," and another he also cowrote simply called "L-O-N-E-L-Y." He could also chime more intricate narratives. "The Days of Sand and Shovels," for instance, tells a time-bending story that combines memories of a childhood sweetheart, a love ruined by infertility, and the reminiscences of "a lonely man who wants to come inside out of the rain."

Without resorting to bluesy histrionics, Vinton managed to pile "heartache on heartache" and win acclaim by exuding anguish while avoiding the toxic backwash associated with nicotine-coated "lounge" singers. And even with a gently swinging backbeat, his songs evoke spooky slow dances, when the ideal prom partner offers a few illusory moments of compassion before strutting away.

England, in the meantime, developed its own Vee and Vinton counterparts—stars who concentrated on grandly orchestrated love ballads, and who featured calibrated dictions that made them sound more American than

Americans. A stellar example is Mark Wynter, who could trill out an amazing Vee-Vinton amalgam in the form of mostly American songs. Born Terry Lewis, he emerged as another "brylcreem boy," a nickname afforded to a crop of young English males who predated the Beatles in teen appeal—and who never went in for all that R&B and skiffle. Sure, the Brits had rock 'n' roll sex symbols, such as Cliff Richard, and pranksters, such as Billy Fury and Marty Wilde, but Wynter was all pop and sunshine, with sparkly elocution, misty blue eyes, and a healthy lack of swagger.

Stylewise, Wynter came close to Craig Douglas, a one-time milkman who, in the late 1950s and early 1960s, entertained youngsters by performing rock 'n' roll with a cleaner vernacular, clearer melodies, and often silky arrangements from bandleaders such as Harry Robinson. Whereas the American gospel-influenced singer Gene McDaniels made the Garden of Eden sound like a sex fest in "A Hundred Pounds of Clay," Douglas converted the same song into one of gilded romance, his delicate and tidy delivery draping Adam and Eve with an audio fig leaf—even before he made an alternate, BBC-friendly version with less suggestive words.

Like Douglas, Wynter had a knack for tune polishing. He also inherited Pat Boone's tendency to sound slightly off-kilter when veering into the higher tenor ranges—an effective method of conveying just how flighty a young man with the romantic shakes can get. But following the commercial success of several songs, including "Dream Girl," his Decca singles started to slow. He switched to Pye Records, where arranger and bandleader Tony Hatch preened his sound all the more. There, Wynter tackled such teen idol fare as "Venus in Blue Jeans," old rock 'n' roll standards like "Only You," Broadway melodies that included Rodgers and Hammerstein's "A Fellow Needs a Girl," and countrypolitan torch songs such as "Love Hurts."

Wynter's presence in the United States was virtually absent, a problem rooted mostly in his penchant for extensively covering American songs. Vee and Vinton had already cornered his American market, at times recording the same material as Wynter. Like many other Bobby Tomorrows, Wynter ended up exercising an appeal in Australia, and he was very comfortable participating with Vee on packaged tours. (They also appeared on the same bill in the 1963 movie *Just for Fun*.) He, like Vee and Vinton, offered teenagers quixotic dreams while satisfying the rules of an old BBC memorandum (which was equally applicable in America) that the optimum entertainment would be "to blend the maximum of wholesome brightness with the atmosphere of quiet leisure about the hearth."

"I feel like everybody's brother," Vee chuckles when assessing his legacy. "People came to me because my music is accessible. But people get to a place in their psyche about when something gets so popular, and they look for something more cutting-edge. It's like in that James Dean movie when the kids have the chicken race. Reckless abandon makes better copy. That's the reason pop music hasn't shown well in the Rock and Roll Hall of Fame. If there's one good quality to the music I made, it was honest. I was doing the best I could do. I'm not a schooled musician or a jazz singer. I just want to hear what's in somebody's heart. I want them to be themselves."

4

Johnny Angelfood

Shivering in Heaven

As her voice flowed through the echo-rich studio like a disembodied wave, Shelley Fabares was anxiety personified. The role of the young Mary Stone on *The Donna Reed Show* may have elevated her to television royalty, but when it came time to make her first single, she felt entirely alone in that isolated chamber. The producers and engineers at Colpix Records were fortunate enough to absorb this panic mode into their circuits the day she recorded "Johnny Angel."

Shelley Fabares was a good example of how some of pop's most memorable stars had no previous musical training. "I'm not a singer," she told one reporter. "I was a very good, very sweet little girl who was not raised to say no, so it took a lot for me to say that." This was obviously not a performer trying to impress upon the listener any virtuoso pretenses, a modesty that may partly account for her delicate, tentative style. Like the early Frankie Avalon ballads, Fabares's "Johnny Angel" was spotless and vulnerable. She sang with a refreshing lack of "technique" that would likely take wizened jazz singers years of *unlearning* to approach.

Like many such ballads that endured through the years, "Johnny Angel" embodied melodic sweetness, romantic yearning, and, for good measure, shiver-inducing suggestions of the afterlife. The arts of over-dubbing and echo that gave the record its power were technological staples at the Colpix studios, where other media-friendly singers including James Darren (and later the Monkees) recorded. Producer Stu Phillips, the studio mastermind who would also arrange and produce impressive records by the Hollyridge Strings and the Doodletown Pipers, served as Fabares's guide into the acoustical unknown.

Phillips started out with different ideas for "Johnny Angel." "These writers gave me a copy of the music while I was on the elevator," he recalls. "In my head I was hearing this thing slightly on the jazzy side. I'm singing it to myself this way. I just had the lead sheet. I sat down and said I had to do it

differently. We went instead for a 'chach' beat—a term I devised for the 'cha-cha-cha.' It had a kind of slightly pop Latin feel that appeared on many up-tempo ballads of the day in the early sixties. The 'chach' is essentially a 'Begin the Beguine' beat done in a rock-pop mode. It was used on Frankie Avalon's 'Venus' and on 'Johnny Angel.' Many of the people in the business were using this. These were the days of Bobby Vee."

The Blossoms, a studio group that provided the actual voices behind such Phil Spector offerings as the Crystals' "He's a Rebel," backed Fabares with an ultra-feminine volley of "sha-lum-da-das." Spector, who usually preferred his music with an R&B rumble, attempted to achieve his own angelic chorus early in his career with the Paris Sisters. But even on songs such as their most famous "I Love How You Love Me," with the flowing violins and airy acoustics, lead singer Priscilla discolored any creamy vanilla potential with shady swirls of sexual innuendo.

Donna Reed's producer-husband Tony Owen would never allow Fabares to communicate such a mixed message. An absolute control monger, he insisted that she do songs that reinforced her television image. Just as Disney exercised enough browbeating power over post-Mouseketeer Annette Funicello to ensure she never exposed her navel in beach movies, Owen nixed Fabares's first planned recording—the rather risqué-sounding "I'll Do Anything You Want." "Johnny Angel" was a more appropriate teen anthem—the brainchild of *Jackie Gleason Show* writer Lyn Duddy and Lee Pockriss (who also wrote "Catch a Falling Star" and "Itsy Bitsy Teenie Weenie Yellow Polka-Dot Bikini").

Stu Phillips remembers how Fabares's musical shortcomings became a strategic asset: "For 'Johnny Angel,' I was working with a singer who had little to offer the performance until we got into the studio, and I discovered there was a song. And then I started to experiment. Shelley could do a double voice perfectly—she was used to looping because she was an actress. All those actors were used to looping on film. But when you asked real singers to double up, they would always sing differently every time."

To convey Fabares's heavenly aspirations, Phillips had her voice scale the trebly heights, stressing what sound engineers call the "high end." "Much of this has also to do with frequency and the high end of the spectrum," he notes. "But starting with the Rolling Stones, the bottom and the bass became the big thing. I used to carry a Rolling Stones record in my briefcase to demonstrate that a low level can be done. The big rage became low-end, but it's easier to control the high and mid-range."

In March 1962, "Johnny Angel" glided across the airwaves and into millions of American ears when Fabares performed it on a special episode of her television series. By the following month, *Billboard* had placed it at #1. Subsequent records, which included her follow-up single, "Johnny Loves Me," and teenage updates of standards such as the Sammy Cahn–Jule Styne favorite "The Things We Did Last Summer," as well as the perk of starring alongside Elvis Presley in three movies, could never eclipse Fabares's initial blip on the pop cultural radar—that ghostly glow of a tune that embodied the best of what would be known as the era's "girl group" sound.

In a 1967 issue of *High Fidelity* magazine, the late, great pianist Glenn Gould identified such singing as part of a "Gidget syndrome." For him, the lack of gutsy grunts "minimizes the emotional metamorphosis implicit in these songs, extracting from the text of each the same message of detachment and sexual circumspection." Oddly, the songbird he had in mind was Petula Clark, who (like her American counterpart, Lesley Gore) seemed more of a husky belter—at least from a Fabares-enhanced perspective. Gould, with a patronizing ear that was prone to regard *all* pop singing as less than "authentic," discerned in Clark the kind of sonic abstraction that Fabares mastered without guile. For Gould, when Clark's voice materialized on his radio, the songs (recorded under her arranger-husband Tony Hatch) emphasized "some aspect of that discrepancy between an adolescent's short-term need to rebel and long-range readiness to conform."

Fabares's near-whispers ironically make the emotions in the song all the more apparent, all the more naked. Perhaps director David Lynch thought of her when he included that waif of a chanteuse Julee Cruise on his *Twin Peaks* series. Standing forlorn in a flowing prom gown and buttressed by Spectorish "Wall of Sound" acoustics, Cruise sang of doomed love and lives, subjects that Lynch made all the more demonic by dressing them in an angel-food exterior that, decades before, was a guilt-free pleasure requiring no patina of "camp" for validation.

Sirens from the Big and Small Screens

Others before Fabares cultivated a similar angel-food approach. Hollywood's paragon of good behavior, Debbie Reynolds, had a more conventionally full voice, but she helped set a precedent for teen appeal with her 1957 release of "Tammy," the Oscar-nominated Jay Livingston–Ray Evans theme from *Tammy and the Bachelor*. Reynolds also tackled the title role of a bayou naif who falls in love with a wounded air pilot (played by the ever-placid Canadian Leslie Nielsen). Although Reynolds affected a heavy Southern accent throughout, the movie pauses for a magic moment when her character stares from an attic window and lapses into romantic reverie, while transmitting the song in good, clear American English. The song was definitive enough to go straight from the film to a single, complete with Joseph Gershenson's orchestra and Henry Mancini's arrangement intact.

Though response to *Tammy and the Bachelor* was initially lackluster, the song went to *Billboard*'s #1 spot by July of that year—a godsend that enticed Universal Studios to rerelease the film. The movie then proceeded to make such a favorable impression that Reynolds became typecast into playing sweet ingenues and benign variations thereof, a trend that culminated in the title role of the movie *The Singing Nun* in 1966. Even many years later, as Reynolds sweated under the Vegas lights with her own hotel, casino, and Hollywood movie museum, audiences continued to assail her with "Tammy" requests. She graciously complied, but most likely abused her fans in her attempt at a rap version.

As early as the mid-1950s, "champagne music" master Lawrence Welk drafted his own counterrebels, the Lennon Sisters, in a low-key musical culture war. When he introduced the singers to his weekly television show on Christmas Eve 1955, Dianne, Peggy, Kathy, and Janet Lennon were extremely well received. The deluge of phone calls, letters, and telegrams that flowed into the ABC network's office made their appearance with Welk mandatory just about every Saturday night for years afterward, as they performed numbers like "Mickey Mouse Mambo" and chimed selections from their 1957 album *Let's Get Acquainted*.

The Lennon Sisters, joined by Welk's "Sparkling Strings," recorded a gleaming version of a Gene Austin tune from the 1920s called "Tonight You Belong to Me." They were upstaged that same year, however, by Patience and Prudence McIntyre, another sister act from Los Angeles. Patience & Prudence's follow-up single, "Gonna Get Along Without You Now" (previously recorded by Teresa Brewer, and later by the Caravelles, Skeeter Davis, and Trini Lopez), was a model of beautiful, plucky orchestration, with the young ladies' enterprising dad, Mark McIntyre, arranging. But they did not have a much easier time in the music business than did the Lennons. Despite their sizeable share of young fans, they somehow could not find a secure niche with promoters, who were seeking a rougher edge. Their offhanded portrayal in the 1978 Alan Freed biopic *American Hot Wax* gives some indication of the contempt that those entrusted with rock 'n' roll history heap upon the lighter 1950s stars who often traveled in the same packaged publicity caravans with the harder ones.

The Lennon Sisters, however, stayed in the public eye, even though other youngsters eventually felt peer pressure to curb their enthusiasm, primarily

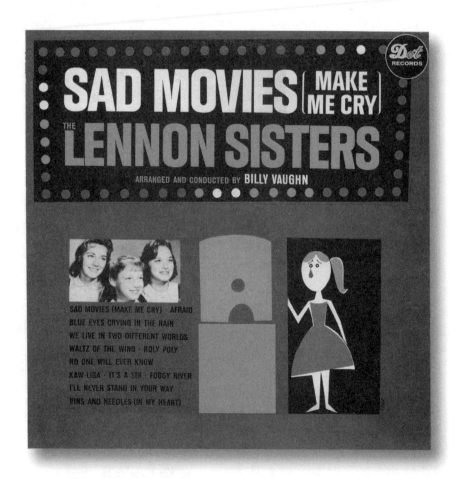

because of their Welk association. In 1961 the Lennon Sisters released "Sad Movies Make Me Cry," a hallmark of precise harmony, yet the country crossover singer Sue Thompson, significantly older than the song implied, managed to hijack listeners' attention with her simultaneous release. Nevertheless, among all the girl groups to emerge in the 1950s and 1960s, the Lennon Sisters had the most contoured tone. Instead of veering off into different pitches in the standard barbershop mode, their voices melded with seemingly no effort; at times listeners had difficulty telling them apart. Their smoothness was not a contrived technique, but the kind of singing attributable to their middle-class Catholic upbringing, and to their adoration of Mantovani and Perry Como.

Layers of Sonic Chiffon

Despite their barbershop quartet ties, the Chordettes layered on spun sonic chiffon when adopting more of a choirgirl stature. When the Sheboygan, Wisconsin, natives started out, Carol Hagedorn (later Buschman) provided baritone, Janet Ertel (later Bleyer) sang the feminine equivalent of bass, Virginia "Jinny" Osborn offered tenor, and Dorothy Hummitzsch (later Schwartz) sang lead. The notion of such an all-girl act was still renegade enough in their province to elicit amazement whenever gaggles of barbershoppers gathered for various conventions. Fortunately, Jinny's father, O. H. King Cole, happened to be president of the Sheboygan chapter of the Society for the Preservation and Encouragement of Barbershop Quartet Singing in America.

Their first albums were done a cappella, and the Chordettes felt a bit awkward with studio instruments when they began recording with arranger-producer Archie Bleyer at Cadence Records. Their first single, released in 1954, was a pretty waltz called "True Love Goes On and On." The group had undergone personnel changes around this time, and it now consisted of Buschman on baritone, Ertel as bass, Margie Needham on tenor, and Lynn Evans providing lead. By April of that year, they proved to be more than Andrews Sisters clones by cultivating a much silkier manner. The McGuire Sisters, who had replaced them as regulars on *Arthur Godfrey's Talent Scouts* by 1953, tended to command a more adult-oriented, Vegas-bound look and style, but the Chordettes' gift for converting songs into childlike lullabies was indisputable once they shined a "magic beam" over the pop landscape with "Mr. Sandman."

"Mr. Sandman" opens with the ear-tickling human chime effect—the celebrated "bum, bum, bum" that Bleyer tried to turn into a Chordettes trademark. It would, through time, show up in other recordings, such as the Browns' 1959 single "The Three Bells," and years later with the Association's "Cherish." The Chordettes piped out more sound effects to complement the instruments on their follow-up release, "Teenage Goodnight"—another candy-coated dream theme full of echo, celestial accompaniment, and those reliably honeyed inflections. Bleyer took great pains to get that lilting, reverberant effect, even shifting the girls from one New York City studio to the next, then playing out the songs in the enormous Webster Hall before transferring the results to tape. "I can remember Archie saying, 'Sound young!' Carol Buschman recalls. "We tried to sound young, and he would say, 'Younger!' "

Though they detoured into the R&B cover route with a dusted-off version of the Teen Queens' 1956 release "Eddie My Love" and a doo-wop permutation called "The Wedding," the Chordettes worked best with more original material. This was especially true when Bleyer gave their sound an almost intergalactic mystique, as he did on "Echo of Love" (cowritten by German pop orchestral giant Werner Mueller). To achieve the desired effects, the Chordettes chimed the lyrics on one track, listened to the playback, and sang an answer echo on track two for an overlapping, otherworldly dazzle.

They continued to refine their sound on "Soft Sands" that same year. The record, which predates 1960s "sunshine pop," is haunting, yet childlike; drifting, yet precise; florally melodic, yet tight on the harmony. Singing lead this time, Jinny Osborn commanded a diaphanous distinction that floats in the kind of curved audio time that would distinguish a song like the Sandpipers' "Come Saturday Morning" (quite a contrast to the guttural wail on that group's 1958 release, "Lollipop"). The Chordettes rebounded in the early 1960s, spending more time among the seraphim with selections such as their version of Manos Hadjidakis's Oscar-winning title theme to the 1960 film *Never on Sunday*, as well as the record's tingly flipside, "Faraway Star." Other songs, which included Hadjidakis's "White Rose of Athens" and their 1962 interpretation of "Wooden Heart" (the Bert Kaempfert tune that Elvis sang to a marionette in the movie *GI Blues*), took the Chordettes far beyond the barbershop.

Nineteen sixty-three was a magical year for other female singers who celebrated the sugarspun over the homespun. Country singer Skeeter Davis put her Southern accent in braces and created, according to *Billboard*'s four major singles tallies, the most successful crossover record of the year, merging themes of doomed romance and cosmic apocalypse on "The End of the World." The record glistened with gleaming strings and an uncannily ingenuous voice, even though the circumstances surrounding the song were as bleak as its subject. Though it was certainly not a "death disc" in the "Leader of the Pack" mode, Skeeter could think of nothing else but her dearly departed friend Betty Jack Davis (with whom she played in an act called the Davis Sisters). Betty Jack died in the same car crash that Skeeter was lucky enough to survive. Although Nashville producer Chet Atkins suggested she record it as just another sad love ballad, Skeeter associated the song with deeper and darker emotions. By singing it in an uncluttered, little-girl voice, she made the sadness seem all the more tragic—and gave the tune a mood of threatened innocence that would have been drowned out had she performed it in the manner of a seasoned country drawler or a pickled lounge diva.

The Murmaids, from Los Angeles, consisted of sisters Carol and Terry Fischer, along with neighborhood friend Sally Gordon. The quirky keyboardist, singer, and songwriter Kim Fowley, who was the in-house producer for Chattahoochee Records, decided they would be right for a composition by future Bread head David Gates called "Popsicles and Icicles." The record complemented lyrical niceties about "bright stars and guitars" and "drive-ins on Friday night" with a captivating melody and a softly percolating rhythm guitar. Gates also wrote the trio's follow-up single, another wraithlike number called "Heartbreak Ahead." It was released early the following year, just as the Murmaids decided to forsake a recording career for college.

Simultaneously in England, the Caravelles, consisting of two working-class London girls named Andrea Simpson and Lois Wilkinson, offered their own breathy harmony variation. Their workmates encouraged them to cut a demo of "You Don't Have to Be a Baby to Cry," a song found on the flip side of Tennessee Ernie Ford's triumphant single "Sixteen Tons." America's lovable country bumpkin, Ernest Tubb, had also recorded it in 1950. By the time Lois and Andrea were finished with it, however, the tune had lost its homegrown twang and vaporized into an ethereal gem. Adopting the name of a French airline, the Caravelles relayed their sweet rendition across the Atlantic, where it had a second life in the United States.

Jackie Ward's Summer Longings

That same year, Barry De Vorzon and Perry Botkin Jr., who had previously produced Shelby Flint's cotton-soft "Angel on My Shoulder" in 1960, sprinkled more sonic sugardust with "Wonderful Summer." Acclaimed session singer Jackie Ward recorded it, using a first-name alias in order to feel more like the teenager she portrayed on the record.

Jackie Ward, born Jacqueline Eloise McDonnell, was the daughter of a navy officer. She was born in Hawaii, grew up in a small Nebraska town, and came from a family of musicians. She began singing, along with her sisters, in her local church, favoring the alto parts. The sisters formed a trio and entered a radio talent contest that famed bandleader Horace Heidt organized and broadcast nationwide. When their daughters took the prize, Mr. and Mrs. McDonnell became instant stage parents and moved the family to Hollywood. By 1954 the McDonnell Sisters were performing on local Los Angeles station KTLA's *Bandstand Revue*, a show that boasted a format similar to *Your Hit Parade.*

As Jackie Ward, Jacqueline surfaced as the strongest of the brood, and stuck to the musical trade. She would soon find work recording demos of new songs, which were sent to producers who, in turn, assigned them to their favorite label artists. The talented voice breezed along the path from faceless demo maker to full-fledged studio singer, providing the high-pitched wail on Pat Boone's "Speedy Gonzalez" as well as the chirp of maternal comfort food that uttered, "Rice-A-Roni, the San Francisco treat!" Frank Sinatra, Jimmie Rodgers, and Bing Crosby would also profit from Ward's feminine background vocals.

"Wonderful Summer," which Botkin cowrote, tells the bittersweet tale of a girl who meets her "boy of summer" and puts on a happy face when she is forced to say good-bye to him in the fall. The song is sad and sentimental, covering the same thematic ground as others of its ilk, but it also reveals emotional quandaries many have secretly felt at least once in life. The sound of waves, the reverberating drumbeat, and the cooing background chorus commingle into a sonic wash not unlike Phil Spector's Wall of Sound. On "Wonderful Summer," Ward, who used the first name of her daughter Robin for this occasion, stares into the face of heartbreak with noble fortitude.

As a studio entity, Robin Ward came across as every bit the wistful and vulnerable dreamer that Fabares portrayed—an effect due partly to the common practice of recording the voice at a slightly higher speed to bring out its brilliance and make the singer sound less advanced in years. Sometimes studios would even triple-track a song to augment this effect. Several other singers of the era, including Linda Scott ("I've Told Every Little Star") and Marcie Blane ("Bobby's Girl"), were also subjected to this dexterous manipulation of studio knobs. (Even that cock-of-the-walk Chuck Berry was alleged to tweak it up a notch or two.)

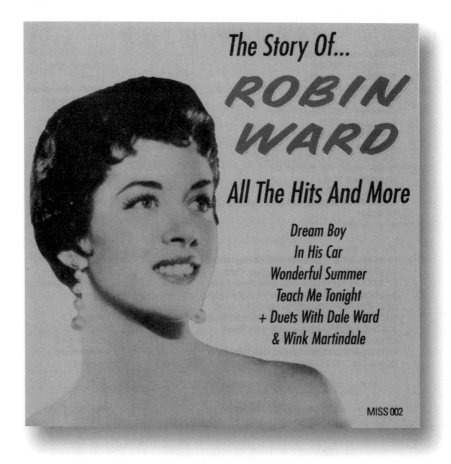

The Story Of...

ROBIN WARD

All The Hits And More

Dream Boy
In His Car
Wonderful Summer
Teach Me Tonight
+ Duets With Dale Ward
& Wink Martindale

MISS 002

As a result of her convincing performance in her role as a teenager in the song, Ward received loads of letters from appreciative young boys who were unaware that the girl sounding sixteen years old was actually a much older woman. Dot Records realized this and released the accompanying *Wonderful Summer* album without her photo—just a sketch drawing of generic teenagers on the beach. Dot also put Ward together with singer Wink Martindale, a man whose clean-cut image and constant presence as a 1960s television announcer suited their duet on a version of the Poni-Tails' 1958 song "Born Too Late." Ward forged ahead in her career as a Hollywood and television ghost voice on *The Carol Burnett Show* and *The Danny Kaye Show*, but her tendency to sound light and sweet posed a bit of a dilemma when she was hired to dub Natalie Wood over Andre Previn's music for *Inside Daisy Clover*. Director Robert Mulligan thought her too slick-sounding for Wood's down-and-out, degenerate character, and Ward was sent back to the studio and told to make her voice sound less innocent.

Ward's career ran the gamut from performing in sessions with the Ray Conniff Singers to singing themes for *Batman* and *Flipper* to participating in backup sessions for stars such as Mama Cass and the first incarnation of the Partridge Family (before David Cassidy stole the show). She appeared on recordings by the Carpenters, Gordon Lightfoot, and Barbra Streisand, as well as on the soundtracks of *Hair* and *Grease*. In the 1970s she chimed the theme to the television show *Maude* and was a background singer on *The Sonny & Cher Show*.

Whether through Fabares's gossamer, the Lennon Sisters' moderate wisps, the Caravelles' near-supernatural cooing, or Jackie Ward's tender exuberance, the Johnny Angelfood years offered palate-pleasing subtleties. "No tricks, no phony stage smiles, no artificial attempts to impress anybody," Lennon Sisters biographer A. H. Parr declares. "Just four sisters, girls with clear, true voices, singing a great song the way the song was written to be sung. The melody filled the room. It seemed to bring everyone sad dreams of things lovely and far away and wonderful."

5

Vanilla Expressionism

Joe Meek's "Paradise Garden"

L ooking like a human ice cream cone with his spindly frame and bleached blond coif, Heinz Burt embodied the teen idol in all his boyish and alien beauty—at least to the eyes and ears of legendary engineer, producer, and songwriter Joe Meek, who peered through the studio glass while Heinz, dubbed "the White Tornado," sang the lines, "I've been told, and I'm sure it's true, that when two lost their hearts, dreams do come true."

Meek wrote "Dreams Do Come True" to celebrate his own auspicious career and to commemorate the cockney-tongued, working-class Brit (of apparent German extraction) who represented nothing less than angelic love. Burt's debut song was also one of Meek's most characteristic offerings—a pretty melody laced with extraterrestrial effects and an electronically enhanced voice that poured across the audio spectrum. Stiff and bracing, lush and sentimental, ornate and wall-bouncing, "Dreams Do Come True" was a plea for a bright future, accented with an edge of dread.

Unfortunately, "Dreams Do Come True" would be a prelude to Meek's worst nightmares. At thirty-three, he was at tether's end. Burt would turn out to be not so much a pop Prince Charming as a smarmy Eddie Cochran imitator who offered only romantic betrayal. Meek's quixotic quests for a soul mate, in a period when British law rendered his passions criminal, proved too frustrating.

Meek made every effort to document this terrified and torn existence in his music. He explored many styles: cheeky novelties about giddy sweethearts; aggressive dirges about coffins, killers, and vampires; Buddy Holly– and Elvis-inspired rockabilly knockoffs; sleazy variations on the Mersey beat; and rollicking instrumentals that brought to mind scenes of the Wild West, the wild surf, and outer space. Meek's most accomplished, ambitious, and biographically inviting works, however, were his glossy ballads.

Due to his incessant use of reverb, his adventures in tape speed alteration, and a penchant for pushing his heavily compressed recordings into the VU meter's red zone, Meek earned a reputation as a musical contortionist. He created his best records and compositions, however, by contrasting elaborate audio layers with often very simple, singsongy airs—a practice more akin to vanilla expressionism. He adopted the sounds and styles of American teen idols but executed them in a much more intense, hysterical fashion. To get a sense of the quintessential Meek ballad, imagine Bobby Vee or Bobby Vinton singing through a tunnel and accompanied by studio musicians who are pumped full of amphetamines.

He was born Robert George Meek on April 5, 1929, in Newent, a rural community near Gloucester, England. A mold-breaker from the start, Meek developed into what his older, more rugged brothers would call "an indoor boy." He was relatively effeminate, preferred putting on skits that involved cross-dressing to sports, liked show tunes, and displayed a dreamy, moody disposition. As expected, his school peers often branded him with the epithet "sissy," but Meek did have at least one decidedly masculine obsession: electronics. He spent much of his boyhood reconfiguring audio appliances, and he enjoyed taping sometimes embarrassing family conversations. Meek had the kind of romantic aspirations usually credited to teenage girls, but his boyish love of horror films intimated a personality teeming with contrasts.

After a stint in the army, he sought his fortunes in London, where in 1955 he took a job as a balance engineer for the International Broadcasting Company (IBC). Within a few months, Meek terrorized his IBC workmates with his bent for sonic unorthodoxy, striking particularly hard at the staid world of "trad jazz." Trad jazz, a variation on Dixieland music, was very popular in postwar England. Most of its players, such as Acker Bilk, Kenny Ball, and Chris Barber, voiced a dislike of any music that smacked of "commercialism," but they were disinclined to shy away from ascending to the pop charts at any given opportunity. Another of the genre's big stars, Humphrey Littleton, recalled in a 1992 BBC Television documentary how, in 1956, Meek cleaned away all of the raw "naturalness" of "Bad Penny Blues" and substituted an array of effects. "Joe over-recorded the drum brushes, and he also did something very peculiar by distorting the left hand of the piano. . . . Had I not gone on holiday, had we all gathered 'round and listened to playback, I would have had a fit. I would have said, 'That's dreadful!' And I would have thrown Joe into one of his sulks. . . . But in fact I wasn't there, and so it all came out like that, and became a hit—I think for those reasons."

With his knob-twisting fixation and desire to stress the trebly high end over the low, Meek became both an innovator and the most popular of IBC's engineers. This did not prevent professional rivals from venting their petty jealousies with catcalls about his erotic proclivities. Sick of the browbeating, Meek abruptly left IBC by 1957. He was again on his own, armed with an expanding repertoire of technical secrets and an obsessive personality guaranteed to ignite more creative sparks and social gaffes.

The imperious Meek did not settle for being a mere engineer or producer. When describing his various recordings, he often implied that he was the actual artist. He had no musical training and was tone-deaf, but his innate sense for catchy commercial melodies gave him license to assume quite a few composer credits. His modus operandi was predictably bizarre. When a tune entered his head, he assigned one of his pianists to transpose his off-key hums onto sheet music.

Meek's aesthetic kinship with Mitch Miller was already evident with his first successful songwriting effort—a softhearted ballad called "Put a Ring on My Finger." Britain's pre-Beatles heartthrob Tommy Steele recorded the song, but the version most remembered is Les Paul's and Mary Ford's echo-redolent American recording, done under Miller's auspices at Columbia. Theirs had reached the *Billboard* Top 40 in 1958 and garnered enough royalties to aid Meek in building his own studio. Meek also incorporated Les Paul's instrumental quirks, brought on primarily by "sound-on-sound" techniques that involved recording one track over another for an otherworldly reverberation, into his own musical repertoire.

Listening to many of Meek's creations, one can sense that the mid-1950s, particularly the years 1956 and 1957, left a major impression on him. Some of his most intriguing early 1960s work reveals a hybrid of two major American releases: Gogi Grant's "The Wayward Wind," with Buddy Bregman's lush strings and horns, and Marty Robbins's "A White Sport Coat (and a Pink Carnation)," with its sparkling Ray Conniff production values. As Dave Adams, who was among Meek's artists and assistants, remembers: "Joe's musical mind was locked in that era, and only the collaboration of a few key musicians, myself included, would bring him at least partway out."

Just as Miller discovered his echo effects through the water closet's reflective tiles, so would Meek refer to his own studio at London's 304 Holloway Road as "the Bathroom." But Miller had the clout of a major label behind him, whereas Meek was essentially England's first independent producer. Instead of investing thousands of pounds in sophisticated equipment, he created ingenious "do-it-yourself" recording methods that years of high-fangled gadgetry and digital maneuvering still cannot duplicate. Dave Adams recalls that, while at the Lansdowne Studio, Meek put up some Lucite folding screen panels to "liven the sound of a very dead room." Among his most notorious crafts, a stretched-out garden gate spring covered in duct tape, was known in Meek circles as the "black box spring reverb."

In Meek's hands, standard studio tools like compressors and limiters, conventionally used to bring the loud and soft tones to a more equalized middle, became dramatic devices. He deployed them to create a belligerent thump that, when paired with sweet strings, constituted a kind of violent vanilla suited to his simultaneously wistful and frantic personality. The end result was sonic overload, purposely fashioned to evoke romantic highs smashing against earthly limits. Meek essentially converted a technological faux pas into an art.

For the record, Meek also played a significant role in the British "string-beat" trend that John Barry jump-started in 1959. Just before he recorded with Adam Faith, Barry brought an Elvis soundalike named Lance Fortune into the Lansdowne Studio. There Meek, still a budding engineer, helped endow the singer with that lilting and reverberant pizzicato backing on a remake of a German song originally titled "All Girls Like to Kiss." Refurbished in English as "Be Mine" (with Barry assuming the name Johnny Prendy), it technically predated Faith's "What Do You Want?" as the first British record to incorporate the Jacobs-Holly innovation.

Charles Blackwell was working as a music copyist when he met Meek in 1957. The two developed a strong professional relationship, which began on a writing collaboration for a song called "Land of Make Believe." Once Meek formed Triumph Records and retained him as his key arranger, the young Blackwell showed an astounding appreciation for ballad orchestrations. And, like Meek, he had a flair for the vanilla extreme, exaggerating the harps, violins, and choirs. "We grew up with the fifties kind of sound," Blackwell reminisces while being interviewed for this book. "It was something we couldn't quite achieve in the English studios. Joe was the first to come up with the goods in that respect. He was very experimental and always tried to achieve loud records—louder than anything else that came on the radio, with lots of compression."

Blackwell helped put Meek on the professional map in 1960 with the highly successful recording of "Angela Jones," a teen theme about schoolboy crushes and stolen kisses that, like other prized Meek productions, resounded with echoing audio. A sleeper of a hit in England, the song was also a vehicle for singer Michael Cox, who gave the lyrics their appropriately twee comportment. Cox was also a rather handsome lad and one of many living testimonies to Meek's apparent conviction that a song is only as pretty as its singer. Many of Meek's vanilla balladeers looked like—and sometimes were—movie stars. In most cases, Meek required his singers to vocalize clearly enough to submit to multiple tape splices and, above all else, literally smile as they sang their words, no matter how lachrymose the subject matter.

Blackwell was there when Meek made a foray into a kind of teenage love song popularly referred to in the early 1960s as a "death disc." The genre's themes, rife with stories about young lovers passing away too early and intimations of a romantic afterlife, were occasionally set to the effects of auto crashes and, more often, the wail of mourning angels. Fate worked in Meek's favor when he forged a friendship with a starry-eyed gentleman and self-styled clairvoyant named Geoff Goddard, who shared Meek's interest in spiritualism. Both were obsessed with Buddy Holly. There was something about the late rock 'n' roller's ghostly voice that enticed them to hold séances, seeking advice (as well as chart and sales predictions) from Holly's spirit. Goddard would even write "A Tribute to Buddy Holly," but the clairvoyant seemed even more possessed by otherworldly forces when he rushed off something that endures as one of Britain's most remarkable pop recordings: "Johnny Remember Me."

John Leyton, a comely actor, had just scored a role in the television series *Harpers West One.* His manager, future Bee Gees maven Robert Stigwood,

wanted to break Leyton into recording and arranged for him to sing Goddard's narrative, which would be produced by Meek and Blackwell. The song's
story was molded right out of Gothic horror: a man relates the passing of the
one he loved, her eerie cries blaring to a jarring rhythm. It galloped to England's #1 spot, and there remained throughout August and September 1961.
Teenagers swallowed the tune up, while some older audiences gave it a mixed
reception best exemplified when comedian Spike Milligan described the
record as "Son of 'Ghost Riders in the Sky'."

Though Leyton's voice on this and some other recordings is too deep and
cowboy compliant to pass itself off as authentic vanilla, the instrumentation, particularly the otherworldly effects, characterizes the gossamer glory of his other,
less strident, ballads. One good example is Leyton's cover of "Tell Laura I Love
Her," which comes across more earnest than America's original 1960 counterpart by the country-influenced, multi-octaved Ray Peterson. The Meek-Black-
well arrangement is more inventive, with touches of Calypso rhythms, dramatic
guitar strums, and cries from Meek's favored soprano, Lissa Gray.

Andy Cavell was another of Meek's pretty-boy discoveries who did not
start out with singerly ambitions. Born Andrew Hatjoulli in Piraeus, Greece,
he initially pursued the photographer's trade. Once again, Meek's instincts
were dead-on when he declared that singing was the lad's higher calling. Cavell
possessed a fragile yet appealing quality, replete with slight traces of a foreign
accent. Including Connie Francis among his favorites, he was comfortable layering tearful affectations on tunes such as "Andy," which Meek composed to
dramatize another amatory rendezvous from beyond the grave. Meek's fascination with the supernatural became so extreme that he took a recording
apparatus into actual graveyards, hoping to capture acoustical delights privy
only to the spirit realm.

Of all the vocal curiosities to emerge from Meek's studio, actor Iain Gregory was perhaps the most controversial. He was already a member of London's Actors Workshop when he met Meek through Robert Stigwood, who
wanted to employ Gregory as both a screen star and a teen idol. Meek agreed
to let him cut a cute, Clavioline-driven ballad called "Time Will Tell," but
Gregory's voice was not conventionally consonant, so Dave Adams assisted as
a guide vocal. Stigwood used "Time Will Tell" to launch a massive publicity
campaign for Gregory, whose next release was the manicured hillbilly treat
"Can't You Hear the Beat of a Broken Heart?" The song was replete with
Blackwell's echoing orchestra, a burnished fiddle, and a regulated beat remi-

niscent of Marty Robbins's "A White Sport Coat." By the time he put out his third Meek single, "Mr. Lovebug," Gregory had established a demure style all his own.

While he often used his own name in song credits, Meek also resorted to pseudonyms such as Robert Baker, Robert Duke, Peter Jacobs, and, to indulge his cheeky sense of humor, Dandy Ward. Many of his tunes were repetitions of childlike patterns that at times suggested the cadence of an off-kilter ice cream truck. His lyrics tended to center on ideal love clad in celestial scenery. In this sense, Meek was engaged in an inner conflict between Heaven and Hell—a spiritual crusade with a renegade battle plan.

"I haven't forgotten how it goes—you meet someone and there's an atomic crash," Pat Boone once wrote to describe his idea of romantic fantasy. "Your heart and knees develop lives of their own and your head gets full of pink cotton. Cupid's guided missile has scored a direct hit. It *must* be True Love." Boone, of course, followed this ecstatic verbiage with a moralistic warning about the hazards of leaping into love too quickly.

Meek was born and grew into the world of pop music at roughly the same time as Boone, but, unlike America's Dean of Clean, who could always lie back on a cushion of Judeo-Christian orthodoxy, Meek had no ideological safety net. This moral challenge made him all the stronger in his resolve never to give up the good fight of remaking the kingdom of Heaven on Earth in his own mind. "All the stars in heaven," one of his songs proclaims, "Can shout we're wrong / But I'll love you forever/ For together we belong."

"I think basically he must have been a religious man," British music publisher Bob Kingston reflected when assessing his time spent with Meek, "because he was searching constantly. He was not a devout churchgoer, but within himself I think he was very much a lost individual. I always thought he was a very lonely person, but you could never really get to know him."

Events in Meek's life make speculations about the homosexual ideal found in his lyrics unavoidable. Many of his ballads may even imply a healthy challenge to the depressing determinism that dictates romance as only a male-female enterprise. "It's difficult to think of more than a handful of Meek songs that are specifically about boy-girl relationships," Frank M. Young writes in his essay "Everybody's Got to Face It One Day: Joe Meek's Songwriting Legacy." "His song lyrics become 'normal' only because those are the expectations of most pop music listeners." Meek's primary biographer, John Repsch, concurs when asked: "I tend to think that some of the songs were written with a boyfriend in mind. You get that impression when you listen to the composing. He would sing sometimes as if he were the girl. It is quite feasible that a lot of his songwriting was stimulated by love for various young men. He had many encounters and quite a lot of food for thought."

One of Meek's very best compositions alluding to such a metaphysical struggle is "Paradise Garden," which scored well in the United Kingdom but unfortunately never made a dent Stateside. Peter Jay, originally Peter Lynch, was in his late teens when Meek discovered him performing in a Mayfair club. Here, Blackwell puts in a session packed with vanilla vigor, opening with an angelic harp and a booming timpani. Pillowy violins and a divine choir lead into Jay's embellishments of Meek's lyrics about a miracle of true romance "so strange and so mysterious." The record's grandeur suggests the loftiness of a Broadway musical performed somewhere over the astral plane; it retains an ambiance closer to Spector's roomy Wall of Sound than is found on other Meek recordings.

Jay's voice had an uncanny similarity to Andy Cavell's, as well as to another in Meek's pop-crooner harem, a former Royal Navy deep-sea diver named Don Charles. Charles had an edge over most of Meek's protégés, however, since he was an actual trained singer. Charles in many ways was the cabaret equivalent of Wally Cleaver and was pictured on his sheet music covers bedecked in preppy sweater attire with immaculately combed waves. He was a big guy, but he delivered his songs like a dignitary. "Most of the young singers today have muscle-bound tonsils," Decca A&R mogul Dick Rowe observed. "Don Charles is different, he tackles a song from the other end of the telescope and concentrates on the words."

Meek enjoyed a positive friendship with Charles and seemed to reserve some of his best original compositions for him. This was apparent when Charles sang another of Meek's invocations to the great beyond. "Walk with Me, My Angel" is arguably Meek's greatest ballad. From the ceremonious drum roll opening, followed by Lissa Gray's high-octave siren call, this is an invocation to celestial companionship like no other. As Charles starts singing, the drums strike a gentle rock-a-ballad beat against the bass and acoustic guitar, while the strings ease into the backdrop and eventually form a countervoice.

Throughout the song, Charles builds the emotional impact into overrecorded mini crescendos, starting with, "No clouds above, no earth below, can hide our love so true." The distortion is apparent each time he reaches the height, such as when he declares, "No blackbird's song can say we're wrong/ The world knows I love only you." As Charles's emotions soar, Meek's VU indicator light flashes in mad crimson. The instrumental interlude gives the violins full control as the choir gets more prominent, all leading to a screeching brilliance and the clarion call of French horns. Like Bobby Vinton, who would achieve a more tempered and less compressed drama on songs like "Coming Home Soldier," Charles invests "Walk with Me, My Angel" with the potent force of a male living out the romantic frenzies that social conventions usually reserved for females.

Another of Meek's more vanilla offerings was Mark Douglas's 1962 single "It Matters Not." Douglas sounds like a teen with a fluttering heart as he utters schoolboy declarations. Meek's in-house band, the Tornados, provides the guitars, which are set against a glockenspiel, a comically clunky clarinet, an angelic choir, iridescent strings arranged by Ivor Raymonde, and lyrics written by Mike Leander (who would become prized for his Mersey beat–era string arrangements for stars like Marianne Faithfull).

In a 1964 interview he gave for a Granada television show, Meek recited a checklist of his prized recording gear essential for such heavenly effects, including a Lyrec twin-track, an EMI TR51 recorder for dubbing, a self-built compressor, a homemade mixer, a Vortexion mixer, a Vortexion tape recorder for tape echo delay, an echo chamber he described as being above his control room, and an electronic echo he had patented. He was particularly proud of his string arrangements. The top-grade musicians accustomed to playing in Mantovani's orchestra would renounce their skepticism about Meek's humble recording quarters once they heard his playbacks:

> The method I use for recording strings is to have a microphone pretty close to them. The four of them sit, two opposite each other, and then the signal I delay with the head of the Vortexion. I feed this back in again, which adds a reflection; which in a way gives you eight strings. And on this, I put my echo-chamber sound and also some of my electronic echo. And this way I seem to get a very big string sound and a very commercial sound. The other instruments are recorded pretty ordinarily. I do add quite a lot of top sometimes to the harp, and a lot of echo on the French horn.

Male balladeers were his specialty, but Meek also had notable girls in his talent pool. Pat Reader is a fine example, though Meek made relatively few sides with her. A direct contrast to Glenda Collins (another Meek songstress, who sang in a rougher manner that was similar to Dusty Springfield), Reader came off soft and gushing. Songs with titles like "May Your Heart Stay Young Forever" combined Connie Francis's teary plaint with the starched-white diction of Vera Lynn. Her frequency blended with the high-pitched violins, rattling drum, and rhapsodizing background chorus of Meek's other major arranger, Ivor Raymonde (who would gain stature primarily for his work with Dusty Springfield).

Even amid the visions of death, rays of vanilla sunshine beckoned from Pamela Blue on another Geoff Goddard "death disc" called "My Friend Bobby," as she sang about a boyfriend whom the Lord took away, in a style not unlike that of America's Marcie Blane or Linda Scott. One music trade magazine provided the ideal endorsement of the song, calling it a "happy sounding tune with deathly lyrics . . . should be a hit, especially if the BBC ban it."

Despite his success in England, Meek is chiefly remembered in America for two songs: the Honeycombs' frenetic stomper "Have I the Right?" and "Telstar," an instrumental by the Meek-formed group the Tornados. Meek was inspired to write the latter after watching a transmission of the first commercial transcontinental satellite beamed through his television on July 10, 1962. Within a half hour, Meek contacted Dave Adams once again to transcribe what was, at the outset, another manic melody.

On "Telstar," Meek melded his romantic and intergalactic yearnings into one heady mixture, full of Clavioline ornamentation and bold strokes of neurotic aggression. A fan of John F. Kennedy and the spaceward era he represented, Meek molded "Telstar" to express his frantic hopes for the world becoming an exciting and technologically immaculate place. Goddard shared Meek's fascination with space. His speeded-up vocals and optimistic regard for interplanetary communication on his 1963 record "Sky Men" left ample impression through the years to inspire an interpretation from the 1990s power pop group the Wondermints.

Given Meek's risky recording approach, however, the actual Tornados members were shocked when returning to the studio from a prior engagement to hear the final results. The redoubtable Heinz Burt, when interviewed about the song many years later, bluntly said that he and his fellow band members thought it "Crap!" The group expected it to be a routine surf-rock guitar number, but it ended up as a tonal wash of high-pitched effects and altered speeds suggesting manic mummers on the moon.

The Tornados' record was too rocky to be vanilla, but Meek ended up putting a creamier texture over the melody when he added words and called it "Magic Star." To perform the song, he chose a fifteen-year-old named Ken Plows, who was singing with a rock 'n' roll band at some coffee bar. Meek renamed him Kenny Hollywood and had him record the song for Decca—a departure for Plows, who was used to bellowing out variations on "Blue Suede Shoes." Mr. Hollywood enjoyed his little brush with fame, even though the single did not sell as well as expected. He was the paragon of the pining "amateur singer"—a factor that enhanced the record's starry-eyed mood.

Sulky and prone to mood swings and outright paranoia about the "rotten pigs" he felt were looming about to steal his technical secrets, Meek could switch from a shy and soft-spoken man into an explosion of accusations and invectives. "One minute he was nice as pie," Hollywood told *Thunderbolt* magazine, "and the next minute you wondered what you'd said, because he suddenly changed. That was the worst thing about Joe. You never knew from one day to the next just how he was going to be. . . . It was great when he was OK, but not so good when he was throwing cups and saucers about."

Meek would also lapse into trances, standing with a blank stare in the middle of the room while those around him stared back in disbelief. But despite these lapses into spiritual darkness, Meek was not a nihilist. Up until his final recording sessions, when he started including more faux R&B-inspired hard rock acts, Meek continued to scoop out as much silky romance as the market permitted.

The Telstar satellite would experience malfunctions and eventually burn out with the earth's nuclear emissions, but Meek retained his space-age optimism with the same sad tenacity with which he held out for honest affection. Legend has it that Meek molded Heinz Burt's peroxided image after the Aryan-like imps who take control of a small town in the 1960 British thriller *Village of the Damned.* Heinz turned out to be, in many respects, Meek's demon child. He not only reinforced his mentor's sense of romantic doom, he also owned the single-barrel shotgun Meek used to shoot himself on February 3, 1967—the eighth anniversary of Buddy Holly's death. Like the insides of that black box that held the secret to his sonic ricochets, Meek left the planet as a tightly pulled wire that finally snapped. A grim story—but one that brings home the deep emotional desperation pervading most vanilla ballads. The listening may be easy, but the stories behind the songs are intense.

6

"Sealed with a Kiss"

America's Shadow Anthem

magine a packed baseball stadium, the eager spectators perched like winged predators, ready at any moment to lash out. For all they know, the guest vocalist entering the heart of the arena is about to kick off the game with another "Star-Spangled Banner," followed by the customary hoots and heckles.

As the unassuming lad grasps the microphone and starts intoning the opening lines to "Sealed with a Kiss," the throng reacts with dead silence all the way through the first verse. But going into the second, and its immortal line, "Guess it's gonna be a cold, lonely summer," the singer triggers an accompanying hum from the bleachers as one onlooker after another starts to sing along. By the time he follows with, "But I'll fill the emptiness," the outpouring of otherwise frustrated voices swells into a gratified chime. The familiar melody and lovelorn words may have been meant for a solitary singer and a lonely guitar, but in this arena, the song has morphed into a far gentler national anthem—one without any of Francis Scott Key's "bombs bursting" bluster.

While waking life has yet to offer such a surreal scenario, Brian Hyland, who introduced "Sealed with a Kiss" to the Top 40 in 1962, relates a remote parallel. "I was down in Florida. Tommy Boyce was my guitar player. We were on a show with Bobby Darin and Marty Robbins. There I was, in the Jacksonville Arena. This had to be the winter of 1962 or 1963. It was a big auditorium across from the Gator Bowl. When I got up there to do 'Sealed,' they hit me with a blue spotlight just as Boyce played the opening guitar spot. I got a standing ovation before I even started singing."

Adopting "Sealed with a Kiss" as his signature song, Hyland, the petite, sweet, and bashful blond who sang from a collective teenage heart, unfurled the definitive breakup ballad—a paean to what psychologists have since labeled "seasonal affective disorder." He also became, without realizing it, a troubadour for his nation with this perfect shadow anthem that encompasses the angst and romantic uncertainty lurking beneath America's otherwise optimistic spirit.

"Sealed with a Kiss" also had a pre-Hyland history. As the 1960s dawned, songwriters Gary Geld and Peter Udell were up-and-coming tunesmiths. Lyricist Udell once worked as a stock boy for a publishing company owned by his mentor, the composer Frank Loesser, before he and Geld formed their own publishing company and collaborated on other Hyland recordings, including "Let Me Belong to You" and "Ginny Come Lately."

During a recent telephone conversation, Udell recollected looking out the window of Geld's Manhattan walk-up apartment near Central Park West when the immortal lyrics rose in his head: "I kept wanting to write a consummate summer romance kind of song. I already had the title in mind, but Geld kept begging me to use the acronym 'S.W.A.K.' I thought to myself, I don't like that. He kept begging me. I said I'd write it but that it should be called 'Sealed with a Kiss.' Those words came very quickly, but up till then it took me six years to write a good summer song. We thought of the Brothers Four, but the Four Voices recorded it. The record was very popular in Cleveland but went nowhere else."

The Four Voices, a Columbia harmony group, made a previous Top 40 appearance in 1956 with "Lonely One." They sounded quite a bit like the Four Lads (especially with Ray Conniff's arrangements), but by 1960 they were ready to explore the folkish vogue. Their interpretation of "Sealed," with just a pensive acoustic guitar for backing, was a beautiful and gentle blend that delivered the melody in a simple yet sweet and affecting manner. This was also the way the composers imagined it sung.

Brian Hyland became a troubadour for his nation with this perfect shadow anthem that encompasses the angst and romantic uncertainty lurking beneath America's otherwise optimistic spirit.

Hyland had previously joined the teen idol roster in 1960 with "Itsy Bitsy Teenie Weenie Yellow Polka-Dot Bikini." This debut ditty became such a symbol of postwar teenage culture that director Billy Wilder used it (sung by another artist) in the comedy *One, Two, Three* to satirize Cold War fears of Communist brainwashing tools. Larry Fine of the Three Stooges, a cousin by marriage, also plugged Brian's song on a local New York television show. Hyland's first album, *The Bashful Blond*, followed, reinforcing the singer's "bikini boy" reputation with other humorous tracks that included "Cozy Little Compact Car" and "Don't Dilly Dally, Sally." Still, his bright and refreshing style helped him project the aura of life's elusive dream date; at times, he even sang with a bit of a country accent, despite the fact that he was bred in Queens, New York. With sweet interludes such as "Rosemary," as well as revivals of chestnuts that included "A—You're Adorable" and "I Don't Know Why (I Just Do)," the album indicated that he was ready to take on more tenderhearted material.

Epic Records wanted Bobby Vinton to record "Sealed with a Kiss," but the future "Polish Prince" declined, leaving Hyland to fill the void as he moved over from Kapp Records to ABC-Paramount. "In 1961 I started working professionally with Geld and Udell," Hyland recalls. "We were looking at 'Sealed.' I liked the chord progression; it was unusual compared to most of the pop records. When the Four Voices did it, they sounded like the Brothers Four, with a 'Greenfields' type of arrangement."

Working with arranger Stan Applebaum, Hyland, Geld, and Udell took a different approach. Anyone who thinks he or she does not remember the song is likely to have instant recall when hearing the first creamy vanilla notes: the tingly electric guitar and acoustic strums, the hypnotic percussion, the delicate bass line, and the moody harmonica that melds so well with the background choir and Hyland's multitracked tenor. As he speculates on the long summer ahead, promises to send more love letters, and voices his "pledge to meet in September," Hyland celebrates a milestone in post–Tin Pan Alley tunesmithery.

Today, Hyland remains enthralled by Applebaum's work on the session: "Whenever I do live gigs, people are under the impression there are violins. It lends itself to that. There are voices doing what the strings should be doing. Geld, the writer, sketched out a lot of that stuff before he brought it to Applebaum. It was all done live at the Bell Sound Studios. I was there on the floor singing in a booth."

Hyland supplies another arena-related anecdote: "We were out on the road around 1991 or '92. We had a day off in Kansas City and parked a renta-car in the Kansas City Royals Stadium, where 'Sealed with a Kiss' was playing over the stadium's PA as we arrived for the game. The biggest and most memorable venues singing 'Sealed with a Kiss' would be the giant, packed soccer stadiums in Buenos Aires that seated 75,000 to 100,000. This was during Carnival in the early to mid-sixties. A truly amazing experience!"

A few years later, Gary Lewis & the Playboys reintroduced "Sealed" in a strained and key-deficient manner that Lewis hates, but even after forty or so years, still transmits all the honesty and sadness that won fans over in the otherwise mean summer of 1968. Even as a personal statement, Lewis's version resonates with an autobiographical dread of departure from familiar places. Being perhaps the only prominent pop star at the time to be a Vietnam-era conscript, this was the first recording he made while on leave.

Santo & Johnny, the Ventures, and the Shadows gave "Sealed" a surf guitar tribute. The Lettermen, the Happenings, and the Everly Brothers harmonized to it. Bobby Vee provided a late 1960s rendition, while Bobby Vinton finally put out his adult contemporary tribute in 1972. International vocalists such as Daniel O'Donnell, Niemen Natalia, and Olympic Bobek spread it across the globe. In 1989 Australian teen idol and soap opera star Jason Donovan took a breather from his usual dance-track repertoire to give it new blood, his sweet voice modulating between power guitars and a softly synthesized backdrop. The early 1980s even saw a predictably sacrilegious send-up from the Surf Punks.

Still, Hyland remains the song's true spokesman: "It has a signature riff at the beginning with the guitar—when I play that riff, there's a hush, and it gets everyone's attention. Girls would be screaming. That would really generate a lot of excitement in the audience. But a lot of the feedback from the song is from people who would come up to me over the years and say they remember a specific incident in their lives when they heard it. It really meant a lot to them. That particular story was their story at the time."

"The concept was thought out for the kids who buy the records," Udell declares with mercenary modesty. "It was for those who have love affairs that end when summer comes and they are headed for camp. I tell the same story in 'Save Your Heart for Me.' Jerry Ragovoy, who wrote rock 'n' roll songs such as 'Time Is on My Side' and 'Piece of My Heart,' used to kid around and say he was very jealous of me because he could never hear his stuff on Muzak. He finally said to me that music is more important than lyrics, because when you go into an elevator you never hear 'Lyrak.' He then called 'Sealed with a Kiss' an elevator song."

Hyland also cherishes the praise he received from professional peers: "In 1969 I went up and saw Elvis in Las Vegas. After the show, we went around the side to meet him. He came out of the dressing room; they introduced me; he told me he loved the song." A few years later, during a New Orleans engagement, Hyland got more encouraging words from Allen Toussaint, the arranger, producer, and all-around musical polyglot known mostly for R&B acts such as Dr. John and Patti Labelle: "He told us he thought the melody for 'Sealed' was so strong, you could play it with a trumpet and it could be a hit."

After "Sealed," Hyland went on to interpret other Geld-Udell creations, including the countrified "Warmed Over Kisses (Left Over Love)" and the lushly orchestrated "If Mary's There"—each with Stanley Applebaum's sugardust embellishments. Geld ended up also handling the arrangements on Hyland's "Save Your Heart for Me" and "I'm Afraid to Go Home"—two songs that reveal the singer's sweet and moody styles, respectively.

In 1966 Hyland went over to Philips Records, under Snuff Garrett's production, and worked with arrangers Al Capps and Leon Russell. According to Garrett, Hyland's comeback song, "The Joker Went Wild," boasted an acoustical gimmick with a cute backstory: "I was working with Al Capps. We're in the studio; we finish the date, and I play the track back. I saw a set of vibes that belonged on *The Lawrence Welk Show*. This was about one or two o'clock in the morning. I asked Al if he ever played vibes. We set up the vibes and played 'The Joker Went Wild.' I called Mr. Welk the next morning and told him I owed him some money for breaking the lock. He gave me a key next time he saw me."

Hyland rode out the rest of the 1960s with other pleasant musical interludes, including "Holiday for Clowns" and "Stay and Love Me All Summer." Then Del Shannon became his producer in 1970 and had him dip into a less amiable direction with "Gypsy Woman." But Hyland retains his rightful place as a sweet-natured balladeer. He likes to conclude interviews by sharing the proud moment when he got kudos from one of the few figures in the 1990s and beyond to promote the dying art of traditional melody: "On our last tour in England, in the fall of 2002, we played the last night at the Palladium, and Andrew Lloyd Webber was in the audience. At a shindig after the show, he said to me that 'Sealed with a Kiss' was a classic, and that it meant a lot to him. He thought the construction of the song and the record had a life of its own, and that the song was going to be around a long time."

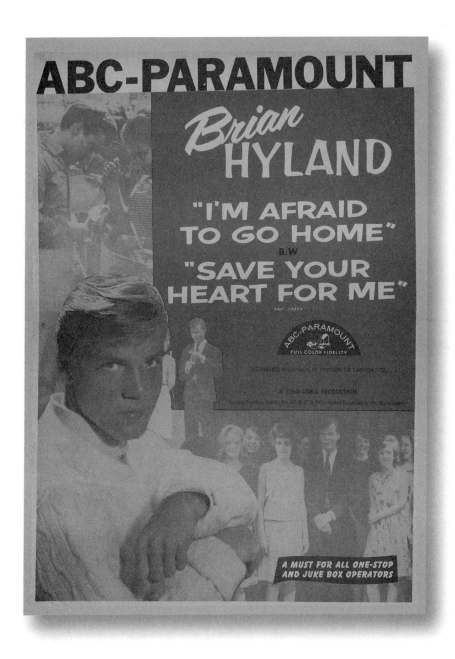

7

Summerchime

Sunshine Pop's Precursors

"Rhythm of the Rain"—The Cascades

Solitary wayfarers, vulnerable to idle thoughts and hallucinations, may occasionally encounter tonal patterns chattering across the sky. Such ciphers result from a combination of bizarre weather patterns and phantom radio signals that still hover in the stratosphere from decades-old broadcasts. Some who encounter them may experience spiritual epiphanies; others have momentary lapses of clairvoyance. But those with the wherewithal to transpose them into a song are specially gifted.

One night in 1961, during his U.S. Navy tour of duty, the musically driven John Claude Gummoe thrived under such an electric sky. Sitting aboard the USS *Jason AR-8*, gazing at the Aleutian Islands and braving the crashing waters, he started feeling misty-eyed for family and friends. The muse finally goosed him with the first thunder crack. Sizing up nature's fury, Gummoe started composing the words and melody to "Rhythm of the Rain."

Gummoe, who today sounds as gentle and youthful as he did the first time he sang the tune with his group, the Cascades, has vivid recollections of those lightning-charged moments. "When you're in a situation like that, it's very dark. You're up there on the bridge of the ship; relatively alone. It's the

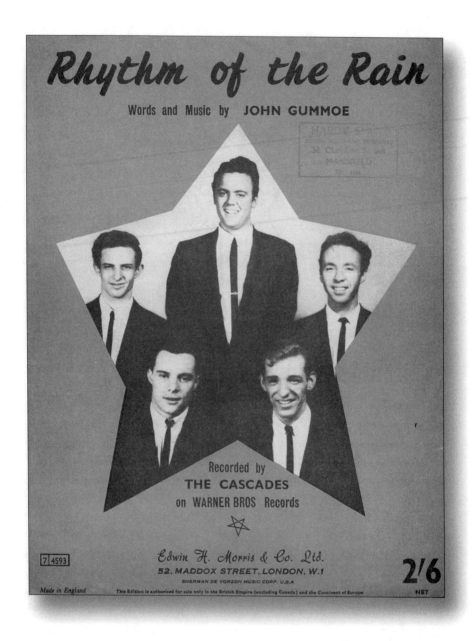

middle of the night and raining. And you're away from home. You're away from everything you're familiar with. That lonely kind of feeling had an effect on me as I was putting everything together. I actually had the lyrics in my head before I wrote chords."

Gummoe's collaboration with climatic foul play forged a lasting impression on American pop. Years after its release in November 1962 and its presence in *Billboard*'s Top 5 by January 1963, "Rhythm of the Rain" received BMI's Special Citation of Achievement in recognition of over six and one half million broadcast performances. BMI also listed it in its Top 100 as the ninth most performed song of the twentieth century.

The Cascades germinated in 1960 during Gummoe's navy days at the San Diego home port. He was enamored with the Silver Strands, a local singing group that entertained at area clubs. Starting as the group's manager, he eventually became a member, lending a dulcet voice to duets with fellow Strand David Wilson. Gummoe and Wilson then formed the Thundernotes and released an instrumental, on Del-Fi Records, called "Thunder Rhythm."

The Thundernotes soon realized that harmonies were their main draw. Until he joined the band, Gummoe, a self-described insecure and shy guy, had never thought he could croon in front of a studio microphone, let alone face an audience. When Len Green left the group to pursue a country music career, bass guitar player David Stevens came along, followed by another guitarist named Eddie Snyder. While Wilson remained on percussion and drums, David Zabo also entered the fray as co-singer and keyboardist. The Cascades were born—a name that Gummoe claims came about not by the image of raindrops, but from the brand name of a dishwashing detergent.

Fortune arrived when the Cascades met a San Diego guitarist named Andy Di Martino, who was, at the time, in search of a young singing ensemble he could manage and mold. Di Martino liked them, and he arranged a meeting with Valiant Records founders Barry De Vorzon and Billy Sherman in Hollywood.

De Vorzon, who composed "Dreamin'" (which Johnny Burnett made famous), joined other talents including songwriter Bodie Chandler and arranger Perry Botkin Jr. to make Valiant an accomplished soft-pop label. They were glad to discover in Gummoe a zealous songwriter who composed devotional ballads such as "There's a Reason," the first Cascades single to enter the radio waves in the summer of 1962. Though it enjoyed mostly regional airplay, the record established the group's method. As Gummoe reflects: "The recording technique had a lot of reverb—special effects on voices to make them sound big, like a church. De Vorzon had his own thing going. And Perry Botkin Jr. had the idea of adding strings to some of the songs."

There was no string section for "Rhythm of the Rain," but the celestial chime sparkled in just the right places to suggest cerebral soda pop. From its opening thunder to the scintillating rhythm guitar blending with Gummoe's sugary voice and the subtle background harmonies, "Rhythm of the Rain" demonstrated how vibrant America's pop scene was before the Fab Four's arrival. Gummoe describes the record as "a jaunty kind of happy sound, in complete contradiction to what the song has to say."

Others attempted "Rhythm of the Rain" with varied success. Among the best examples is Percy Faith and His Orchestra's instrumental version from the album *Themes for Young Lovers*, complete with pizzicato rainfall and other string flourishes. Floyd Cramer applied his "slurred note" technique, while Lawrence Welk included a wordless female chorus on the album *1963's Early Hits*. Gary Lewis & the Playboys, Johnny Tillotson, and France's Sylvie Vartan met Gummoe's challenge with their melodic best. In contrast to Dan Fogelberg, who grounded it with a "down-home" version in the early 1990s, the 1980s Australian teen idol Jason Donovan freshened it up for synth-pop audiences with the required vanilla zest.

The Cascades continued their sonic excursions on their first album, an effort aided by engineer Stan Ross, who assisted in the creation of Phil Spector's Wall of Sound. The sessions included "Wrecking Crew" stalwarts Hal Blaine on drums and Carol Kaye on bass guitar, as well as Glen Campbell, whose rhythm guitar provided acoustic radiance. The Cascades' follow-up single was no less haunting and hypnotic, turning out to be a double-sided treat with "The Last Leaf" and "Shy Girl." On "The Last Leaf," Campbell's rhythm guitar dominates, while Gummoe's voice dramatizes (without *over*-dramatizing) the story of a broken heart.

The rippling style remained when the Cascades continued their efforts on the RCA Victor label with Burt Bacharach and Bob Hilliard's "Little Betty Falling Star," Harold Spina's "How Much Do I Love You," a honeyed version of J. J. Cale's "Awake," along with Gummoe originals "Vicki (My Love)" and the gentle rocker "Those Were the Good Old Days." Some personnel changes ensued, with Tony Grasso and Ron Lynch replacing Stevens and Zabo. But by the late 1960s, when Gabe Lapano replaced Gummoe as the lead singer, the Cascades went in a grittier direction with the single "Maybe the Rain Will Fall." Still, the celesta-driven "Rhythm of the Rain" lingers, especially in Japan and some other parts of Asia that appear to outwit Americans when it comes to appreciating the lighter aspects of American pop.

The Cascades: John Gummoe, Eddie Snyder, Ron Lynch, Tony Grasso, and Dave Wilson (Photo courtesy and by permission of John C. Gummoe)

"'Rhythm of the Rain' was #1 in Japan, the Philippines, Hong Kong, and Singapore," Gummoe continues. "Even to this day, it's a huge, very popular song in Thailand. It is still popular in Japan. I was on a cruise in the Baltic; the waiter was from the Philippines. He couldn't believe he was meeting me. The Cascades are like the Beatles in the Philippines. It's always done well in the Orient; it has kind of a Chinese-sounding melody."

"Lazy Summer Night"—The Four Preps

By the early 1960s, when the Cascades made their Top 40 entry, the art of soft, tightly woven harmony groups was still strong. Gummoe admits to drawing from many sources—the Lettermen, the Brothers Four, the Fleetwoods, and the group that helped start it all: the Four Preps.

In 1956, while the Crew Cuts recorded songs with titles like "Honey Hair, Sugar Lips, Eyes of Blue," four young men entered and won a talent contest held at Hollywood High. Apart from their musical acumen, they relished the extra advantage of being the competition's only male entry. They were also lucky enough to catch the eye of Capitol Records producer Voyle Gilmore, who soon made them the youngest vocal quartet ever to secure a major label contract.

They consisted of Bruce Belland on lead tenor, Ed Cobb on bass, Marvin Inabnett (sometimes Ingraham) following Belland on high tenor, and Glen Larson on baritone—a combination that mustered all the brightness and stainless integrity of a toothpaste commercial jingle. Their first record—a rock-a-ballad called "Dreamy Eyes"—was released in early 1957. It had much of the Crew Cuts' helium-pitched appeal (minus the big-band blasts) and a lustrous texture provided by Van Alexander and His Orchestra. "They got 'It' with a capital 'I'," Louis Armstrong declared to television viewers when he appeared with them that same year on the *The Edsel Show*.

The Four Preps arrived at a juncture in the 1950s when male vocal ensembles provided smooth background choruses on a number of records. "I had the inclination to have men sing in a velvety low unison," Les Baxter told author Joe Smith in *Off the Record*. Baxter's 1955 version of "Unchained Melody" was a splendid example of this. Such precise harmonies were everywhere—they had become an essential part of the cultural fabric. Norman Luboff was another major player in the genre with his Norman Luboff Choir, which was among the most recognized and regarded pop chorales. In this sense, the Four Preps, the Lettermen, and others were not really like barbershop quartets.

To get a better appreciation of the difference, here's a brief barbershop history. From the mid-nineteenth century onward, barbershop quartets have conveyed time-honored, quasi–Norman Rockwell visions of jovial guys with straw hats, pinstriped suits, and a repertoire of chestnuts such as "A Bicycle Built for Two," "By the Light of the Silvery Moon," "While Strolling Through the Park One Day," and "Meet Me Tonight in Dreamland"—all of which celebrate a gilded age of courtship, replete with cakes and dainties on the seaside.

Apart from an affinity for close harmonies and sweetly textured renditions, however, the similarities tend to end there. Tradition dictates that barbershoppers assign each member a strict role and range allocation. Right alongside the top tenor, the second tenor takes the lead and supports the melody; the bottom bass provides those sometimes-humorous low-end hums, while the more ambiguous baritone acts as filler. Together, they tend to sound like a human harmonica that flows softly one moment, then undulates along the scale to create a forward, swooping effect the next. Groups like the Four Preps and the Lettermen did not usually indulge in such conceits.

With the onset of popular records and their ensuing volley of *Your Hit Parade* fare, the vocal harmony offerings varied. Fred Waring had his ever-popular glee club, while the Mills Brothers tended to favor tight barbershop traditions over gospel. Into the 1940s, the Andrews Sisters performed some sweet tunes, but they were often too awash in "boogie woogie" rhythms to retain consistent sonic chastity. The Ames Brothers arrived by the late 1940s, but their deep-chested vocals were too viscous to pass the vanilla taste test. The Pied Pipers, however, came much closer, especially when chiming in unison with Paul Weston and His Orchestra on their gossamer 1945 recording of "Dream."

What the Pied Pipers exuded, and what other vocal combos subsequently continued, was more akin to a mini-choir. The Four Lads began cultivating this technique with Mitch Miller on the Columbia label, while at Decca the Four Aces attempted the same with varying results, layering their refinements on cinemelodies such as "Three Coins in the Fountain" and "Love Is a Many-Splendored Thing." The Aces' lead singer, Al Albertini, also known as Al Alberts, tended toward vocal muscularity, but the results proved more satisfying when the group made that extra effort to chime a lighter, more assonant accord. A good example is their title song to the 1957 movie *Written on the Wind*. The single sported a bouncier rock 'n' roll backbeat, whereas the version heard in the movie's opening credits is creamier and, fundamentally, more satisfying to the type of romantic who would be drawn into Douglas Sirk's melodrama.

The Four Aces were *relatively* vanilla compared to the Four Freshmen, the group that Brian Wilson often touts as a major Beach Boys influence. For those attuned to the vanilla vibe, the Freshmen had a noisome habit of using "open" harmonies, with various chord notes wavering higher or lower. This slip-sliding approach made them more congenial with jazzier vocal groups such as Mel Tormé and his Mel-Tones, the Hi-Lo's, and, later, the Singers Unlimited and the Manhattan Transfer—performances tailored for a smoky, New York supper club ambiance favoring dry martinis over vanilla shakes.

The Four Preps continued the Aces' embellishments with even cleaner results. They developed a group image that merged the teenage dreamer with the collegiate smart aleck, making a strong impression on songs that expressed summer heartbreak interspersed with summer fun. As creatures of Southern California, the Preps found their ultimate muse on the beach, where Belland and Larson (the group's songwriting team) drifted on the soft sands just prior to their first recording sessions. They started collaborating on verses about "a tropical heaven out in the ocean," and, several months later (and a mere fifteen minutes before their session ended), recorded what would become the starry-eyed "26 Miles (Santa Catalina)." With peppy harmonies and backing by Joe Maphis and His Orchestra and an Yma Sumac soundalike, "26 Miles" sailed from "the island of romance" up to *Billboard*'s #2 spot by January 1958. It even showed up as a rendition on *Your Hit Parade* by March of that same year.

Lincoln Mayorga, a well-regarded pianist (and essential "Fifth Prep"), was the group's chief arranger and conductor. In addition to going on to work with such acts as Chad & Jeremy and the Association, he became a cofounder of the audiophile company Sheffield Lab. Mayorga backed the Preps on their next major release—another Belland-Larson number called "Big Man." The song's blustery piano chords befitted its subject, a braggart who takes his love for granted and ends up in the romantic doghouse.

Mayorga's arrangements are all the more alluring on their 1958 summer release "Lazy Summer Night." Harold Spina, an eerie-minded composer with a penchant for titles such as "Haunted Ball Room" and "It's Dark on Observatory Hill," penned it for the MGM film *Andy Hardy Comes Home*. Its B-side carried on the seasonal celebration with a more sobering reflection on warm weather and cold hearts called "Summertime Lies," in which the voices try to buoy the dejected spirit implied in Mayorga's almost staggering piano accompaniment.

One of the Preps' finest achievements was the album *The Things We Did Last Summer*, which included luminous renditions of Sammy Cahn's and Jule Styne's title track, "Love Letters in the Sand," "A Tree in the Meadow," "Graduation Day," and a honky-tonk rendition of "In the Good Old Summer Time." Rock 'n' roll ringmaster Dick Clark, who contributed the album's back cover notes, trumpets how *Cash Box* magazine "named them the most promising vocal group of 1958." By then, with Don Clarke temporarily replacing Inabnett as the high tenor, they had cultivated a style as breezy and luminous as their mythological sandscapes. Their excursions to tropical islands of romance and their dedication of whole albums to summer and surf made

The "It" boys. Of all the pop harmony groups to emerge from the 1950s, the Four Preps probably had the biggest impact on acts like the Association and the Arbors.

them a logical addition to the 1959 CinemaScope movie *Gidget*, the first of several sagas about the "half-girl/half-midget" beachcomber and her acne-age dilemmas.

Living up to their name, they staged many sold-out concerts on the campus circuit and demonstrated a flair for often self-parodying humor. In 1961, *The Four Preps on Campus* arrived with earnest songs about love and war, tempered with unsoiled jokes and sophomoric routines. They seemed at times to be passing themselves off as more of a folk-era comedy act like the Smothers Brothers, with tracks such as "More Money for You and Me," a hilarious and shameless five-minute Belland-Larson medley that mocks the Fleetwoods, the Kingston Trio, and others who vied for their moments in the Top 40 sun. Such novelty numbers did tend to wear on the nerves, primarily because the quartet was so talented with the more serious ballads.

All humor aside, the Preps continued to excel in amiable moon/June ditties such as "The Seine," a 1961 single that told of amorous moments "one light above the moonlight" by the celebrated French river. Many fans sighed with relief when the group decided to get more earnest with the 1963 release *Songs for a Campus Party.* On it they interpreted songs that included Richard Chamberlain's "Theme from *Dr. Kildare* (Three Stars Will Shine Tonight)," Kyu Sakamoto's "Sukiyaki," and Henry Mancini's downhearted screen theme "Days of Wine and Roses."

In May 1963, the Preps recorded "Charmaine," a waltz tune dating back to the 1926 silent-movie war epic *What Price Glory?* Mantovani had already released a "cascading strings" version of the song with great success in 1951. In 1962 the Bachelors, a Dublin-based trio, retained the basic melody but charged it up with a trendier up-tempo beat that the Preps also adopted, yet made more salutary by scraping away the Bachelors' rustic, Celtic twang.

As the British Isles waged their invasion on American music the following year, the Preps (who would hold together until 1967) responded by slipping out a gripe-about-the-competition track called "A Letter to the Beatles." The story goes that the Beatles' management pressured Capitol Records into letting the Preps' disc die its own death. Oddly, Stu Phillips—who would make several ectoplasmic instrumental albums of Beatles songs under the rubric the Hollyridge Strings—produced the session.

By the mid-1960s, David Somerville (formerly of the Diamonds) had replaced Ed Cobb. The Preps crashed against the Beatlemania monsoon, but they managed to retain much of their fair-weather luminosity. "I'll Set My Love to Music," a Nino Oliviero melody they turned into a prom-boy ballad, showed up as the incongruous opening theme to the American version of the 1965 Italian shockumentary *Mondo Cane 2.* Released in the summer of 1966, "The Girl in the Shade of the Striped Umbrella" boasted a Perry Botkin Jr. arrangement and captured the Preps in their best high-voiced, beachcomber luster.

Bruce Belland went on to write songs for a variety of performers, including Johnny Mathis, Willie Nelson, Donny Osmond, and the Mormon Tabernacle Choir. He also became a television scriptwriter, received three Emmy nominations, and won the Presidential Medal of the Arts by cowriting the official anthem of the bicentennial of the U.S. Constitution. Glen Larson's post-Preps work included cowriting the theme to the 1980s television series *The Fall Guy*. Ed Cobb also kept writing songs, venturing into unexpected directions with the Standells' "Dirty Water" and Gloria Jones's "Tainted Love," which would resurface in the 1980s thanks to the band Soft Cell. In the mid-1980s, the Preps reunited, with Belland, Cobb, and Somerville joined by Jim Pike (formerly of the Lettermen). Jim Yester would emerge from his veteran status with the Association a few years later to replace Pike as a quarter of the New Four Preps.

"Greenfields"—The Brothers Four

While the Four Preps deployed a collegiate name to reinforce an image, the Brothers Four were actual members of the Phi Gamma Delta fraternity at the University of Washington. Each Brother also had a distinct identity. Bob Flick, on baritone-bass and bass fiddle, wanted to study television production. As an eleven-year-old child, he'd performed in USO shows, and he was valedictorian of his high school class. Dick Foley, the lead tenor who played guitar and cymbals, once aspired to be an electrical engineer. John Paine, a trooper who stayed with the quartet through its subsequent permutations, was the most traveled. He majored in Russian and Far East studies before serving with the band as a baritone and master of the banjo and guitar. Finally, there was Mike Kirkland, the crew-cut tenor who also played guitar and banjo and who once served at his university's homecoming chairman. As the group's spokesman, he conveyed enough good spirit to dispel any unseemly jock image the quartet might otherwise have displayed.

To underscore how much the group's sweater vestments went with the music, the four band members made their initial dip into show business as a result of a college prank. A rival fraternity fooled them into answering a fake audition call from someone identifying herself as a secretary from Seattle's fashionable Colony Club. When they arrived, there was no one there to hear them, but a magnanimous proprietor, seeing how all four arrived with instruments in hand and irresistible smiles, gave them a chance.

After playing the Colony Club through much of 1958, they traveled to San Francisco, where quirky places with quirky names like the hungry i and The Purple Onion showcased the Kingston Trio and other rising folk stars. They got their recording break when Mort Lewis, who was managing West

Coast jazz mogul Dave Brubeck, took a shine to one of their shows. He brought them to the attention of Bob Morgan at Columbia. Both Morgan and Mitch Miller liked how the quartet's good looks matched its smooth vocal flow. The added novelty of two baritones was another distinction. They perceived the group as a new variation on the Four Lads, with instant appeal for young folks looking ahead to what history would call a "New Frontier."

"I was the producer," Morgan explains. "That got me my wings. I was purported to be the next name in folk. They were called the Marksmen at the time. They had a tape; I liked it and sent it to Mitch Miller in New York. I used to listen to all the stuff he didn't want to be bothered listening to. He realized there was already a Kingston Trio, and Columbia had the Easy Riders, but he saw enough quality in them to tell me, 'If you like them, see what you can do.' I had them come into New York on their summer break, where they stayed at the Great Northern Hotel on 56th Street. We were down the road at the old building on 799 7th Avenue. On the top floor, we had two smaller studios. They'd come up there, and we would spend two or three afternoons per week working on their material. When they learned they couldn't call themselves the Marksmen, they came up with the Brothers Four, taking their name from a Woody Herman recording ["Four Brothers"]."

A native of Buffalo, New York, Morgan moved down to New York City when he was about thirteen. Initially a jazz enthusiast, he also became fascinated by pop choruses. "I worked out of New York. I had this stiff choir with Jimmy Carroll arrangements behind it. They were stiff, not relaxed. They would sing with an open throat from the bottom of the diaphragm, similar to the Ray Conniff Singers. It may have sounded old-fashioned, but the stiffness was a tradition."

Morgan illustrates the difference between jazz and pop harmonizing with an instrumental example. "In the early seventies, I had a commission from the Columbia Record Club to re-record the Glenn Miller Orchestra. Buddy De Franco led the band. I did a reasonable re-creation. We used the younger players from the road band, but it was very hard for them to play on the beat the way the Glenn Miller stuff was done in the forties. That's the way they grew up with music. The younger ones had to work harder to get on the beat. Being on the beat was considered square."

In vocal terms, this very "squareness" gave the Brothers Four their allure. They were even more clean-cut than their relatively clean-cut contemporaries, the Kingston Trio, singing with an unruffled clarity that may have riled hard-core folkies, but that struck others as endearing and inspiring. "They were folk music people," Morgan continues, "but they didn't come through the Weavers tradition. They were college kids who liked to sing those songs and sang them very well. They had no pretensions to being Bob Dylan."

The Brothers Four broke through with their recording of a beautiful but desolate offering that Terry Gilkyson, Richard Dehr, and Frank Miller (who comprised the Easy Riders) wrote called "Greenfields." They converted it into a Mitch Miller–era masterpiece, produced with a minimal amount of instrumentation: just acoustic guitars and bass, double-tracked voices, and Foley's solo corralling the background harmonies. With the voices gleaming out in front, the quartet had the bearing of historical overseers cooing out reminders of "the valleys where rivers used to run" and "the lovers who let their dreams depart." The reassuring voices ringing out the otherwise heartrending lyrics made it one of the most singular radio releases to inaugurate the post-Eisenhower years, prompting *Cash Box* magazine to dub the Brothers Four "one of the biggest success stories of 1960."

"Greenfields" co-composer Gilkyson is one example of someone who wedded folk styles to commercial song formulas. A Phoenixville, Pennsylvania, native, he abandoned academic music studies to pursue guitar and songwriting at a friend's ranch in Tucson, Arizona, before heading to Los Angeles. There, he eventually teamed up with Dehr and Miller. As the Easy Riders, the three adapted and recorded a Bahamian tune that the world would know as "Marianne," and they wrote other chart wonders, including Dean Martin's croony "Memories Are Made of This." Gilkyson, careful not to push any "Red Scare" buttons, favored novelty and nostalgia themes to overt political messages—a factor that made him a congenial choice to later work on *The Wonderful World of Disney*, as well as on the 1967 Disney animated feature *The Jungle Book*.

The Brothers Four were most becoming when they augmented "Greenfields" with other songs about lost summer days—a favored theme since the time when Stephen Foster wrote songs with titles like "Summer Longings." That second baritone reinforced the group's melancholy mood on Stuart Gotz's "Summer Days Alone," Dimitri Tiomkin's and Paul Francis Webster's "The Green Leaves of Summer" (the theme from the 1960 film *The Alamo*), and "Try to Remember," which composers Tom Jones and Harvey Schmidt introduced in their early 1960s musical *The Fantasticks* as a swan song to America's vanishing innocence.

By 1964, the Brothers Four became the United States' "unofficial good-will ambassadors," due mainly to their impressive overseas tours. They usually skirted overt politics, but they stuck their necks out by traveling the country on behalf of Lyndon Johnson's presidential campaign. They'd also expanded their sound by 1965, retaining an acoustic backbone but introducing orchestral stringsweeps, which were arranged mostly by Tommy Newsom. The *Try to Remember* album more than justified this switch. The tracks varied from an unassuming rendition of the Japanese folk tune "Sakura" to the string-laden "The Song from *Moulin Rouge* (Where Is Your Heart?)" and the eerie "I Remember When I Loved Her." The closing song, "When Ev'rything Was Green," continued the "Greenfields" theme about an idealized, ever-receding past.

Teo Macero had come onboard by 1964 as the group's producer. Macero began as a saxophonist, and he later made a name in jazz by recording the likes of Miles Davis. Taking executive responsibilities with Columbia, he worked with pop luminaries, including Johnny Mathis and Simon & Garfunkel, while producing several exceptional albums by Andre Kostelanetz. On *The Brothers Four Sing Lennon/McCartney* and *A New World's Record*, Macero reinforced the Brothers Four's wistful side, with selections including an early version of "The First Time Ever I Saw Your Face," the lushly constructed Burt Bacharach–Hal David entry "Walkin' Backwards Down the Road," and even the raga-tinctured pop of "Umbrellas in the Rain."

The Brothers Four—as both a sound and an image—served as paragons of sorts. Lawrence Welk, in some of his 1960s shows, featured a clean-cut male quartet called the Blenders, whose presentation was obviously patterned on the "Greenfields" Gang of Four. When Frankie Avalon and Annette Funicello introduced them on the February 5, 1965, installment of *Hullabaloo*, the Brothers Four performed their lush tribute to "Somewhere" from *West Side Story* in suits and ties—a vivid contrast to the Kinks, who shared the bill.

"Come Softly to Me"—The Fleetwoods

Hailing from the Brothers Four's state of Washington, the Fleetwoods became part of a West Coast trend that, by the early 1960s, had a significant influence on the billowy sunshine harmonies that would thrive through the rest of the decade. Serendipity was on their side the day Barbara Ellis and Gretchen Christopher (allegedly born nine days apart, wailing together in the same maternity ward) decided to switch from cheerleading to performing as a girl duet at their Olympia High School.

The girls initially envisioned including a third member in their all-girl band, and they planned to use the doo-wop song "In the Still of the Night (I Remember)" as their audition piece. But, as David Dasch wrote in his notes to the EMI compilation *The Very Best of the Fleetwoods*, the girls "found that the applicants' seismic renditions of the Five Satins tune didn't match Christopher's 'audio-vision' of a warm, soft sound." Ellis and Christopher continued their pursuit, biding their time at the piano and composing a whispery number called "Come Softly"—the tune that would soon change their fortunes. A young trumpeter and charmer named Gary Troxel then entered their lives.

Ellis and Christopher were looking for a horn to accent their voices, but Troxel was inept at trumpeting in their key. He did, however, manage to win Christopher over with his singing voice one day while walking her to ballet class. The trio developed an inimitable style, securing a fan base at Olympia High assemblies before reaching the ear of record producer Bob Reisdorff.

At graduation time in June 1958, Ellis, Christopher, and Troxel, under Reisdorff's supervision, started recording for real, albeit in the rather humble confines of a Seattle basement studio. Ellis and Christopher's "Come Softly" still needed some tailoring. The most significant addition was Troxel's new lyrics, which replaced the part where he had been relegated to a wordless chorister. The result was the augmented "Come Softly to Me." Of course, the trio now had to agree upon a catchier name than "Two Girls and a Guy." They found their answer emblazoned on an Olympia telephone book that listed "Fleetwood" as an area prefix.

"Come Softly to Me" finally christened Reisdorff's homegrown Dolphin label (which was distributed by Liberty Records). The name changed to Dolton, so as not to rankle a religious record company that had already adopted the aquatic mammal as a mascot. KFWB in Los Angeles had only to play "Come Softly to Me" a couple of times before the station was flooded with ecstatic callers. By March 1959, the Fleetwoods' first radio coup soared on downy feathers to *Billboard*'s peak, where it remained for four love-struck weeks. The trio performed the song on Dick Clark's *American Bandstand*, on which they received a warm greeting from Frankie Avalon—a magnanimous gesture, considering that "Come Softly to Me" knocked "Venus" out of the #1 spot on the charts. England's Craig Douglas, meanwhile, had also recorded a cover of the hit song. Years later, author Jay Warner would, perhaps somewhat begrudgingly, admit that the Fleetwoods' "lily-white rhythm ballad" proved a winner for even R&B audiences.

The next Fleetwoods single was another Ellis-Christopher creation, this time in honor of their transition from high school to the uncertainties of semiadulthood. "Graduation's Here" celebrated all that was preppy about their image. The lyrics, which possessed a prematurely nostalgic ring, even for the 1950s, arrived on the airwaves between the spring and summer of 1959. While boasting the same formula of feminine voices playing against Troxel's dulcet "doo-dah-dees," the song also demonstrated how the more streetwise style of doo-wop could profit from marshmallow enhancements.

A "guardian star" next guided the Fleetwoods on what, judging by its lyrics alone, could have easily been one of the era's most depressing ditties. "Mr. Blue" was the first of their big releases composed by an outside writer, a gentleman named Dewayne Blackwell, who had once pitched it to the Platters. Although Troxel sang the weepy lead, he was not initially thrilled with the tune. Nevertheless, drawing inspiration from a vast history of downhearted crooners who warbled before him, he did an excellent job of portraying the wistful swain in the midst of an amorous meltdown.

Instrumentally, "Mr. Blue" tried to exude more "cool," with jazz guitarist Roy Lanham plucking out the introductory notes, and the otherwise swing-happy Si Zentner playing a woozy trombone. Despite this, the record survived through the years as a malt-shop mood setter. The album *Mr. Blue* served up more examples of how the Fleetwoods could dress up the most lyrically

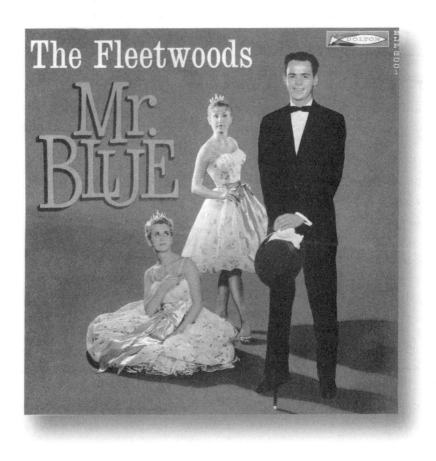

depressing songs, including a downright spooky version of "Unchained Melody," in sonic chiffon.

The Top 40 atmosphere was rife with other melancholic airs. Parallel to the Fleetwoods, a group from Pittsburgh made up of Mike Lazo, Gene Schachter, Jim Drake, and Tom Minoto changed their name from the Four Larks to the Tempos (not to be confused with the West African percussion group of that name). By the summer of 1959, they'd made their one and only mark on American hearts with the Sherman Edwards–Sid Wayne composition "See You in September."

Edwards proved equally resourceful for the Fleetwoods when he collaborated with Hal David on "Outside My Window," a recording that suggests a mild-mannered precursor to the Mamas and the Papas. But the sad spell of September struck again in 1960, when *Teen* magazine featured a photo of Ellis and Christopher looking a bit glum. The accompanying feature story, titled "Two Lost Girls," imparted news that Troxel had been drafted. The occasion inspired a now faintly remembered single (coproduced by Lou Christie) called "Since Gary Went into the Navy."

Even after Mr. Blue donned navy blue, the group's efforts continued. By the summer of 1961, the trio released the album *Deep in a Dream*. Its cover featured Troxel in his sailor garb, lying back in blissful repose as the images of Ellis and Christopher hovered above him in a ghostly blur. One of the Fleetwoods' very best recordings of this period was "Lavender Blue (Dilly Dilly)." Theirs was a diaphanous interpretation of the traditional English folk tune, which had previously appeared in the 1949 Disney film *So Dear to My Heart* and that Dinah Shore and Danny Kaye recorded in the late 1940s to great success.

Around this time, an aspiring songwriter named Randy Newman was scouting for a break. He would later credit the Fleetwoods for that chance when they recorded his "Tell Me It's Summer," another weather-sensitive love plaint that ended up on the B-side of the 1962 single "Lovers by Night, Strangers by Day." The latter was just one of the treats offered on *The Fleetwoods Sing for Lovers by Night*, which was released in January 1963. The album included "My Special Lover," penned by a pre-Bread David Gates, who also wrote the Murmaids' "Popsicles and Icicles" from that same year.

In January 1965, the Fleetwoods released *Before and After*, which consisted primarily of covers of songs previously recorded by such easy-listening contemporaries as Andy Williams ("Almost There"), Steve Lawrence ("Go

Away Little Girl"), and one of the first recordings of a fine Italian melody set to English lyrics called "Softly, As I Leave You." The Fleetwoods performed the album's title song (which was written by Van McCoy, years before he went on to hog the international disco stage with "The Hustle") to mixed effect. The blend of the male and female voices with the strings was exemplary. But when Troxel arrived at the bridge, he broke the mysterious mood by lapsing into some pseudo-soul. Hard-core vanilla aficionados are likely to conclude that Chad & Jeremy (who recorded it on the Columbia label several months later) offered a more definitive interpretation.

"Everyone's Gone to the Moon"—Chad & Jeremy

When Chad & Jeremy emerged from the United Kingdom and eventually relocated to America's West Coast, the duo became an important sunshine pop influence as well. They bore an uncanny physical likeness to another duo of the time, Peter & Gordon. Each featured a bespectacled, demure, and sensitive member, who offered a contrast to his slightly more aggressive, slightly more "rock 'n' roll" partner. There were noticeable differences, however, beyond each act's surface appearances. Even with easy-listening maestro Geoff Love's arrangements, Peter & Gordon stayed smugly ensconced in the British Invasion. Peter Waller's groaning, low tones on the remake of Buddy Holly's "True Love Ways," for example, showed their somewhat grainier texture. Peter & Gordon could do some pretty harmonizing, but they did not really chime like Chad & Jeremy.

Chad & Jeremy had softer harmonies, more pillow-rich orchestrations, and a misfit stature among their Carnaby Street contemporaries. David Stuart Chadwick, who came from the modest English town of Windermere, commanded the duo's musical direction. Michael Thomas Jeremy Clyde, on the other hand, was a product of snootier Dorney, Buckinghamshire—the offspring of shipping magnates, the beneficiary of an Eton education, and the Duke of Wellington's grandson. But both shared experiences as schoolboy choristers, and they found common ground as aspiring thespians when they met in the early 1960s at London's Central School of Speech and Drama.

Realizing that music was more their calling, they formed a duo. From the start, Chad had the musical smarts, and he tutored Jeremy on the guitar. The two played at local clubs that catered to the folk scene, which had started in America and quickly found succor among espresso-addicted Brits. They also played for a while in a band called the Jerks, in which they performed at a coming-out party for the Duke of Wellington's niece.

Meanwhile, John Barry, already immersed in composing music for the James Bond movies, was busy with his own group, the John Barry Seven. By 1963 he was also an associate producer and A&R scout for the independent Ember label. One night a Barry representative saw Chad & Jeremy perform at a West End coffeehouse and recommended them. Barry liked the act enough to sign them up and produce some sessions. That summer, in the face of limited resources and distribution problems, the duo plugged away at material that would typify much of their edible and spreadable output.

Barry took pride in adopting Chad & Jeremy as his Ember protégés. The first single he backed for them was Chad's country-influenced "Yesterday's Gone" (which Barry also let Chad arrange), along with an intimate rendition of "Lemon Tree" as the B-side. British audiences gave "Yesterday's Gone" a favorable reception, despite Ember's promotional shortcomings. But the early 1964 follow-up single, "Like I Love You Today" (backed by "Early in the Morning"), did not get as much attention—a situation that prompted the impatient Barry to shift his efforts elsewhere and leave the duo's fate in the hands of their producer, Shel Talmy.

In spite of his early abandonment, Barry was among those who encouraged Chad & Jeremy to develop their whispery singing approach. Even with Talmy's aggressive pitching, however, the duo had difficulty competing with the mounting "beat" style of the Animals and the Rolling Stones. Bud when Ember leased the duo's recordings to World Artists Music, a fledgling label located in Pittsburgh, Pennsylvania, they became American favorites, despite the fact that they remained, at least according to Chad, "two characters in search of a musical identity!"

Chad & Jeremy's debut album, a quaint collection of folk tunes and Tin Pan Alley chestnuts, was released in the United States under the title *Yesterday's Gone*. The title track quickly entered America's Top 40, but it was the gorgeously arranged "A Summer Song" that stood out as their quintessential piece as it entered *Billboard*'s Top 10 by the summer of 1964. The combination of acoustic guitar and strings also worked favorably for their updates of Harry Warren and Al Dubin's "September in the Rain," as well as Rodgers & Hammerstein's "If I Loved You," from *Carousel*.

One of the duo's best achievements on record was their version of one of America's more original and enigmatic tunes, Ann Ronell's "Willow Weep for

Me." Recording it was a bold move that paid off commercially and helped to vindicate the musical traditions that rougher Mersey beat denizens tried to supplant. Chad & Jeremy not only revived Ronell's classic, but also arguably recorded the best version of all time, taking it into America's Top 20. They were indeed a lighter alternative to the British Invasion.

Ember released the same collection in England, but the Merseyside masses' reaction to the album ranged from indifferent to mildly hostile. Even the duo's "A Summer Song" received scant favorable response. Were it not for the sole positive vote of panelist Ringo Starr, who predicted its success in America, the other prickly judges on BBC-TV's *Jukebox Jury* would have consigned it to oblivion. Chad & Jeremy incurred an additional problem when

the *Daily Express* published an embarrassing photo of a young, velvet-clad Jeremy dressed as a page at Queen Elizabeth's 1952 coronation. It seems the rebel factions were too enchanted with working-class heroes to tolerate a hipster aristocrat.

In America, where fears of "commercialism" and musical lightness had not yet defiled pop sensibility, Chad & Jeremy's finger-sandwich scandal had little to no meaning. If anything, their polite, starched-collar demeanor filled a void. Going where the love was, Chad & Jeremy severed their English roots and bustled across the Atlantic to set up house in California. There, they acclimated to an atmosphere dominated by the Beach Boys' surf music and the Byrds' folk-rock—influences that, while unavoidable, were not strong enough to poke holes in the transplanted Redcoats' delicate aura.

The credits on the back of the World Artists album *Chad & Jeremy Sing for You* include many respected American session players. Lettermen arranger Jim Haskell was the producer; guitarist Al Caiola acted as orchestra leader; George Tipton and Ian Freebairn shared arranger credits; and David Nadien, Max Pollikoff, and Paul Winter were among the seven violinists. But despite artistic integrity, Worlds Artists' business practices were not to Chad & Jeremy's liking. In 1965 they switched to Columbia.

Before and After, their first Columbia venture, offered a mixed bag. The dulcet tones for which they were most admired were present, but they made some gangly attempts to incorporate rock 'n' roll into their style. The breezy and silky title tune made a respectable showing on *Billboard*'s pop chart, and it was among the album's highlights. It, like some of the other, better tracks, was arranged and conducted by Frank Hunter, a respected orchestral pop figure who worked extensively with Roger Williams and whose talents ranged from exotic instrumental albums to *Music by Muzak*®. Under Hunter's baton, Chad & Jeremy crafted another amalgam between youthful pop and easy listening with a variation on the Andy Williams charmer "Can't Get Used to Losing You." "I would categorize *Before and After* as the Americanization of Chad & Jeremy," Chad later affirmed. "It was a slick production, with 'Brill Building' written all over it."

Guest spots on *The Dick Van Dyke Show* and *The Patty Duke Show* helped their exposure. Soon they were media personalities fit for *Hullabaloo*, *Shindig*, and that most venerable of prime-time institutions, *The Andy Williams Show*. Their follow-up album, *I Don't Wanna Lose You Baby*, which was typified by the Righteous Brothers–style title single, was, in the duo's own estimation, a misfire. "So, here we are, folks," Chad recalls, "with Jeremy screaming at the top of his range—grumbling all the time." The album did include one diamond in the rough, a Chad-arranged rendition (recorded during the *Before and After* sessions) of Rodgers and Hammerstein's "I Have Dreamed" from *The King and I*.

The *Before and After* album reflected Chad & Jeremy's mounting interpersonal tensions, especially as Jeremy's acting ambitions loomed. One story has them scheduled to perform at Chicago's McCormick Place. With tickets already purchased and derrieres planted in the seats, the audience waited as Chad coped with a Jeremy who was too involved with his role in a London production of *Passion Flower Hotel* to get to the concert in time. Improvising in a manner that would have made Andy Warhol proud, Chad appeared on stage with a cardboard likeness of Jeremy by his side. Chad's wife, Jill, joined him onstage in a rendition of "I Got You Babe." Chad and Jill later went on to record Peter Yarrow's and Paul Stookey's "The Cruel War," with a string arrangement that, according to Chad, impressed Yarrow enough to rush a similar backing onto Peter, Paul & Mary's 1966 recording.

Chad & Jeremy reconnoitered and returned to Columbia to record *Distant Shores* in 1965. Clyde's musical tastes were hyperdriving at the same rate as his passion for sports cars. He urged Chad to take their sound on a cacophonous crash course with a mess called "Teenage Failure," which they dutifully performed on an episode of *Batman*. The record's flip side, a benign cover of Gordon Lightfoot's "Early Morning Rain," better reflected their calling. Around this time, a young gentleman named Larry Marks replaced Lor Crane as their producer and somehow struck up a better rapport with the duo. Their bass player and future manager, James William Guercio, wrote the moody title entry that sported raga-style folk picking, pastoral woodwinds, and the duo's trademark dual vocals. It would be their last Top 40 hurrah. Chad did much of the album's arranging, an effort that culminated in a nice rendition of Jerome Kern's "The Way You Look Tonight."

Distant Shores arrived in stores roughly one week after the Beatles introduced their psychedelic *Revolver*. Though Chad & Jeremy's album adhered to their combination of original songs and standards, subtle textures indicated more cerebral forays. The one track that sticks out in this regard is their cover of Jonathan King's "Everyone's Gone to the Moon."

Like Chad & Jeremy, Jonathan King was a gentle wind during the British Invasion typhoon. Eric Burdon, Steve Winwood, and Mick Jagger may have been emulating backwoods Mississippi moans, but King was apparently channeling William Wordsworth when he wrote and recorded the song while still a Cambridge undergrad. Released by the autumn of 1965, "Everyone's Gone to the Moon" packed a set of verses that were unapologetically arcane and mauve. The beguiling melody, coupled with a childlike voice that King would call a "rather tuneless whisper boosted by mechanical processes," triggered a transatlantic thrill.

Speaking through his mask, King later claimed that he intended "Everyone's Gone to the Moon" to be "a satire of the Dylan school of 'meaningful' lyrics." Regardless, its candyland observations about "streets full of people all alone" and "roads full of houses never home," made it a surefire favorite among folks such as Bobby Vinton. Dan Burr, in a compilation of King's material on Wounded Bird Records, astutely pointed out that King's singing resembled "a middle ground between Chad and Al Stewart, displaying sensitivity and excellent phrasing that makes one feel he believed in the words being sung."

Chad & Jeremy were the only artists who could equal King's lunar lyricism. Their version of "Everyone's Gone to the Moon" boasted another Chad arrangement that included some extra zany sound effects but retained fealty to the composer's presumed intent. Like King, they were not timid about entering a melodic time warp that played against fashion. "Coolness" may have eluded them, but they, like the other artists addressed in this chapter, best represent the soft-harmony art. Each has at least one tune that 1960s pop devotees can recall with a minimum of memory jogging.

"Summer's Come and Gone"—The Lettermen

The harmonic balm that calmed the 1960s. Adult contemporary's preeminent troubadours. However one describes them, the Lettermen always have a way of wrapping any kind of song in their choral cocoon. When jazz or doo-wop vocal groups stretched tunes beyond recognition, the Lettermen could be counted on to pull them back into shape.

They, like the Four Lads and the Crew Cuts, had roots in church choirs. If their music sounds vanilla, it is not due to the absence of R&B, but to the presence of their own musical culture, primarily that of the Lettermen's founding member, Tony Butala. Raised in Sharon, Pennsylvania (the future home of his Vocal Group Hall of Fame), Butala started singing at age four and performed on Pittsburgh's KDKA radio station by age eight. Two years later, he was chosen out of hundreds of other hopeful lads to be a member of the Mitchell Boys Choir.

Once the family moved westward, Butala appeared with the choir in some noteworthy Hollywood moments, including a pivotal Christmas-carol scene with Doris Day and Gordon MacRae in the 1951 film *On Moonlight Bay*. As a ghost voice, he sang behind some of the animated characters that chimed the television commercials for Sugar Krisps and Krinkles cereals. He also accompanied the "Lost Boys" in the Walt Disney animated version of *Peter Pan*.

While a student at Hollywood Professional High School, Butala put together his first vocal group. The Fourmosts consisted of Mitchell Boys Choir alumni Jimmie Blaine and Dan Witt, along with vivacious classmate Concetta Rosalie Ann Ingolia. Ingolia harmonized with them for a couple of years before venturing into a career, in movies and on television, as Connie Stevens. The Fourmosts continued as a trio in various capacities—always with Butala at the helm. But by 1958, the Lettermen had their first incarnation with Butala, Mike Barnett, and Talmadge Russell. Jim Pike (who had previously performed with Louis Prima at Hollywood's Moulin Rouge club) and Bob Engemann (who happened to be the brother of a man Connie was dating) replaced Barnett and Russell to become two-thirds of the official trio.

The first Lettermen singles—"The Magic Sound" and "Their Hearts Were Full of Spring"—were really tryouts. But in 1960, Capitol's Nick Venet gave them the opportunity to make another recording in the few studio minutes that the Four Preps left open as they argued over their next song. On Preps time, the Lettermen squeezed in four tracks: "Glory of Love," "When," "That's My Desire," and their first Top 20 hit—a gauzy rendition of the Jerome Kern–Dorothy Fields Oscar-winning composition, "The Way You Look Tonight" (originally from the 1936 movie *Swing Time*). These tracks provided ample evidence of the "Lettermen blend"—that delicate acoustical drapery few can ever forget.

The Lettermen could pour themselves into any genre, from Broadway show tunes and Hollywood movie themes to rock-a-ballads and traditional love songs. They also betrayed a fondness for folk balladeering—a propensity that stayed intact even amid flashy brass and orchestral grandeur. Through the years, they would perfect the art of covering current songs— from folk to Broadway to even Motown—bringing new interpretations and somehow winning over

young audiences, who were otherwise averse to "mushy stuff." In 1961 their follow-up to "The Way You Look Tonight" and their most successful single, a
reinterpretation of the Victor Young–Edward Heyman song "When I Fall in
Love," typified the dreamlike way the Lettermen sauntered over the lyrics,
pushing the higher notes on words and phrases that packed the most sentimental meaning. The title track that opens the Lettermen's first album, *A Song
for Young Love*, incorporates a mandolin, acoustic guitar, and Jim Haskell's
strings, all wrapped around the voices that linger on near-listless poeticisms. The
effect is gorgeous and mildly frightening.

Their second album, *Once Upon a Time*, dedicated to themes about smit-
ten hearts and shifting seasons, paid a Brill Building nod to Cynthia Weil and

Barry Mann's "Remembering Last Summer" and to Paul Anka's dramatic "Summer's Gone." The "summer longings" premise cropped up time and again in the Lettermen songbook. In the summer of 1965 they seduced teenagers by bravely adapting Mack Discant's words to Max Steiner's "Theme from *A Summer Place*." Later that year they released the album *Jim, Tony and Bob*, which included "Summer's Come and Gone," another Gilkyson-Dehr-Miller lament over love lost and times past that bolsters the Lettermen's folk connections. It also includes a self-referential line about "three lonely boys on a lonely shore."

As the 1960s progressed, the Lettermen stayed with their auspicious format to earn a place as America's #1 adult contemporary vocal group of that decade. Engemann left the lineup by the end of 1967. He was replaced by Jim Pike's brother Gary, who helped the trio launch into a more Vegas-inspired mode on such records as "Shangri-La," Paul Anka's "Put Your Head on My Shoulder," and the medley of "Goin' Out of My Head / Can't Take My Eyes Off You."

Their 1967 album *Warm* included songs by the Association ("Don't Blame It on Me"), the Beatles ("For No One," "Here, There and Everywhere"), Jerome Kern ("Smoke Gets in Your Eyes)," and a lyrics-added elucidation of the Santo & Johnny instrumental "Sleep Walk." Subsequent endeavors would show an affinity with their fellow summerchimers on versions of "Graduation Day, "A Summer Song," and "Everyone's Gone to the Moon." "Together with the creative instrumental backing of arranger-conductor Perry Botkin, Jr.," the back-cover notes declare, "the Lettermen mold each song to melodic and lyric perfection and create a romantic atmosphere in which the entire world of Lettermen love songs flourishes with magnificent oneness."

That "magnificent oneness" was part of the harmonic convergence that permeated the alien radio signals on the night John Gummoe communed with his "Rhythm of the Rain." He still appreciates his mentors. "I was brought up on the Four Aces, the Four Lads, and the Lettermen. We did a couple of concerts with them in the sixties. I always loved what they did. I have always been very proud of my sound. If one wants to call it vanilla, that's a compliment. It was commercial; it had a universal appeal. When I think of vanilla, I think of an acoustic guitar, a gentle voice. Music that doesn't hurt. I never growled on a song in my life."

8

Vanilla Psychedelia

Curt Boettcher's "Upholstered Folk"

"**A**ll alone am I, in my world." This refrain from "Dancing Dandelion," a song Curt Boettcher recorded in 1968, encapsulates all that was marvelous and unsettling about the man's career and life. Its lyrics tell of an unattached visionary, blessed with an illuminated mind but pressured nonetheless to close himself off every time he reaches from his solitary fortress.

Barricaded behind rosy dreams and thorny obsessions, Boettcher at least had an easy time filling the contradictory roles of misanthrope and adept. As a person, he remained an enigma to many who worked with and attempted to love him. But Boettcher's cravings for spiritual certitude, despite all odds, made him one of the more remarkable characters in late 1960s West Coast harmony pop.

Sharing Joe Meek's autocratic quirks and (likely) his emotional quandaries, Boettcher broke through the societal noose by expanding his auditory horizons, even if this meant symbolically smashing his head against the studio soundboard. Bold ribbons of audio candyfloss adorned his circuitry as he devised sounds that would impact artists including the Association and Tommy Roe, as well as Chad & Jeremy in their psychedelic phase.

The Boettcher story properly begins in the mid-1960s, when rock and pop were going through an identity shift. The Beatles evolved from the primitive Mersey beat as Lennon and McCartney walked the melancholy mile required to cultivate their lyrical gifts. While songs like Count Five's "Psychotic Reaction" confirmed parental fears about rock 'n' roll's baleful blow, other tunes, such as the Beatles' "Yesterday," the Left Banke's "Walk Away Renee," and Bob Lind's "Elusive Butterfly" offered encouragement.

At the time, the term "folk-rock" was the catchall category as electric guitars merged with their acoustic counterparts. While those entrenched in purist folk politics spewed forth shopworn canards about the evils of going "commercial," Bob Dylan twitted audiences at the 1965 Newport Folk Festival by taking his electric guitar onstage. Future Doors producer Paul Rothchild, who handled Dylan's console that day, recalls the peace-loving Pete Seeger becoming so livid he grabbed an axe and threatened to sever the cables if the gravel-voiced bard proceeded with such a heinous act.

If folk purists thought that Dylan squealing out his electrified (but still raw) lyrics was a step into Mammon's jaws, they were in for paroxysms when groups such as the New Christy Minstrels (and to some extent even the Byrds) processed folk textures into proud, pretty, and echoey pop confections every bit as "commercial" as Mitch Miller's sing-alongs.

The New Christy Minstrels were a special bone of contention among the folk movement's left wing, many of whose comrades scorned the group's escapist fare of old railroad songs, love tunes, and Broadway and Hollywood themes. But, along with the Kingston Trio and Peter, Paul & Mary (whom the pickers and strummers considered more "real"), the New Christy Minstrels were among the most popular, albeit processed, folk acts.

From the time he formed the New Christy Minstrels in 1961, Randy Sparks had no apologies about his goal to forge "a compromise between the Norman Luboff Choir and the Kingston Trio." The lineup usually consisted of ten members, but the personnel changed constantly; its alumni including Jerry Yester (later of the Modern Folk Quartet and the Lovin' Spoonful), Gene Clark (who would join the Byrds), future Association member Larry Ramos, Barry McGuire (who charted solo with "Eve of Destruction") and Kim Carnes (who found her niche in the early 1980s with "Bette Davis Eyes").

Though named after the notorious nineteenth-century minstrel troupe, the New Christy Minstrels were far from being "Ethiopian song" pretenders. They attained Top 40 prominence with the 1963 single "Green Green," with Ray Conniffied harmonies offset only by Barry McGuire's foghorn lead. They went on to record more burnished songs, flouting those levying the ultra-commercialism stigma with ultra-commercial fare such as "Saturday Night" and an adorable version of the *Mary Poppins* classic, "Chim-Chim Cheree."

Years later, director Christopher Guest's mockumentary *A Mighty Wind* parodied the inane browbeaters who thought themselves too "authentic" to give the New Christy Minstrels the time of day. Here, a group called the Folksmen (modeled after the Kingston Trio) and the New Main Street Singers (patterned on the New Christy Minstrels) are at aesthetic loggerheads when vying for the spotlight in a Public Television reunion concert. One scene, of a preconcert cocktail party, speaks volumes as a Folksmen member sidles up to the only visibly black guest, making a desperate camaraderie pitch by singling out the New Main Street Singers as the commercialized fakes.

By 1962, Curt Boettcher, apparently oblivious to such "authenticity" fetishes, had plans to go the New Christy Minstrels route while attending the University of Minnesota. In a scenario almost paralleling that of the Fleetwoods, he met two sisters—Dotti and Sheri Holmberg—who shared his musical predilections. The Holmbergs (also Twin Cities denizens) had been harmonizing at church gatherings and various charity socials under the name the Holmberg Hi-Lite Sisters. Boettcher met them at Le Zoo, a Minneapolis coffeehouse tailored to a folk clientele. There, the elfish seer strummed guitar and piped out his gravity-defying tenor. Though the lousy weather resulted in scant attendance that night, he refused to let the limp response deter him and asked the audience to join in a rendition of "Puff, the Magic Dragon." Sensing a moment of drama and possible fame, Dotti and Sherri Holmberg made sure they were the loudest in the crowd and immediately secured their place in Boettcher's heart. They joined him, along with Ron Neilson, to form the GoldeBriars.

The group's oddly spelled name was just another example of Boettcher's idiosyncrasies. He intended the name to imply an alchemistic fusion of opposites: the precious element of gold merging with earth's prickly briars. One night, during another coffeehouse engagement, a headhunter named John Haeny approached the group about record prospects. Haeny, who would become a respected engineer, secured the first GoldeBriars contract. Bob Morgan had since gone from being Mitch Miller's assistant producer to overseeing Epic Records and, considering his Brothers Four work, was the logical choice to nurture the GoldeBriars' tight harmonies. To Morgan, Boettcher stood out with a voice that seemed processed through helium, a mode that was refreshing in its unrepentant dandyism.

"Boettcher was the magic in the group," Morgan remembers. "He surrounded himself with good people like Dotti, Sheri, and Ron. But Curt was the one who told them what they should do. He had his own thoughts about flowing tones, modular up and down scales, interweaving suspensions that were light and airy. They were very, very young; Curt couldn't have been more than maybe nineteen. Their sound was high-pitched and kind of floated. Even the up-tempo material floated back and forth. They played on top of the beat and were precise, as opposed to jazz or swing people who played behind the beat."

Back in England, at roughly the same time, Joe Meek also sought a similar "Everly Chipmunks" effect with a high-pitched brother duo called the Dowlands, but they came nowhere near the GoldeBriars in terms of pushing the sonic envelope. In February 1964, during the same week that *Meet the Beatles* appeared in record stores, the GoldeBriars released their first album, *The GoldeBriars*. "Railroad Boy," the opening track, leads right into that bright sound—a contrast to the dark lyrics about a heartbroken young girl who, after falling for a boy from the wrong side of the tracks, devastates her parents when Dad walks into the attic one day to find her "hanging by a rope."

Structurally, most of the GoldeBriars' material did not waver from the standard folk formula of songs such as "Old Time Religion" and "Shenandoah," but acoustically their style blended the homespun and the sugarspun. The Holmberg sisters wrote most of the songs that appeared on the group's second album, *Straight Ahead!*, which came out in late summer of 1964. The GoldeBriars' feminine allure continued, with Dotti's little-girl voice sparkling on tunes such as the Boettcher-Goldsteinn composition "Sea of Tears." The album's liner notes even mention how the first album's "three female voices (Ron doesn't sing) made the group sound very much like The Lennon Sisters doing work songs."

Boettcher's songwriting also surfaced on *Straight Ahead!* with "Haiku," which is among the album's standouts. His short but effectual solo, "deep in thought of memories forgotten," is likely a reflection of his youth, which he spent in Japan. "He was a navy brat," Morgan remembers, "and showed his travels in some of his writing. The first time I ever heard the term 'haiku' is when he wrote that title. This was when they were still trying to find themselves. Then, Bobb Goldsteinn came along. He hooked up with Curt and became more of an influence on them. Curt then went into a different direction and got more Tin Pan Alley."

The GoldeBriars: Curt Boettcher (left) cultivated a style that blended the homespun and the sugarspun.

Bobb Goldsteinn—who would become Boettcher's manager, confidant, and probably the best raconteur on all things Boettcher—was also an accomplished songwriter. Best known for composing the Village Stompers' 1963 instrumental "Washington Square," Goldsteinn was there in the early days when Greenwich Villagers flocked to coffeehouses and clubs. This is when "authentic" folk, like "authentic" jazz, gave many mostly white, middle-class audiences a chance to fulminate against things white and middle-class. Purists may have been less than enthusiastic when Gordon Jenkins's string orchestra embossed some of the Weavers' recordings, but Goldsteinn intuited a new and exciting direction with what he calls "upholstered folk." He elucidates that "upholstered," in this sense, means echo, double-tracking, and "anything that inflates or cushions."

Among Goldsteinn's favorite GoldeBriars recordings is "Castle on the Corner," another variation on the theme of unreachable love.

> This kind of song was a big Brill Building fad when I was there around 1961, '62, and '63. Unattainable love was the winning theme. We used every metaphor possible. John Gluck wrote a version of that with the song "Mecca" and went on to write "It's My Party" for Lesley Gore. These fads would sweep through the business like the garment industry. "Castle on the Corner" was like many songs that say: "She loves me but she doesn't know I exist, I'm really shy and don't want to approach her."

Deemed "too odd" by 1964 pop standards and with too much of a processed flavor to pass muster with folk's hard-core hickory nuts, neither album proved salable. Even when attempting to blend with the Greenwich Village folk scene, the GoldeBriars came across as strange and a bit precious, especially with their gypsy shirts with tunics. The boys also had the temerity to wear earrings. (They were asked to leave a Charleston, South Carolina, hotel when their exotic look scared some of the guests.)

"They are sorta 'folk,' but with a distinctive twist," Dotti Holmberg and Bobb Goldsteinn claim when summarizing the group's effect, stressing how Boettcher's "oriental exposure bastes the group's sound like a soy and ginger marinade." Boettcher's vaunting ego also did little to encourage any future GoldeBriars projects. After recording a third album, which was not released, the GoldeBriars parted ways in mid-1965.

As under-the-radar as they may seem in retrospect, the GoldeBriars, with their balance of girl and near-girl voices, left an impression. "Without Boettcher," Goldsteinn insists, "we would have had no Mamas and Papas as we know them. Cass was his biggest fan. She imported his sound into the Mugwumps. And when they invited her to join the Mamas and the Papas, she brought the Boettcher sound with her." Boettcher himself, in a 1974 interview for *ZigZag* magazine, concurs. "I think we were the first folk rock group."

The art of sweetening folk music with twinkling studio effects, string orchestras, and electric guitars would undergo several permutations in the next few years, both in America and in the United Kingdom. This cross-pollination—"the Cascades meet Chad & Jeremy"—would produce what history would deem "sunshine pop." In this sense, Boettcher was ahead of the game, using electronic gadgets to prefigure psychedelia before its major advent on the pop charts.

Boettcher's utmost sunshine venture materialized when he brought a demo he'd made to Vee-Jay Records executive Steve Clark. Won over by the demo's sprightly textures, Clark soon joined Boettcher and Victoria Winston to form Our Productions. One of Boettcher's first assignments was to produce—and add his pixie dust to—Tommy Roe. In 1966 Roe was going through stylistic fluctuations, imitating Buddy Holly with songs like "Sheila," but gladly joining Boettcher for such light and bouncy fare as "Sweet Pea" and "Hooray for Hazel," as well as for more heady material for the 1967 album *It's Now Winter's Day*. Boettcher added psychedelic innovations to GoldeBriars-style chirps with the Our Productions release of his composition "Milk and Honey," as well as to a song, written by Roe, called "Too Young to Marry." "Milk and Honey" is particularly disarming in its gorgeous naïveté, and is coated with lyrics that pine away for a special and spectral territory where "lovers last forever."

Enamored of the band the moment he witnessed their performance at Pasadena's Ice House, Boettcher played a major role in molding the sound of the Association, intuiting that they were more of a studio phenomenon than a live act. Valiant, which established vanilla credentials with the Cascades, also wanted to take the nice-boy approach into the psychotropic frontier. Stipulating that professional studio musicians would do the basic backup work, Valiant head Barry De Vorzon allowed Boettcher to produce the group's first LP: *And Then . . . Along Comes the Association*. The album, which included the ultimate prom song, "Cherish," jolted Boettcher's harmonic finesse, and his enthusiasm for stereo separation, up several notches.

By the end of 1966, when the Dancing Dandelion became one of Los Angeles's most sought-after independent producers, Boettcher accelerated his harmonic ambitions by forming the Ballroom. At the time, he attempted to align the music with his spiritual leanings, identifying with the loosely defined organization Subud, through which he met much of the Ballroom's personnel. Along with Jim Bell and Michele O'Malley, there was Sandy Salisbury, a smiley California blond (and a future writer of children's fiction) who provided another fine tenor foundation.

The going was not often as smooth as the music, however, when Boettcher tried getting his fellow musicians to play the songs exactly as he heard them in his head. He would deploy terms like "snappy, snappy" and "cherry, cherry" to describe the luminosity he expected to hear. Fond of those hallucinogenic sugar cubes, Boettcher intended his Ballroom recordings to re-create the cerebral carnivals, altering and enhancing the GoldeBriars-style "upholstered" folk with devices such as a tape-looping Mellotron for an optimum phantasmagoria.

The Urantia Book was also a likely stimulant in Boettcher's acoustical game plan. This grand tome, found abandoned in a Chicago bus station in the 1930s, has intrigued and inspired millions since its first publication in 1955. It attempts, in often-recondite language, to explain concepts as vast as the creation of the universe, the life and teachings of Christ, the genesis and destiny of mankind, and the nature of reality as conceived by "seraphim" and "midway creatures" that act as liaisons between Heaven and Earth to aid mortals on an ever-ascending spiritual evolution.

Boettcher's music and munchkin voice conveyed some kind of communion with such midway creatures. These celestial fantasies may not have taught him the infinite wisdom of human interaction, but they likely informed his recurring themes about trying to break out of a "space-fettered," "time-bound" shell. His quest for eternal Eden came across on "Spinning Spinning Spinning," "Would You Like to Go?" "Love's Fatal Way," and even the self-evidently dour "It's a Sad World," which evoked images of flower children scaling the psychic altitudes and romping in daisy-splayed meadows—the musical equivalent of Day-Glo balloons.

"Boettcher offered a tingly sound," Bobb Goldsteinn recalls. "It was a mentholated, wintergreen sound—something that clears the sinuses. It was spongy and cut by a certain intellectual precision that kept it from being sentimental; that was a leaning of Curt's. Brian Wilson confirmed how much he revered Curt's vocal sense. You can hear something like Curt's voice in the Sandpipers. You can also hear it in Harpers Bizarre, although they were too self-conscious about their work. And he could have easily worked with a singer like Brian Hyland."

By seeking refuge in such ethereal cream, Boettcher also found a way to escape his twitchy, demanding, and, at times, demonic self. Future Boettcher collaborator Joey Stec summarized Boettcher's personality with the term "control freak." "Boettcher was manic," Bobb Goldsteinn remembers of the Golde-Briars days. "He would fritter around, wave his fingertips as if they were burned. He had a private language that was not shaped by the rules of English. He was despotic—the classic Napoleon martinet complex."

One nutty genius was plenty for the world to absorb, but two plotting side by side was a recipe for the type of human combustion that occurred in the spring of 1966, when Boettcher met Gary Usher. Usher recalled he was working at Studio Three West with Brian Wilson when he heard curious, high-end noises coming from an adjacent room. He and Wilson edged down the corridor, getting closer and closer to the source until they finally came upon the diminutive cherub with the earring. The envious shade of white on Brian Wilson's face when encountering Boettcher's studio craft has become legendary among many soft rock enthusiasts. The moment Usher and Boettcher became soul mates, 1960s pop was never the same.

At first glance, Usher's background might seem to have made him an improbable addition to Boettcher's world. In addition to his involvement with such Samuel Arkoff cinema fare as *Muscle Beach Party* and his role in the early 1960s monster craze with groups such as the Ghouls and the Weird-Ohs, Usher basked in a pampered Beach Boys lifestyle full of surf, cars, and girls. Though California born, he spent a childhood in New England before rebounding to the place where it never rains, living in the Inglewood area, not far from Brian Wilson's hometown of Hawthorne. Usher collaborated with Wilson on adolescent fodder that included "409" and "Pom Pom Playgirl," but he also shared songwriting credit on two of the Beach Boys' better early offerings, "In My Room" and "The Lonely Sea."

As the tanning lotion inevitably started to itch, Usher became frustrated. He wanted to make new music. Inspired by ideas that would later be given the "new age" imprimatur, he experimented with sounds that promoted inner healing and outer harmony. He got a chance to nurture some of his ambitions as a producer at Columbia Records, where he was on hand for recordings by Chad & Jeremy, Simon & Garfunkel, and the Byrds.

Chad & Jeremy could be persnickety about song selections, but Usher was sure the duo would leap at the chance to reinterpret an unusual and clever tune, previously recorded by the UK group the Ivy League, that equated unrequited love with global decay. Heartbroken but undaunted when Chad & Jeremy balked, Usher recorded "My World Fell Down" himself, using his own choice of studio musicians and relying upon Boettcher's spiritual counsel. He also employed Wrecking Crew pal Hal Blaine at the drums, with Doris Day's son Terry Melcher and Beach Boy Bruce Johnston singing the choral parts. Boettcher was not present for this particular recording; the song's wraithlike lead singer was none other than Glen Campbell.

With "My World Fell Down" ready for release, Usher now only needed a nod from Columbia honcho Clive Davis for the unveiling. Davis would go bonkers over progressive rock following his trip to the 1967 Monterey International Pop Festival, but he was still open-minded enough to appreciate Usher's potentially commercial enterprise. Davis gave his blessing, even though the group still did not exist. Usher at last found an ensemble, which he christened with the name of his astrological sign. Sagittarius took shape less as a bona fide band and more as a coven of excellent studio talent, with Boettcher its principal player.

When Usher got Boettcher a staff producer job at Columbia, he was also able to help him get out of his Our Productions obligations. In the process, Columbia became the owner of Boettcher's Ballroom recordings, which explains why the Sagittarius album *Present Tense* contains two slightly altered Ballroom numbers: "Would You Like to Go?" and "Musty Dusty." The Ballroom and Sagittarius songs were so congenial in exposing the splendor of twee that their juxtaposition was seamless. "Musty Dusty" is the best example. In it, Boettcher looks back on childhood "memories shattered and gone," with "all the maple trees, butterflies, and bees banished away." Here, he reminisces about toys—"lost little friends" like "Teddy Bear and Bobo the Clown"—as his multitracked voice joins an acoustic guitar and an electronic keyboard to conjure the melodic wisps of a vanishing carnival.

Boettcher was now more determined than ever to imbue the music with what Usher has called "the vibratory element." Both men were serious in their beliefs about the effects that certain types of music have on the "etheric bodies." This is where the *Urantia* influence on *Present Tense* is most apparent. Boettcher appears to have enjoyed intercommunication with some higher intelligence when he wrote the opening song (and the group's first single), "Another Time." Loaded with enough otherworldly grandeur to match the aerated tone, it suggests a solitary but bemused time-drifter. While tracks like "Glass" (which the Sandpipers also recorded) triggered raga-pop trances, the album's pretty atmosphere is sabotaged with the creeping nihilism of "The Truth Is Not Real"—Usher's only songwriting effort in the collection.

The voices, tweaked higher and ever reverberant, offered the same cerebral prickle in "Would You Like to Go?"—which Boettcher cowrote with the Association's Gary Alexander. It is among the most airy-fairy of the Sagittarius sessions, the lyrics offering a return to a long-lost paradise, where "choruses of angelic hosts sing hallelujah." "The Keeper of the Games" is packed with

Celebrating the splendor of twee, Sagittarius's *Present Tense* combined multitracking, glistening effects, and wraithlike voices to evoke both nostalgic and psychedelic themes.

Urantian references as well, mainly to those sometimes frustrating "Thought Adjusters" that the book claims dwell inside every individual:

> Adjusters are playing the sacred and superb game of the ages; they are engaged in one of the supreme adventures of time in space. And how happy they are when your co-operation permits them to lend assistance in your short struggles of time as they continue to prosecute their larger tasks of eternity. But usually, when your Adjuster attempts to communicate with you, the message is lost in

the material currents of the energy streams of human mind; only occasionally do you catch an echo, a faint and distant echo, of the divine voice.

All along, Boettcher was mixing bits and pieces of his harmonic obsessions into other projects. With the band Eternity's Children, he went more into folk-rock mode and—despite the group's desire to sound heavier—managed to keep them buoyant through most of their debut album. The group's most remembered single, "Mrs. Bluebird," exemplified the compromise between pretty folk-pop and an oddly fitting fuzz guitar blare.

Finally, with his next group, the Millennium, Boettcher veered into areas that would be better appreciated decades later, when "sunshine pop" fans understood that "lightweight" need not be a pejorative term. Along with engineer and coproducer Keith Olsen, the Millennium consisted of Boettcher, Mike Fennelly, Joey Stec, Sandy Salisbury, Doug Rhodes, Lee Mallory, and onetime GoldeBriars drummer Ron Edgar. Edgar, in a comparison to the rock-hard fare he previously offered with the Music Machine, fondly called the Millennium's music "soft serve."

Sessions began in 1968 on *Begin*, the Millennium's only officially released album. Boettcher's knack for reversed echoes and catchy yet dreamy structures continued. At this juncture, he would assemble up to fifteen harmony layers and whip them up into a reverse-echo soufflé. "I Just Want to Be Your Friend," for example, is ever gentle and spacey—full of innocent pleadings for companionship, but tempered with lingering suspicions that such intimacies are beyond reach. The message at least subdues listeners with the impression that even those unsuccessful connections may entail amicable departures and "finally leave me transcending." But the Millennium's lofty messages about superbeings and a Universal Mind incurred an expensive tally that some honchos at Columbia found insufferable.

Usher, with some of Boettcher's help, made a noble effort to continue that luminescent spirit on the second Sagittarius album, *The Blue Marble*, which was released in 1969 on Together Records. He reclaimed his co-composition "In My Room" by layering on multitracked acoustic arpeggios, an "I Am the Walrus" cello, and enough helium intonation to indicate that the group still hovered in Boettcher's orbit. This mélange of effects resulted in a much more enchanting and stargazing version of the song than the Beach Boys' original, especially as it ricochets off both ends of the stereo continuum. *The Blue Marble* appeared just as the Moog synthesizer had begun making inroads on more and more pop recordings. Usher used the device not really to synthesize so much as to create the ghostly textures that listeners might expect of a "space age" apparatus. Despite a few harbingers of country-tinged vocals that would be the vogue in the coming years, most of the tracks orchestrate glistened dreams. "I See in You" sounds every bit like its "crystal sea where the two of us can be alone," while "I Sing My Song" has all the cherubic qualities of the version that Boettcher recorded for Dotti Holmberg in 1966.

Though he was miffed when Chad & Jeremy refused to record "My World Fell Down," Usher still kept the duo in mind for other projects. Peter & Gordon disbanded by 1968, but Chad & Jeremy sang on for a little while longer, despite the onslaught of bluesier Columbia acts, like Big Brother and the Holding Company, that started to upstage the sweet psychedelia. Soon, Chad & Jeremy ventured into the *Sgt. Pepper*–inspired "concept album" *Of Cabbages and Kings* to mixed response. The press once portrayed them as aristocratic oddballs among a Beat generation; now they were accused of intellectual pomp. Around this time they recorded "Sister Marie," which had the obvious presence of what Chad refers to as Boettcher's "higher-than-high voice." As to be expected, Clyde hated the "ear candy."

Usher's "My World Fell Down" arrangement, a mixture of Baroque-styled acoustical sound effects, became the sound template he pursued on Chad & Jeremy's follow-up LP *The Ark*. Usher is listed as the official producer and Chad Stuart the arranger, but the album (despite the occasional grainy guitar) has the mark of Boettcher all over it—with multitracking, echoes, ebullient woodwinds, and whimsical songs telling whimsical stories. The Columbia bean counters were predictably antsy about scaling back costs, but Usher ignored such tics.

When *The Ark* disembarked before a fickle world in 1969, the net result was Usher getting fired and Chad & Jeremy's careers capsizing in the gales of changing tastes. Nineteen sixty-nine was, after all, the year in which the granolafication of pop music began, as more and more whole-wheat warblers of country and soul eclipsed sugarspun choruses. Today, *The Ark* commands appreciation for its dazzling acoustics, trippy humor, and, especially, those Boettcher-esque soprano layers on songs such as "Painted Dayglow Smile." "Paxton Quigley's Had the Course" (from Chad's score to the 1968 film *Three in the Attic*) includes choral mists—even melodic phrases—that foreshadow Queen's "Bohemian Rhapsody." Looking back, the album, even with its wry humor, seems just a shade of the old apple tree from "olde tyme" tunes about reverie and romance. Boettcher was the good fairy who aroused such endearing dalliances.

For Boettcher, there was life after the Millennium, as he continued to sing and produce. Among his best endeavors was a coproduction with Keith Olsen on Sandy Salisbury's 1969 recording, "Come Softly." Salisbury's style often leaned more toward California country, but the harmonic surges on this update of the Fleetwoods' "Come Softly to Me" proved a beatific studio moment. After lapsing into granolafied pop with the 1973 solo LP *There's an Innocent Face*, Boettcher sang backup on the 1976 Elton John album *Blue Moves*, as well as on the Elton John–Kiki Dee single "Don't Go Breaking My Heart." He also contributed session vocals to some late 1970s and early 1980s Beach Boys records. Fiddling with disco, he at least got a chance to explore more openly gay themes. Though nurturing the muse until his death in 1987, Boettcher never recaptured that 1960s "painted Day-Glo" poise.

"Curt was Peter Pan," Bob Goldsteinn concludes. "He considered himself the founder of a cult. The cult was founded on him being the absolute guru. He did this with every group he was involved with. Curt knew about chakras. He may not have known the word 'etheric' at the time, but he embodied it. There is an Italian word—*putti*—for angels: the little cupids and sprites that hang around the edges of the canvasses. As devilish as he could be, and he had some very deep, vengeful undercurrents, Curt's sound was totally '*putti*.' His angels' testicles had not descended yet. That's the Curt Boettcher sound: It goes from heart up and does not descend to the abdomen—and certainly not to the groin!"

9

A Name That's Lighter than Air

The Association Machine

The Association was in a cheeky mood when it opened the Monterey International Pop Festival on June 16, 1967. Brian Cole, the group's resident jokester, introduced the act as "a machine of our own construction," pointing out the ensemble's "many integral parts" to the accompaniment of a robotic beat. When he finished, the six components switched gears and launched into the wacky rhythm of "Along Comes Mary."

There they were: a six-man melody unit, wearing jackets and ties while facing the more ornately clad flower children. They worked to clockwork perfection as their guitars, percussion, intermittent flute, and voices commanded uncommon polish. Their onstage formation, as precise and comely as the harmonies, made the bedlam inherent in the driving tempo and alleged drug references in "Along Comes Mary" seem ordered, professional, and perhaps too "square" for the mélange of self-styled miscreants, such as the Who and Jimi Hendrix, who followed them. The crowd apparently liked them, but somehow the Association still seemed like the proverbial strangers in a strange land.

Years after the Association assembled at Monterey, melodies such as "Windy," "Never My Love," and, of course, "Cherish" have—in both their original and interpreted versions—quelled frayed nerves on oldies and adult contemporary radio formats. Many now look back on how the group's harmonic convergence cast a benevolent glow over what would become the Woodstock Nation's creeping apocalypse.

The career, however, was never as easy as the listening. It may be lumped in with many 1960s rock luminaries, but a closer listen to most of the group's material, including album cuts, reveals a vocal ensemble more anchored in conventional choral discipline than most of its contemporaries. They often used the same session musicians, and promulgated lyrics with similar controversies as the Mamas and the Papas, but the members of the Association always seemed better craftsmen and, therefore, less hip.

The group's originators, Jules (sometimes Gary) Alexander, whom Cole designated as the "new transistorized model primal digit flexing calculator," and Terry Kirkman, the "elongated fluting vocalizator," began their serendipitous friendship at a party in 1962. Kirkman had studied music and knew how to play several instruments; Alexander had had a naval tour of duty in Hawaii. By 1964 they had reunited in Pomona, California, where Kirkman managed a coffeehouse. From there, they migrated to Los Angeles and entered a thriving music scene, the hub of which was the Troubadour, a folk establishment that featured Monday night hootenannies. Here, an informally assembled house group called the Inner Tubes gave patrons such as Cass Elliott and David Crosby (along with more inhibited audience members) a chance to ham it up.

The Troubadour's owner, Doug Weston, was impressed by the group, and he offered the musicians a professional chance. The thirteen male members of the Inner Tubes came to the scheduled event and, out of default, dubbed themselves the Men. The band experienced several permutations before seven of the thirteen got testy and bailed out. And then there were six. In search of a new name, the surviving crew debated over "the Neo-Renaissance Singers" and "the Aristocrats." One member's girlfriend decided to look up "aristocrat" in the dictionary, but she instead fixed her eye on "association." It encapsulated the group's interdependent and structured nature, from the way they organized their vocal blend to the parliamentary manner (a process they called "the hanging") in which they determined which members' original compositions would appear on each album.

Though lumped with the Southern California sound, the Association was truly a regional potpourri, its members hailing from at least six different states.

Alexander came from Chattanooga, Tennessee, and Terry from Salina, Kansas. The other members included the "semi-reclined percussive invertebrator" (or drummer) Ted Bluechel Jr., from San Pedro, California; Russ Giguere, the "manifold bifurcated tambouriner" from Portsmouth, New Hampshire, on vocals and guitar; Jim Yester, the "flexible rhythm instrumentator" from Birmingham, Alabama, who sang and played rhythm guitar; and Brian Cole, the "consistent low-range modulator" from Tacoma, Washington, who handled the bass and the heady humor.

Although they auditioned to perform at the Ice House in Pasadena, they were more intent on grooming themselves for the recording studios. Even then, their music was not readily subject to a category. A small label called Jubilee (which put out such material as Rusty Warren's party records) took them under its wing for an A-side: a rather despairing and acoustically muddy version of "Babe I'm Gonna Leave You" (predating Led Zeppelin's rock 'n' roll arrangement) that made few commercial inroads. Valiant Records, however, offered better times.

The label that had christened the Cascades sent representatives to the Troubadour to watch the group. They took a liking to its version of Bob Dylan's "One Too Many Mornings" and promptly released it in October 1965 as the Association's A-side. Despite production values from Valiant's president Barry De Vorzon, as well as a vocal arrangement by Clark Burroughs (formerly of the Hi-Los), the record sounded earnest, but fuzzy by Association standards. Except for an appearance on the *Hollywood A Go Go* television variety show and some local airplay, it did not travel well. Then Curt Boettcher came along to shed his guiding light.

With Boettcher, the Association brightened its sound considerably. He was relatively green as a producer but still insisted on exerting his control. Alexander was most enthused over "Along Comes Mary," which he had previously recorded with Boettcher on a demo session. When the song was released as a single in March 1966, the group inspired the Association Admiration Aggregation, a group of fans whose members harangued radio stations to air it (and all of its marijuana implications) as often as possible.

Despite its resin-coated undertones, "Along Comes Mary" also inspired nuns to interpret it as a paean to "Mother Mary." At one point they swamped the group during a performance at Disneyland. Ted Bluechel told *Goldmine*: "The song became so popular that all the St. Mary parochial schools in the country taped it for the pep rallies. I don't think that would have happened if they thought the song was about drugs."

In addition to Boettcher, the Association had another influence. Just as San Francisco boasted a mystic map to the media-friendly Summer of Love, the Los Angeles area hosted various pop-friendly cults. Like Boettcher, the Association found succor in Subud. Its founder, Muhammad Subuh Sumo-hadiwidjojo, who originated in Indonesia's Central Java area, went by the nickname "Bapak" and espoused pathways to enlightenment based on Sanskrit principles. Some of the Association members were so impressed with Subud's invocations to inner divinity that they presented five of the album's tracks to the cult's Elders, who were especially impressed with "Along Comes Mary" and "Your Own Love." Sure enough, Valiant released them as A- and B-sides, respectively.

The 1966 appearance of their first album, *And Then . . . Along Comes the Association,* heralded the band's dissociation from their surroundings. They had a sound that captured the best of its generation, but they projected an aura and style of another time. Kirkman was twenty-five when he composed the opening track "Enter the Young"—a rebel yell to teenagers from an older but sympathetic outsider. On this and, more obviously, the overbearing antiwar opus, "Requiem for the Masses," the Association's prepared harmonies spawned images of pacifist military cadets chiming advisories on brotherhood and social change.

Even as a package, *And Then . . . Along Comes the Association* conveyed contradictions. Though *Teen* magazine's Phyllis Burgess opened her gushing liner notes to the album with the sentence "Some people think musicians are weird, and many would think the Association weird," the back cover photo showed the group in front of an antique limousine, in starched-collar, three-piece suits that made them look less like "weirdoes" and more like long-haired Fleet Street accountants. Musically, the collection combined pretty melodies and harmonies with searching lyrics and, thanks mostly to Boettcher's studio technology, daring (and "weird") instrumentation.

The album's entire second side displays the Association in top form, starting with the second single. Released in August 1966, "Cherish" reached *Billboard*'s #1 spot the following month. The song harbors the secret thoughts of every shy, sullen, and nerdy kid who at last finds (perhaps for the only time in his or her life) the chance to declare romantic passion. In contrast to Dylan's relentless relevance, "Cherish" sported lyrics that borrowed from a reputable lexicon of tried-and-true sentiments. Some Association members had qualms about this nobly un-ironic song receiving prominence on the airwaves. Fortunately, they did not prevail. The recording transmitted "just the right sound" to allay weary romantics across the globe.

New Christy Minstrel Mike Whelan wanted to record and introduce it, but the Association turned "Cherish" into an acoustical labor of love. The meticulous vocal parts, with human bells reminiscent of the Chordettes' "Mr. Sandman," were recorded at Columbia's highly regarded Studio D. The song's background glistens with bells and a celesta—a tonic that Perry Botkin Jr. had already prescribed to great success with "Rhythm of the Rain."

After "Cherish," the album's remaining minutes unravel into an alternately pensive and jocular journey. Ted Bluechel's lyrics to "Standing Still" speak of "tender phrases proven true" and dreams of kissing in "a timeless eternal bliss," while "Message of Our Love," a Boettcher and Tandyn Almer composition, includes a fairy-light chorus, a quasi-raga instrumental interlude, the sound of a Theremin, and themes of otherworldly communion with Urantian overtones.

Alexander, the group's official metaphysician, was already threatening to make good on his plans to travel to India and live out his mystic ambitions, but he did contribute the album's final three tracks. "Round Again" is another celestial experiment, this time set to a dreamy waltz beat; the haunting and low-key "Remember" pairs lilting guitar chords with an ominous electronic hum, imparting the wisdom of love "out of time and space." "Changes" closes the album with a peppier mood and Ted Bluechel's impersonation of a tonally tenuous Ricky Nelson. In 1967 the group performed this song on *The Andy Williams Show*, clad in dark suits similar to those they sport on the album photo. They looked prim and stylish compared to the casually dressed Williams, who sang right along with them.

Once *And Then . . . Along Comes the Association* was finished, the group, for some arcane reason, fired Boettcher. He may have been officially out of the picture, but the group preserved the Dancing Dandelion's cherubic acoustics and harmonic clarity. Jim Yester's brother Jerry, a former New Christy Minstrel and future Lovin' Spoonful, acted as the group's new producer.

"Pandora's Golden Heebie Jeebies" was the initial single to emerge from the Yester sessions for the follow-up album, *Renaissance*. Alexander crafted it to reflect his Eastern contemplations. From the moment it leaps out with a Japanese koto, it delivers on a promise of a "heady" excursion about lost love and morbid desires that, like a moody Stephen Foster piece, slips gloomy thoughts into an otherwise pretty package. Some, including Association members themselves, deemed "Pandora" "that weird song," even though it comes across as dark but sweet at the same time.

Valiant courted radio play with "Looking Glass," another Alexander piece that would survive as one of the group's best efforts—a combination of bright harmonies and themes about self-reflection and doomed love, tweaked with psychedelic fuzz guitar. More than any other Association track, this earns the band the sobriquet that *Goldmine* writer Marty Natchez would later use when deeming the group "cerebral choirboys." Although "Looking Glass," like "Pandora," proved vanilla at heart, it was too esoteric for the mainstream. Valiant then offered "No Fair at All," which, according to its composer Jim Yester, was written with Dimitri Tiomkin's 1953 theme "Return to Paradise" in mind. The harmonies, consistently soft and roomy, are much like those of the Sandpipers, who were coming to the fore at about the same time.

By the end of 1966, folk rock was a foregone conclusion. The Mamas & the Papas cornered the market on the ultracommercial variety, while Jefferson Airplane embraced a sugar-free and much more stripped-down version. The honchos at Valiant, disappointed that *Renaissance* failed to produce a successful single, bolstered their hopes for the next Association album by relying more on seasoned studio players.

Bones Howe, who at the time was establishing a solid reputation as a producer with the Mamas & the Papas and the Turtles, began the project as an engineer but ended up serving as the producer as well. There were also significant changes taking place with the record label, as Valiant got absorbed into Warner Bros. Still reeling from "Pandora," Alexander predated the Beatles and Donovan by consummating his India-or-bust quest, temporarily rescinding his Association commitment.

Alexander's successor was Larry Ramos Jr., an ex–New Christy Minstrel as well as an ex–child star who was seven when he appeared in the Esther Williams movie *Pagan Love Song*. He also had a way with the ukulele that enabled him to appear on one of Arthur Godfrey's talent shows. Born in Hawaii's West Kauai region, Ramos knew Terry Kirkman from the old days with the Men and arrived just in time to perform on the Association's *Insight Out* album. From then on, he was the band's "digit-flexing instrumentator, stamped 'Made in Japan.'"

Though *Insight Out* had Clark Burroughs returning as vocal arranger, the Association (unlike the Beach Boys) did not as a rule resort to the jazzy cater-wauling of the Hi-Los. The album opens with "Wasn't It a Bit Like Now (Parallel '23)," a rollicking attempt to equate the excesses of the 1960s with the straw-hats-and-roadster days of the Roaring Twenties. Other songs, such as P. F. Sloan's "On a Quiet Night," retained Boettcher's influence, its glistening vocals offset by a harpsichord, a thumping bass guitar, and some backward looping. Bluechel's sunshine voice returned with "We Love Us," while Yester supplied sprightlier insights about romance and dreams on "When Love Comes to Me."

Ruthann Friedman, a folk singer who was trying to build a name in a fickle business, got her break with "Windy," which she dedicated to a rather shy individual who was too timid to express his crush on her. Friedman wrote "Windy" to envision this man's alter ego—a free, soaring spirit leaping out from a taciturn milquetoast. The "Windy" session players congregated at about 1:00 P.M., and the recording culminated in a crowded harmonic closing in which studio engineers, friends, significant others, and Friedman herself sang away. "Windy" was nominated for a 1967 Grammy, but it lost out to the Fifth Dimension's "Up, Up and Away."

The group would achieve a new level of pop immortality on "Never My Love," on which its composers Dick and Don Addrisi impressed Howe by beginning with an unforgettable opening electric guitar riff. The choirboy harmonies were never grander, the romantic connections never sweeter. Notwithstanding the bluesy organ that wiggles in and out of the melody like a randy drunk slinking from bar to bar, "Never My Love" stood tall in the midst of psychedelia's heyday. By August of that year, *Cash Box* magazine ran an ad that also summed up the song's beatific mood, capturing the group in its much-remembered tableau beneath blossoming branches.

One of *Insight Out*'s best tracks is a version of "Happiness Is," another Dick and Don Addrisi tune. Compared to the Anita Kerr Singers, who recorded it with shades of pop-jazz, the Association members stuck to their unified voices, unfettered by any urban "sophistication" pretenses. They, in a sense, let the song breathe with an auditory sensation that, as the lyrics go, "paints a smile on everybody's face." Once again, Bluechel's voice exudes childlike charisma, setting a tone very similar to the vanilla psychedelia of other 1967 fare, including the Yellow Balloon's "Yellow Balloon," the New Christy Minstrels' "I'll Coat Your Mind with Honey," and "Happy," by both the Blades of Grass and the Sunshine Company.

While claiming such innovations as the introduction of the flugelhorn to pop rock, the Association also included names like Marty Paitch (formerly with Stan Kenton) and Bud Shank on their sessions. Yet, even with these seasoned jazz veterans, the group favored a slip-proof vocal mode that was closer to the Four Preps than to the Four Freshmen. As Jules Alexander said an interviewer in 1983: "We tend, in a funny way, and I don't know if you can even quantify it, but we tend to sound like each other."

Compared to less tailored L.A. acts like the Doors, the Association lacked any detectable street credentials. By and large, they were perceived as non-threatening and were more comfortable performing on *The Andy Williams Show* or at the Cocoanut Grove and Greek Theater—places where the likes of Tony Bennett, Frank Sinatra, opera stars, and transplanted Borscht Belt comedians usually headlined—than at more "hip" rock 'n' roll venues. Their success and "good boy" demeanor translated favorably to middle America—a feat that paid off when they upstaged the Beatles in 1967 as the #1 vocal group in Bill Gavin's Radio Record Promotion Association Award poll.

The sweet dreams soured a bit, however, in the aftermath of their impressive Monterey opening. Mamas & Papas member John Phillips, whose autobiography would rhapsodize over "the flowering of a new consciousness founded on sex, drugs, rock, and the renunciation of Americana," was there at the festival's planning stages, negotiating with the dodgy rock managers, quelling members of the peaceful Northern California community, who were leery of hippies invading their turf, and even pulling the laces on Otis Redding's corset just before the singer went on stage.

Phillips opened his roster to non-pop acts that he thought were "cool" (Hugh Masekela), and he sniffed at actual pop stars that he thought were not (the Monkees). He also hired filmmaker D. A. Pennebaker to document the event in *cinema verité*. Papa John, perhaps assuming the Association did not fit the image he was trying to promote to future rock historians, snipped their set from *Monterey Pop*'s final print. (Footage would surface years later as part of the added features on the film's digitally restored version.)

The Monterey Pop Festival represents a "tipping point" by which pop music fashions started undergoing irreparable changes. This is the event, after all, at which Columbia's pop potentate Clive Davis fancied he had undergone a revelation so profound that it affected many of his subsequent releases. The scene in Pennebaker's film in which relatively melodic singer Cass Elliott gapes at a grunting Janis Joplin with self-effacing admiration augured things to come.

In some ways, the Association shared creative frustrations with the less tidy Turtles. Led by Howard Kaylan and Mark Volman, the Turtles straddled a fragile fence between "authentic" folk rock and the modernized music-hall masterworks of "Happy Together" and "She'd Rather Be with Me"—highly commercial "schmaltz" for which many Jefferson Airheads bore a secret love.

On the 1968 album *Birthday*, the Association seemed preoccupied with selective themes about personal growth. "Everything That Touches You" builds voice upon voice until it climaxes with harmonic intricacies that would be ideal for a pantheistic high mass. Tracks like "Rose Petals, Incense and a Kitten" and "Barefoot Gentleman" make one wonder why the group did not use Bill Holman's string arrangements more often. The wistful "Birthday Morning" heralded the addition of a new lyric writer named Skip Carmel, an anthropology major who pulled inspiration from C. G. Jung's book *Man and His Symbols*.

"Time for Livin'" was another Addrisi brothers contribution, and one of the band's final attempts at a sunshine sound. Ramos, who maintained a special attachment to the number, dismisses some of the other Associates' charges that it smacks of "bubblegum." Some have argued that the record was a victim of its time—it was released in April 1968, close to the dates of America's political assassinations and unprecedented unrest. Today, the song's cheery potency outlives such topical anxieties. One piece of missing material from the album rates an "if only" story. Howe secured the rights to use a twenty-four-minute Jim Webb "cantata" consisting of several melodies that included what would soon become "Mac Arthur Park."

In retrospect, many Association tracks bring to mind those fictional psychedelic groups that Hollywood portrayed to convey the music and the ambiance of the "young generation" in an audio-visual language readily accessible to those not "in the know." Such bands would appear in pseudo discotheques or as background in party scenes, looking and sounding as if they had been carefully burnished and toned by producers and engineers versed in the showbiz refinements. One moment the carefully coiffed players could be wielding electric guitars; the next they could dust themselves off after the day's shoot to join an immaculate song and dance troupe on any number of television variety shows. Far from being a disparaging observation, this suggests that the Association had enough talent to last not only outside of—but adjacent to—the expendable trends.

The Association had no way of knowing this in the summer of 1968. With Howe no longer their producer and the road to riches less certain, the group grew more resistant to the "soft rock" label. Their harsh, desperate, and outwardly biographical song, "Six Man Band," is sufficient evidence of that. Meanwhile, Jules Alexander recovered from his mystic mood to rejoin the group, making the Association a band of seven. On their modestly titled *The Association*, one can hear the granolafication process settling in. The Association's singing began to sound less processed as the lure of whole-grain country proved irresistible.

Their last spark occurred when director Larry Peerce solicited the group to provide a theme to his filmed version of Philip Roth's novel, *Goodbye, Columbus*. A contest ensued among the members, with Yester's title song winning out. Nominated for the Golden Globe's 1969 Best Song Award, "Goodbye, Columbus" would also be one of few post-1968 Association records to stick in the public's memory, retaining the easy-breezy quality for which they will always be remembered.

The Association recombined and regrouped for several years thereafter. Brian Cole would die from a heroin overdose in 1972, while Ted Bluechel Jr. would be the only original member to remain with the band. Albums such as the 1971 releases *Stop Your Motor* and *Waterbeds in Trinidad!* saw the group branching out into different, at times unrecognizable, directions. Their 1973 release, "Names, Tags, Numbers & Labels," was a brighter spot that included lush string arrangements by Lettermen arranger Jimmie Haskell.

While Yester would go on to tour with Bruce Belland of the Four Preps and the Diamonds' David Somerville, others carried the Association torch. After eight cold and lonely years, the surviving Association members reconvened and came back to the airwaves with the granolafied "Dreamer." But in 1981, the release of "Across the Persian Gulf" rekindled memories of the Association as harmony's refined avatars.

"Actually, we didn't really fit in too well," Ted Bluechel recalled in a 1982 radio interview. "At the time that we hit we were coined a ballad group, which we didn't think we were, but that's how people started to relate. . . . And we tried to do some harder music when the acid rock came in and things like that, but it really didn't catch on." A couple of years later, Larry Ramos would be even more forthright in explaining the group's paradox: "The problem has always been that our music has always been more popular than we ever were."

After nearly four decades, and with spells of self-doubt hopefully behind them, the Association can embellish pop history with no apologies. When BMI came out with its tally of the "Top 100 Songs" of the twentieth century, "Cherish," "Never My Love," and "Windy" were there to compete with works by the Beatles and Simon & Garfunkel. In September 2003 the Association was inducted into the Vocal Group Hall of Fame. Given that the group was an organization of seven different fully functioning parts, one is bound to get a different interpretation from each member regarding the music, the band's popularity, and the mechanisms behind its demise. Larry Ramos shares the keenest perspective: "We gave people something they didn't get in other acts. But a lot of people hated us because we were too squeaky-clean."

10

The Doodletown Dimension

oodletown—the word might conjure visions of amusement parks, playgrounds, and cotton candy cloud patterns, but it's really a here-and-now adjacent to our quotidian reality: an ideal, parallel universe where people are freed from constraining elemental forces as they move about with equipoise. Here, terms like "diaphanous," "light," and "lightweight" are high praise, not censure. Like that melancholy man in the aforementioned *Twilight Zone* episode who takes the train to the imaginary town of Willoughby, Doodletown residents are protected from life's rhythmic wallops with bright, sweet, and airy sounds.

Those with some affinity for 1960s pop may also remember the word "Doodletown" because of the Doodletown Pipers—a young, perky, and vanilla-intensive vocal ensemble that—in the Mitch Miller–Ray Conniff tradition—chimed out clear, one-note-per-syllable, quaver-free tones. They may not have graced the Top 40, but the Doodletown Pipers continue to signify the clean-cut choruses that once populated mainstream entertainment. They are remembered because of their frequent appearances on *The Ed Sullivan Show, The Red Skelton Show,* and, more regularly, on the 1967 CBS summer replacement program *Our Place.* Decades later, on an episode of *The Simpsons,* they were evoked in typical smart-ass fashion to summarize Homer Simpson's "low-brow" musical tastes.

Choreographer Ward Ellis and musical director George Wilkins worked to showcase the song-and-dance troupe's creamy pop chorales, which were deliberately groomed and engineered to sound as brilliant and silky as the background scrims that embellished the era's television variety shows. While being among the first prominent harmony groups with a multiracial cast (including future *Laugh-In* and *Get Christie Love* star Teresa Graves), the Pipers embodied a style that many still call (for better or worse) "white-bread." Listening to their recordings today, one can easily understand how the group represented a distant, and now largely unheard, world.

In Doodletown, diaphanous music plays everywhere. Many of the tuneful confections that once lined Memory Lane are even more aerated and palatable. No tune better establishes this Doodletown depth-of-sound than their 1966 single "A Summer Song," a reworking of Chad & Jeremy's 1964 release. It epitomizes the Doodletown gleam—that charged moment when the precise voices chime amid the slap-back echo. The Pipers were certainly not the gleam's originators. The sound was already in place on recordings by the likes of the Ray Conniff Singers, Mitch Miller's sing-along gang, the New Christy Minstrels rejoicing with "Green Green," and the Ralph Carmichael Chorus harmonizing to a rippling piano on Roger Williams's 1966 version of "Born Free." But, thanks in large measure to vocal arrangers such as Al Capps and George Wilkins, as well as to Stu Phillips's studio enhancements, the Doodletown Pipers perfected the technique.

A reverberating piano, an eerie electronic sting (either a guitar or a treated keyboard), and light drums lead into the male half's opening verse to establish the melody; a tambourine and the females follow. The second verse introduces horns and electric strums, with all the voices alternating in unison one moment and in a yin/yang counterpoint the next. The gleam shines brightest on lines such as "trees swaying in the summer breeze," as the men stress the long ē vowels, or "soft kisses on a summer's day," which features the women's voices defying the elements with their iridescent highs. On this and most other Doodletown endeavors, the group's resonant voices make up for the absence of strings.

Phillips, who guided Shelley Fabares into her "Johnny Angel" echo chamber, produced "A Summer Song" and much of the group's other material, including their highly collectible and most representative album, *Sing-Along '67*. Here, the Pipers thrived inside a rarefied studio enclosure, a Doodletown Dimension that allowed the voices to beam on such 1960s favorites as "Music to Watch Girls By," "Winchester Cathedral," and a perky version of "Spanish Flea" that was somewhat daring in its preference for regimented Ray Conniff decorum over the "hip" suburban exoticism of Herb Alpert and His Tijuana Brass. The album's sparse arrangements leave plenty of room for the expansive voices, with each track retaining a Christmas carol–style immersion despite all the "contemporary" instruments.

The Doodletown Pipers call to mind the chirpy "upholstered folk" of the New Christy Minstrels (without the Barry McGuire gravel). But they also

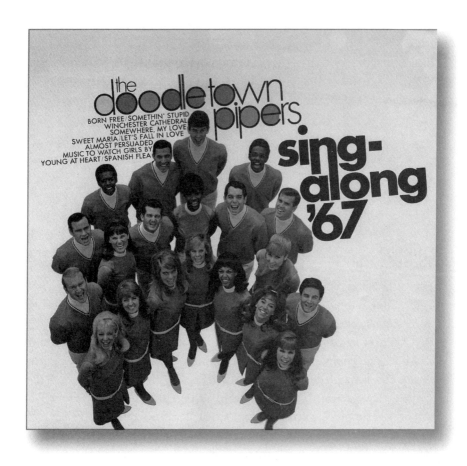

commanded the clarity of the Ray Charles Singers—a pop chorale that adorned America's Top 40 in 1964 with the single "Love Me with All Your Heart," wooed television audiences on *Your Hit Parade,* and provided radio jingles for products ranging from S&H Green Stamps and Lipton Tea to Lucky Strike cigarettes and Cover Girl cosmetics. While the Ray Charles Singers sang backup in Perry Como's television show, the Doodletown Pipers carried the torch by piping backdrops to Como's live performances at Las Vegas's International Hotel in 1970 and 1971.

At their worst, however, the Doodletown Pipers could stoop to pseudo-soul, as they did on interpretations of the Righteous Brothers' "You've Lost That Lovin' Feelin'" and Bobby Hebb's "Sunny." Their style incurred more vanilla depletions in mid-1971, when they revamped into the New Doodle-town Pipers and made regular appearances on the Karen and Richard Car-penter–hosted NBC-TV summer replacement show *Make Your Own Kind of Music.* The voice of one member, Tom McKenzie, was used in a mid-1970s incarnation of the Archies. As the decade continued, the Pipers performed at venues in Las Vegas, Reno, and Tahoe, but exposure to and knowledge of the Doodletown Pipers waned with the increasingly sugar-deprived times.

"Open a New Window"—The Arbors

Many 1960s pop vocal groups—both those that were adult contemporary and more pop rock–oriented—made Doodletown crossovers. The Arbors, for instance, amplified their four-man act into a mini-chorale. Unlike the Pipers, who redoubled their echoing choruses in the absence of strings, the Arbors established an affinity for watertight harmonies set to lush orchestrations in 1966 with their first single, "A Symphony for Susan." Decades after "A Sym-phony for Susan" embroidered the airwaves, the notes to volume one of Varese Sarabande's *Sunshine Days* series aptly describe the Arbors as having "all of the Association's collegiate harmonies, with none of that messy Mary."

The Arbors consisted of two sets of brothers who met at the University of Michigan: Thomas and Scott Herrick, from Grand Rapids, Michigan, and twins Edward and Fred Farran, of East Lansing, Michigan. In 1966 they formed their quartet, named it after their cherished college town of Ann Arbor, and groomed themselves for Date Records, a Columbia affiliate.

Even when delving into the Brazilian beat on songs such as "*Mas Que Nada* (Pow Pow Pow)" and "So Nice (Summer Samba)," the Arbors lanolized

the rhythm with clipped diction and sweetened acoustics. They were, of course, right at home with Broadway songs, such as Jerry Herman's "Open a New Window," from *Mame*, and with Chip Taylor and Trade Martin's celestial "Just Let It Happen." They, too, belied the Four Freshmen Fallacy, claiming jazz influences but almost always embellishing their records with a clean and tidy Four Preps stature.

The Arbors also participated in some backstage Hollywood history. Author Jacqueline Susann gave them the nod to record a theme that the Four Seasons' Bob Gaudio wrote for the screen adaptation of *Valley of the Dolls*. But competition surfaced, with Andre Previn's version ending up the winner—circumstances that doled out one more title for Dionne Warwick's MOR trove. Possibly because Gaudio had given her co-composer credit on his song, Susann continued to endorse Gaudio's tune. "I wrote words that tell the story," she professed on the back cover of the album *The Arbors Sing Valley of the Dolls*, "and the total sound of this recording by the Arbors is three-dimensional—book, words, music. . . . That's why I chose their performance to use as theme music on my television special."

The Arbors Sing Valley of the Dolls offered an adaptation of Tchaikovsky's First Piano Concerto called "You Are the Music," a starched-collar samba on "That's the Way It Is," a rendition of "Graduation Day" that tossed associations of Eisenhower-era goldfish gulpers smack into the Summer of Love, and a closing track called "Endless Summer," written by Bill Stegmeyer (who wrote "A Symphony for Susan"), that features haunting undertones offset by seemingly bright lyrics.

In 1969 the Arbors underwent some sonic alterations. Pleasantly surprised fans marveled at how the quartet remolded the Box Tops' faux R&B record "The Letter" into a celebration of spacey psychedelia—a mix of acoustic guitar, phase-shifts that mimic the whir of a departing plane, and a focused tenor that make the harmonies sound more like those of Harpers Bizarre. Among the best moments on the accompanying album, *The Arbors: Featuring "I Can't Quit Her" / "The Letter,"* is a Gregorian-inspired introduction leading to a marriage of folk guitar, strings, and harmonic cushions in a revisionist interpretation of the Doors' "Touch Me."

With the aid of engineer Roy Cicala (who worked on the Four Seasons' psychedelic foray, *Genuine Imitation Life Gazette* and, later, John Lennon's *Imagine* and *Mind Games* albums) and his wife, singer Lori Burton, the Arbors set Bob Dylan's "Like a Rolling Stone" to a waltz beat. This pop-symphonic manicure of violins, harpsichord, horns, and the requisite electric guitar leads into a brassy crescendo, which the group repeated on their medley of Blood, Sweat & Tears' "I Can't Quit Her" and Simon & Garfunkel's "For Emily, Wherever I May Find Her."

"Feather Canyons Everywhere"—Harpers Bizarre

In the 1970s the Arbors found a second life in ad jingles. Television viewers could hear their voices in commercials for Green Giant, McDonald's, Texaco, and United Airlines. Like the Arbors, Harpers Bizarre blurred the line between soft pop and catchy jingles. Long before irony became safe, Harpers Bizarre was arty and at times facetious about its clean-cut image and sound. One writer may have described them as "a white-bread quartet who performed Beatle songs in Bermuda shorts and madras jackets," but they were manipulative brats who knew exactly what they were doing, and they deserve kudos for being effective at it. Harpers Bizarre pushed the proper emotional buttons to bring out a summertime-in-the-amusement-park sensation.

The cast—a tightly structured yet motley bunch that originated in the calm and sunny environs of Santa Cruz, California—consisted of Ed James on lead guitar; Dick Yount on bass and vocals; John Petersen (formerly of San Francisco's the Beau Brummels) as the percussionist and drummer; Ted Templeman, lead singer and rhythm guitarist; and Dick Scoppettone, who served as lead singer, rhythm guitarist, songwriter, and spokesperson. They began as the Tikis, turning out a somewhat hard-edged sound, thanks to the clangor of electric guitars and primeval engineering, but a breezier muse purred in their direction.

Much credit for the band's rehabilitation into cuter, more nostalgic fare goes to producer Lenny Waronker. At the time, Top 40 was riding a wave of pop nostalgia with the New Vaudeville Band's "Winchester Cathedral" while the Sopwith Camel crooned "Hello Hello." The Cyrkle was also mixing folk rock with wistful summer lad harmonies on songs like "Turn-Down Day." When the latter group passed up a chance to record a cover of Simon & Garfunkel's "The 59th Bridge Song (Feelin' Groovy)," Harpers Bizarre entered the picture.

Waronker wanted to make "The 59th Street Bridge Song" a harmonists' cornucopia, primarily by incorporating some of those strategically mapped baroque "bah bahs" and "dah dahs" that the Swingle Singers championed. One more detail was in order. With the record ready for release, Waronker

wanted a name to replace the Tikis. He sniffed at pompous suggestions like "The Bells of St. Mary's" and "The Archdiocese," but he liked the wordplay on the title of *Harper's Bazaar*, a magazine that dated back to 1867.

The goal was to combine the choirboy purity that audiences subconsciously craved with wisps of palatable cynicism. "The 59th Street Bridge Song" soared across the airwaves in the spring of 1967. The band remained airborne with its follow-up single, "Come to the Sunshine," written by another of the great soft pop composers, Van Dyke Parks, and arranged by Perry Botkin Jr. Here, the madras-clad melodists had a theme song fraught with images of sunbeams and sundaes.

Songwriter Randy Newman offered Harpers Bizarre a little more of a jaundiced perspective. But even he, who would go on to pen more and more clever odes to disenchantment, almost lapsed into believing the cotton-candy sunset illusions on compositions such as "The Debutante's Ball," "Simon Smith and the Amazing Dancing Bear," and the boldly lovable "Happyland." Newman's traipse-along-the-midway arrangement on the latter made the act of suspending disbelief easier, despite the song's assertion that: "Everything is far too real."

Alternately sweet and puckish, Harpers Bizarre marched on with updated chestnuts that included Harry Warren's "Chattanooga Choo Choo" and Cole Porter's already wry "Anything Goes." "Sentimental Journey," that bluesy number that even Doris Day could not sweeten to satisfaction, at last got its creamy-on-the-melody due, especially with female background cooing to add more glaze to Templeman's already feminine tone.

The accompanying *Anything Goes* album ambled further down Memory Lane with Porter's "Two Little Babes in the Wood" and the Jimmy Van Heusen–Sammy Cahn standard "Pocketful of Miracles." As the group's pillowy graces came to the fore by 1969, one could swear that Harpers Bizarre worked closely with psychological engineers on "Witchi Tai To." The Jim Pepper number, which is featured on group's final album, *Harpers Bizarre 4*, was a simultaneously eerie and sunshiny rain dance that packed in an optimal audio seduction of bells and beats. Again, Botkin's windswept strings, teasingly prominent only in the track's final moments, added the proper foam layer.

Harpers Bizarre was comfortable describing its overall effect as "fun-loving easy listening." The group's counterrebellion became more intrepid when Templeman twitted the rock cognoscenti, predicting that the era of hippiedom "will leave nothing but a pleasant memory." Meanwhile, celebrity hippie Joni Mitchell wrote "Both Sides Now," a song that was designed to blast the romanticism of "feather canyons" and "ice cream castles." Judy Collins immortalized it for MOR radio's eternal playlist, but Harpers Bizarre subverted Mitchell's subversive message according to their own worldview. With cherubic voices and Botkin's orchestrations, Harpers Bizzare turned the "clouds' illusions" into a guilt-free perk.

"One-Way Ticket to Happy"—The Cowsills

Like the Association's "Cherish," the Cowsills' "The Rain, the Park, and Other Things" was a producer's pearl. This marvel of studio engineering gave listeners a neural nudge whether their ears were glued to a stereo console or a transistor radio, with every note, every sound, and every vocal inflection tailored to produce a "happy, happy" sensation.

Recorded at New York's A&R Studios and cowritten by their producer, Artie Kornfeld, this first Cowsills hit single cast its raindrops over the fall of 1967. Natives of Newport, Rhode Island, the Cowsills—Barry, Bill, Bob, John, and mother Barbara—were paragons of suburban propriety. They did not seem to have the formal training of the Doodletown Pipers or the Arbors, but their harmonies sounded crystal clear and lucid, especially in contrast to lead singer Bill's twangy tendencies. Kornfeld had caught the family act on *The Tonight Show* and vowed to push them to success.

When recording the follow-up release "We Can Fly," the Cowsills added two more sibling tykes, Paul and Susan. The song, imbued with the antigravity allure of Jimmy Webb's "Up, Up and Away," met the needs of young fans while sating the emotions of older folks who, if not ordinarily exposed to the Cowsills' version, could enjoy Lawrence Welk's instrumental interpretation.

Bill and Bob Cowsill had become producers as well as performers when the group arrived in the spring of 1968 with its most remarkable tune, an unusual ballad about estranged boyhood called "In Need of a Friend." The song is essentially a straightforward call for companionship in a creepy world. Embellished with baroque touches of strings and harpsichord, the lyrics are simultaneously poignant and obscure. Images of a hand groping in the dark may have curdled the crumpets of a few gutter-minded censors, but the likely platonic theme about reaching for a soul mate had universal allure.

Wes Farrell, who would go on to become the musical director for *The Partridge Family*, produced the Cowsills' "Indian Lake," a song that evoked some of the New Christy Minstrels' summer-camp zest. Even when the grainy male leads overshadowed the angel chorus on "Poor Baby," the song's line about a "one-way ticket to happy" still resounded with audio-visions of Doodletown utopia. The Cowsills attempted to sound a bit heavier on a successful version of "Hair," but apocalyptic numbers, such as "The Prophecy of Daniel and John the Divine," suggested a self-induced death knell for the band.

The Cowsills rebounded a bit with their version of the television show theme "Love American Style"—the B-side to the 1969 single "Silver Threads and Golden Needles." But the days when their milk-fed looks and sentiments elected them spokespersons for the American Dairy Association were numbered. Columbia Pictures sent out a camera and crew to follow the group's

daily lives. But by 1970, what had been conceived as a show about the Cowsills had ended up (with much doctoring) as *The Partridge Family*.

"Groovy Summertime"—The Love Generation

As the first Haight-Ashbury pilgrims staged a "Death of Hippie" media event on October 6, 1967, and the Beatles' *Sgt. Pepper's Lonely Hearts Club Band* touched stereo styluses across the nation, the Love Generation offered an over-the-counter version of the "way-out" sound. Brothers Tom and John Bahler were show business adepts when they formed the band, a studio concoction that merged folk pop and choral singing. Song titles such as "Candy," "A Touch of Love," "Love and Sunshine," "Let the Good Times In," and "Sunrise Highway" stressed the upbeat, but the group balanced this out with such reflective pieces as "Love Is a Rainy Sunday."

The Love Generation's first incarnation was as the Hometown Singers, a vocal ensemble that appeared with Roy Clark on a Los Angeles television program called *Swingin' Country*. John Bahler, who served as the show's musical director, worked double duty, singing for the Good Time Singers on *The Andy Williams Show* as well. Along with Mitch Gordon and Jim Watson, the group also had Annie White, a former New Christy Minstrel, and Marilyn Miller, who supplied vocals whenever Sally Field pretended to sing in the television series *Gidget*. In 1967, when they signed with Imperial, the Love Generation was official and ready to fashion easy-listening for kaleidoscope ears.

The 1967 release "Groovy Summertime" may not have been an outstanding commercial success, but its harmonies were powerful enough to cause ripples in Europe, where the Hep Stars (a group that included future ABBA keyboardist Benny Andersson) recorded a Swedish version. The Love Generation followed "Groovy Summertime" that same year with "Meet Me at the Love-In"—an equally gallant stab at vanilla psychedelia featuring bits of Brian Wilsonian falsetto. Both tunes appeared on the group's self-titled debut album, which blended a fluorescent chorus with multitracked vocals and bits of baroque strings and oboe.

Their second album, *A Generation of Love*, had the brothers alternating once again on the arrangements. "Fluffy Rain," with the female voices in the forefront, had brilliant echoes and pizzicato—a fairy-light sound that made it one of the group's best-executed tracks. *A Generation of Love* included a substantial number of moodier items, such as "Leaves Grow Grey," which

takes a gentle look back on a time when "my heart was filled with dancing strings of starlight." The theme of a lovelorn wayfarer calling out from a "secret world buried deep inside" permeates "The Bummer (Guide Me Home)," and "Epitaph (A World Without Love)" borrows baroque bits from "Eleanor Rigby" as it struggles for insights in "a world of shadows."

The Bahlers never felt that commercial sounds and relevant lyrics were mutually exclusive. They shared a conviction that mainstream pop music could truly change the world. In 1969 they came out with the Tommy Oliver and Joe Saraceno–produced *Montage*, which took on topical time bombs like "The Pill" and featured one song with an overdubbed Robert F. Kennedy impersonator reading out portions of the late senator's actual speeches. "Consciousness

Expansion" suggested some form of nostalgic fantasy spiked with themes of psychotropic adjustment.

The group, which had already started to splinter after its second album, made a respectable foray into *Billboard*'s adult contemporary roster with a Jimmy Webb theme from a Debbie Reynolds movie, a wistful melody called "Montage from *How Sweet It Is* (I Know That You Know)." John and Tom Bahler rerecorded the Love Generation's last single, the Neil Sedaka–Carol Bayer song "Let the Good Times In," for the pilot episode of *The Partridge Family*. But they ended up forsaking their original plans to define the Partridge sound once David Cassidy stole the show with his teenybopper grin and pseudo-soul singing. But the Love Generation's demise was no great loss to the Brothers Bahler, both of whom were in heavy demand as studio performers. The brothers would go on to chime behind Frank Sinatra and Johnny Mathis, as well as on Elvis's 1968 comeback television special and with the Going Thing, a traveling troupe of jingle singers for the Ford Motor Company.

The Love Generation spirit pervaded some late 1960s television moments when the Bahlers sang over theme songs for both *That Girl* and *Love American Style*. Whipping folk rock ingredients together with a rich choral accent, the Bahlers' recordings paralleled a notable single from another brother team— Danny and Jimmy Faragher, who formed the Peppermint Trolley Company and enhanced the summer of 1968 with "Baby You Come Rollin' Across My Mind."

"A World of Whispers"—The Lennon Sisters and Percy Faith, His Orchestra & Chorus

Like many who made their advent in the psychedelic 1960s, the Bahlers had older inspirations. John Bahler's grandmother, for instance, encouraged him to imbibe a steady television diet of the Lennon Sisters during his growing years. In 1971, while conducting for Andy Williams, he finally met the actual sisters, and he ended up marrying Janet Lennon in 1976.

America's favorite sister act did not exactly sit the late 1960s out. By 1968 they had ended their honeymoon with the king of bubbly. Lawrence Welk was kind to them in his own way, but his penury and mood swings forced the sisters to break their ties with him. Another vital reason for their split was Welk's refusal to let them perform the welter of new songs, such as "Never My Love," that the Lennons fancied. In 1967 they escaped the champagne master martinet with their Dot album *On the Groovy Side.* The following year they released the Mercury album *The Lennon Sisters Today!!* Arranged by Al Capps, it offered simultaneously mellow and percolating covers of the Association's "Everything That Touches You," "Green Tambourine," and "Elusive Butterfly." Along with the Lennons, two other television personalities had their own chorale endeavors. While Don Grady supplemented his day job as Robbie Douglas on *My Three Sons* with the choir-friendly group the Yellow Balloon, Tina Cole, who played his wife on the television show, was part of the Four King Cousins.

Other, more middle-of-the-road choristers showed an affinity for youthful material. Pop orchestral doyen Percy Faith, who kept his ears open for shifting trends and who even attended rock concerts, assembled his all-female

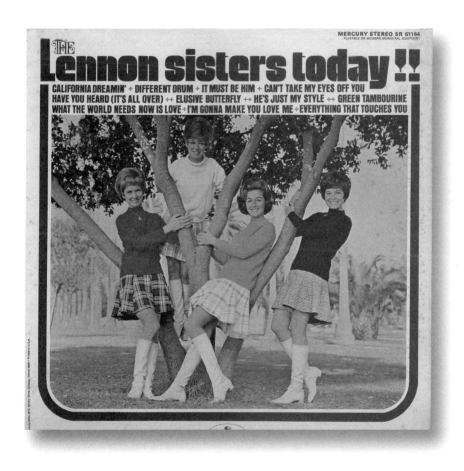

chorus for stellar performances that were geared toward the older market. Faith's 1967 album *Today's Themes for Young Lovers* included fairy-light, sun-swept versions of "The 59th Street Bridge Song (Feelin' Groovy)," "There's a Kind of Hush (All Over the World)," "Windy," and an especially satisfying version of "Happy Together." Another track, "Summer Days," had a prominent place on the adult contemporary charts that same year, while "A World of Whispers" paired Paul Francis Webster's lyrics and a melody that Faith had previously written and called "Our Love."

This was the same year in which Bill Holman, Bones Howe, and Ray Pohlman received Grammy nominations for Best Arrangement Accompanying Vocalist(s) or Instrumentalist(s) for their work on the Association's "Windy," while Faith received a nomination for Best Performance by a Chorus on its version of the same song.

"Make It Real Sharp and Clean!"—The Living Voices and the New Classic Singers

Producer Ethel Gabriel grasped a new approach to harmonic protocol when she assembled the Living Voices. As part of the RCA Camden *Living* series of albums, which also put out many Living Strings volumes, the Living Voices adapted naturally to romantic standards, Broadway tunes, and movie themes. Gabriel met a Herculean challenge, however, with the advent of post-Dylan folk rock—and rock 'n' roll in general.

Among the more daring Living Voices albums was *Positively Fourth Street and Other Message Folk Songs,* in which gritty protest plaints such as "Eve of Destruction" and the Dylan-written title tune were entirely genetically reengineered. As Gabriel explains:

> To begin with, the Living Voices were dependent on the sign of the times. We were mid-America, catering to an age range of about twenty-five and up. In those days, that's when they started to create songs for the real younger generation. We picked it up for the ones who were past the teenage years—the twenties-and-thirties people who were trying to understand the dilemmas. The softer versions helped them relate to what it was about. They wanted to hear versions where the melodic line was pretty consistent; whereas when you take vocalists with more freedom of expression, they will not necessarily sing it in a continuity form that the average person will sing it in. They will hesitate; jump a note.

The majority of people sing it straight, they can't sing it with all these variations that a soloist would. Today singers are not even on pitch. They are selling their emotion, not the song.

Other pop orchestral maestros were using unison voices to reconstitute pop favorites as well. One of them was Hank Levine, an arranger/conductor who worked extensively in Hollywood and who had studied film music composition with Miklos Rozsa. Levine was also known for providing background arrangements for many pop artists. His group, the New Classic Singers, began as vocal instrumentalists. Their first album featured "flowing one-syllable *sounds* that emphasize and enhance the melody's appeal." The chorus, consisting of "four boys and four girls," joined a small rhythm section, adding "ba-ba-baaas" and "byyy-yups" on their reinterpretations of easy bossa nova

standards such as "Call Me," melancholy pop tunes that included "As Tears Go By," and even the zany Alka-Seltzer jingle, "No Matter What Shape (Your Stomach's In)." Their self-titled first album's liner notes share humorous moments, such as when Levine spoke to his singers from inside the engineer's booth, instructing them to "Make your diction more percussive. Make it real sharp and clean!" Levine is also noted as telling them, "Your sound won't smile unless your lips are smiling. Let's see a big smile all through this one!"

Following an extended engagement at Disneyland, the New Classic Singers voiced the lyrics on a follow-up album, *Big Hit Sounds of the New Classic Singers*, which featured Levine's crisp arrangements of selections including "Cherish," "Guantanamera," and "See You in September." The opening track is a dauntless interpretation of Nat Adderley's "Work Song" that replaced the hard bop of the original version with a mentholated march tempo.

"The World's a Nicer Place"—The Johnny Mann Singers

Though they were intended to appeal to an older crowd, the Johnny Mann Singers also chimed the ever-mutating American songbook on albums such as *Don't Look Back* and *We Can Fly*. Their voices and arrangements were a bit less trebly than those of Percy Faith's group as they covered, in a mellow style, a new generation of "classics" that ranged from the Association's "Never My Love" and the Box Tops' "Neon Rainbow" to the Yardbirds' "Heart Full of Soul."

The Johnny Mann Singers also competed (unsuccessfully) on the charts with the Fifth Dimension on "Up, Up and Away," but their version did win the 1967 Grammy for Best Performance by a Chorus. The Jimmy Webb composition proved a springboard for several choral pop variations. Perhaps the best-remembered one, the Fifth Dimension's rendition of the tune is probably that group's most vanilla output, yet its lower tones, bolder brass, and overall slickness of a Vegas revue gave it a more adult aura. In contrast, the Sunshine Company countered with a more vanilla-intensive version, with much of the credit going to Mary Nance's childlike lead vocals. The Johnny Mann Singers offered a happy middle ground. Their rendition features less strident brass, and veers more toward that of the Sunshine Company. The predominantly feminine voices provided a stellar pitch, while the masculine counterparts were obviously schooled in starched-collar choral convention.

Mann was just five years old when, in 1932, he joined the choir at St. Paul's School for Boys in Baltimore. This Episcopalian environment was, according to him, the divine inspiration for his vocal passions. His calling drove him to Hollywood, where he worked as musical director for *The Danny Kaye Show* and *The Joey Bishop Show*, as the host of the weekly Chevrolet-sponsored series *Stand Up and Cheer*, and, with his singers, as an expert in the art of radio jingles.

According to Mann, "cleanliness, accuracy, and pitch" are the essence of his and any worthwhile pop chorale. "No matter what kind of material we did," he insists, "we would not sound as if we were yelling or screaming. A soloist can get away with a lot more, but a choir requires all singing together, immaculately. When one gets louder, everyone gets louder. To understand that kind of pure singing, you go back to 'Dream,' by the Pied Pipers. They had a cluster of voices. The Pied Pipers always stayed together; they didn't spread out. I'm a great believer in a choral sound, with a big fat beautiful mix of voices. It is more beautiful, more lush and desirable than a solo voice. I get more from a beautiful choral sound, all the harmony notes around it. That's what sparked me to doing choral arrangements. You can't do improvisation when you have eighteen people sing."

The Johnny Mann Singers won two of their five Grammy nominations for Best Performance by a Vocal Group. They also performed at the White House during the Nixon administration, serenading both Imelda Marcos and Soviet titan Leonid Breznev. Mann went on to host several celebrity golf tournaments, emcee Palm Springs charity events, and produce a compact disc called *Let the Games Begin* for the National Senior Olympics. Mann later assembled a new generation of Johnny Mann Singers, available to deliver jingles for adult contemporary and oldies radio stations.

"A Carnival Balloon"—The Gunter Kallmann Chorus

The Doodletown Dimension's parameters extended into Europe. The Gunter Kallmann Chorus was soft and brisk, invariably romantic, and often mysterious. Effervescent one moment and haunting the next, its angelic harmonies wandered across magic and moody places with the grace of the "carnival balloon" the group invokes in its exemplary version of Michel Legrand's theme "The Windmills of Your Mind." Even in photographs, Kallmann's chorus suggested the flip side of German expressionism, its members sporting a look to match a musical fashion that replaced shadows and sneers with sweetness and light.

The Gunter Kallmann Chorus: the flip side of German expressionism. (Photo by Lothar Winkler, reproduced by permission of Universal Music Germany)

The choir's evolution dates back to the mid-1950s, when Gunter Kall-mann was a respected studio trumpeter working with some of Europe's best arrangers. Assembling his own chorus, Kallmann intended to craft alluring backgrounds for movie scores and radio ads. His choir soon became a staple of the Cologne studio, where Hans Bertram (one of Germany's enterprising MOR pop producers) employed it to great advantage.

After hearing the British light instrumental "Elisabethan Serenade," Bertram immediately solicited Kallmann's ensemble to record a German vocal version. Released by Polydor in 1964 to worldwide success, the single secured the group an additional contract with America's Kapp label, which marketed it as "The Gunter Kallmann Chorus."

In the late 1960s and early 1970s Norrie Paramor, the head of Polydor's A&R division, pointed Kallmann toward glossy adaptations of pop and rock songs. Of the many choruses to emerge from this period, Kallmann's proved to be among the most distinctive, as it melded the styles of older easy-listening stars like the Ray Conniff Singers with younger "sunshine pop" harmonists. The group had an extra, albeit more or less inadvertent, advantage: the German chorus sang the English lyrics phonetically, lending amiable Teutonic accents to otherwise distinctively American tunes such as "Aquarius" and "By the Time I Get to Phoenix."

Kallmann's singers invoked melodic images full of "rockets, bells, and poetry" in their cover of Cass Elliott's "It's Getting Better," while their take on "The Windmills of Your Mind" is far spookier than the original, with whirling voices, violins, and a taunting flute re-creating the song's "circle in the spiral." The inspirational "Happy Heart," penned by German pop orchestral maestro James Last, boasts an arrangement by Bernard Ebbinghouse that features velvety strings contrasting with the discreet rhythm of a rock-inflected organ, while an amalgam of masculine and feminine tones rejoices over satisfied love, but hints ever so slightly at future melancholia.

"It's a Small World"—The Mike Curb Congregation and Its "Holy" Successors

After writing the feel-good 1960s jingle for the "You Meet the Nicest People on a Honda" ad campaign (for which he also assembled the group the Hondells), record producer and California's future lieutenant governor Mike Curb was intent on keeping his muse hanging from the money tree. Though a conservative, he did not shy away from assembling soundtrack albums for Hollywood hippie fare like *The Wild Angels*, *The Trip*, and the prophetic story about baby-boomer tyranny *Wild in the Streets*. But Curb made a ruckus in 1969 when, upon becoming MGM Records' president, he fired everyone on the A&R staff. He then threatened to dismiss any artists on his roster who used illegal substances. Even this silent majority stickler had a softer side, which he indulged through the Mike Curb Congregation—a chorale that appeared on venues such as *The Glen Campbell Good Time Hour*. They may have sung in a manner that, by the late 1960s, became identified with his conservative Republican sensibility, but he could also please those of various political persuasions with his universal appeals to brotherhood and romance.

In 1970, Curb's Congregation had a successful single with "Burning Bridges," a theme from the Clint Eastwood film *Kelly's Heroes,* and proceeded to revive standbys that included "You Belong to Me," "See You in September," and "Sealed with a Kiss." Their sound tended to be unapologetically child-like, especially on songs like Michel Legrand and Alan and Marilyn Bergman's, "Sweet Gingerbread Man" (from *The Magic Garden of Stanley Sweetheart*), and "It's a Small World," which became the official theme song to the Disneyland attraction of the same name.

The Mike Curb Congregation also provided those sunshine voices behind Sammy Davis Jr. ("Candy Man"), Hank Williams Jr. ("All for the Love of Sunshine"), and Steve Lawrence and Eydie Gorme ("Hallelujah"). They, like the Johnny Mann Singers and the Carpenters, earned the controversial distinction of having performed at the White House during the Nixon administration. For many, Nixon represented a line drawn in the sand when it came to musical aesthetics. The fashion was for harder, earthier sounds, while more conservative elements had no recourse but to promote the sweeter, Doodletown chimes a little while longer.

In 1974 Philip K. Dick released the dystopian novel *Flow My Tears, the Policeman Said.* Dick, who experienced sanity-stretching epiphanies of his own, believed in parallel time travels and "irreal" universes. He fashioned his story within the framework of a future police-state America in which student dissidents are shipped to slave labor camps and Richard Nixon is a national hero. Dick's view of what he called a "black iron prison" would ricochet years later in an episode of the sci-fi television series *Sliders.* In it, a J. Edgar Hoover–ruled alternate world spawns militantly sober teenagers who dance to the lull of easy-listening instrumentals. In the past, some gutter-romancing critics may have stigmatized what Dick refers to in the novel as "pop ballads and sweet—sickeningly sweet—strings," but by the 1960s' end, such vanilla sounds were hyper-politicized. Their proscription became a tenet of the counterculture's counter-religion.

Throughout the 1960s, pop acts were able to express their Doodletown instincts regardless of political or apolitical persuasions, but the early 1970s saw Doodletown aesthetics cordoned off as conservative soundmarks. Harpers Bizarre's "Happyland" got refigured into the Holy Land as born-again Christian groups, enamored of traditional church choirs, retained vanilla forms in their worship music.

The Maranatha! Singers were among the most influential vocal ensembles to grow out of the "Jesus Movement." Lured previously by trendy armatures of peace and love, they gathered at Calvary Chapel Costa Mesa and, led by pastor Chuck Smith Sr., started playing at Smith's weekly services. The Maranatha! Singers became a fifty-person chorus, formed around 1970 and consisting primarily of alumni from the University of Florida and Santa Fe Community College.

In 1971 Smith lent the group money to produce the first Maranatha! albums. The profits, made from sales of the albums at church concerts, went into subsequent studio sessions. In their earlier work, the Maranatha! Singers sported all of the clear and angelic qualities that had once been common to a great deal of mainstream pop. Songs with titles like the 1976 hymn "He Has Made Me Glad" (among the first major Maranatha! releases) and "I Love You, Lord" commanded a unison style that called to mind the Hillside Singers' early 1970s Coca-Cola jingle "I'd Like to Teach the World to Sing (in Perfect Harmony)."

More and more mainstream pop artists abandoned the whipped cream chorales, but religious groups adhered to them after considering the harder musical alternatives. This was a situation that left many vanilla-friendly romantics, with no overwhelming ecumenical affiliations, disenfranchised. Vanilla pop once converted the religious inspiration of choral music into secular hymns about romantic love; now congregations of "the faithful" reclaimed those hymns by default.

This situation also changed as the 1970s wore on. Outfits such as Maranatha! and Randy Rothwell's Hosana! Music veered out of the Doodletown Dimension to incorporate gospel, R&B, and even heavy metal rock into their musical doctrines. Up until the end of the 1990s, however, one could turn on a Christian radio station or watch Christian music videos on cable television to hear beautiful sounds that—if the religious subjects were substituted with romantic themes—would not be much different from the pop chorales of yesteryear. Still, nothing could replace the secular magic of Doodletown, where angelic acoustics orchestrated the search for an approximate Heaven on this "small world."

11

"Come Saturday Morning"

The Rarefied Worlds of Claudine Longet and the Sandpipers

Music
For the
Tiny hours . . .
Songs
For the sad
Easy lazy softly . . .
An anchor
For
The gentle ear . . .

—Derek Taylor, from the
back cover of the Sandpipers album *Guantanamera*

As he looks into the eyes of a seal, Rex Harrison, who played the title character in the 1967 film *Doctor Dolittle*, tries to reconcile himself to a loveless existence. Seeing in this cuddly and confused animal all of the qualities he wishes he could find in humans, he sings Leslie Bricusse's haunting ballad, "When I Look in Your Eyes," likening the creature's expression to "the passing of the years" and "the sadness of a thousand goodbyes." But with the song's final line, "Isn't it a pity you're a seal," he acknowledges that this intimacy, too, must end. Dolittle gently tosses the animal back into the sea, where (if all goes well) it will pursue a mate.

This was the most memorable moment of a children's film that somehow catered more to the whims of adults, and Harrison's romantic moment with an aquatic creature seems both touching and bizarre. While several middle-of-the road balladeers, such as Andy Williams, later recorded the tune as a straight love song without the trans-species reference, Claudine Longet has been the only singer of note to leave "When I Look in Your Eyes" with the seal intact.

This was an intrepid move for someone who seemed otherwise reluctant to step out of the ordinary; someone ever so reticent about performing. The fact that her singing career began on a television series called *Run for Your Life* summarizes the initial reaction she had to her newfound role as pop chanteuse. Expressing the same fragile solitude she sang about on ballads such as "All Alone Am I," Longet reminisced (in an interview I originally conducted in 2000 for the Varese Sarabande release *The Very Best of Claudine Longet*): "This was a time when the world of records was as foreign to me as a faraway land; a time when a sound booth was a little box within a box, where I could mostly hear the sound of my own heart and where I could observe in astonishment my own state of panic."

The story behind *Run for Your Life* involved the plight of its protagonist, played by Ben Gazzara, who tries to squeeze the most out of existence after learning he is terminally ill. "I had appeared in a TV show," Longet recollects, " one of my first television roles . . . in which I sang 'Meditation' to Ben Gazzara. From what I've heard, it got a lot of response from viewers, who wanted to know where to buy the record. Of course, there was none; but it came to the attention of Herb Alpert and Jerry Moss, who were starting a recording company called A&M in the old Charlie Chaplin studios."

Longet's career epitomizes the strange world of A&M Records from the mid-1960s to the early 1970s. The label that cornered the market on suburban chic with Herb Alpert & the Tijuana Brass still managed to put out artists like Longet and the Sandpipers, whose luscious vanilla mesmerized even those who were not inclined to lend an ear toward the middle of the road. Of all the label's progeny, Longet and the Sandpipers came across as unique, their styles nearly oblivious to the worldly changes occurring around them.

By 1966, A&M had purchased the libraries of the Irving Berlin and Almo Music companies and acquired more than two hundred copyrights. The company's founders, Alpert and Moss, nourished an array of artists that included Sergio Mendes & Brasil '66, We Five, Burt Bacharach, Liza Minnelli, Chris Montez, and the singing-songwriting team of Tommy Boyce and Bobby Hart. This was an intriguing time in pop music, as easy listening adopted soft-focus Franco-Brazilian textures, to which Claudine added little girl wisps. Compared to Astrud Gilberto, whose soft and haunting voice still connoted smoky nightclubs open only to adults, Claudine's interpretations evoked the beaches, sunshine, and soda pop of a child's postcard memories.

Alpert and Moss contacted Longet soon after her television performance. She accepted their offer to record her, and the label released the Antonio Carlos Jobim bossa nova ballad "Meditation" as her initial single that same year. Fortunately, Longet also had good people on her side and she retains fond memories of how Alpert "would often poke his nose into the recording studio with words of encouragement." Producer Tommy Li Puma and arranger Nick De Caro were also there "to correct, to fix, to make beautiful sounds, to make me laugh, and occasionally, to hold my hand."

Whether she was singing a chiffon lullaby or kittenish pop, she struck an instant rapport with her studio technology. The reverberation did not "enhance" her voice so much as complement the beatific vapor her voice already possessed. The simultaneously tender and eerie technique reflected the tentative relationship she had to her craft. Unlike singers who practice and preen for a swipe at the limelight, Claudine acquired her wraithlike charms by happenstance.

Born on January 29, 1942, in Paris's Fourteenth District, the art-student center of town where existentialism once thrived, Longet grew up to be what guitarist, composer, and sometime collaborator Mason Williams describes as "the French girl next door." She was schooled in ballet and drama, but she never regarded singing among her show business aspirations. By age eighteen, she'd moved to America and to the now legendary Las Vegas of the early 1960s. There, she became a dancer with the Folies Bergere.

French vanilla: Claudine Longet

Longet's parents were not thrilled about their daughter's casino cancan period and demanded she leave the painted desert's rhinestone cowboys behind and return to France. She was back in Paris when she encountered the gentleman who would turn her life around. On what she recalls as a "glorious morning," Longet experienced car trouble and, like a hyper-congenial hero appearing out of thin air, Andy Williams came to assist her. It was easy-listening kismet from that moment on. Marriage followed in 1961, and Longet assumed a life of connubial bliss and motherhood. Her only public appearances were with her three children on Andy's annual Christmas specials.

Mason Williams looks back on how this modicum of exposure soon lured her out of the background: "When the public got a good look at Claudine, they were captivated. Not only was she warm and friendly, but gorgeous, wonderful, and compelling to look at. She began to get fan letters and more or less started to develop a following of her own."

Longet peeped into the television frame for sundry parts on such shows as *Combat* and *Hogan's Heroes* before her *Run for Your Life* appearance. She had no idea that two years later she would be dancing in a pool of bubbles with Peter Sellers in Blake Edwards's film *The Party*.

After "Meditation," Claudine released a ghostly version of the Beatles' "Here, There and Everywhere," and followed that with a cover of that truffle of mid-1960s whimsy, "Hello, Hello." On the latter, she showed her flair for vaudevillian-style cheek—the perfect doppelganger to the Rudy Vallee croon-alike on the Sopwith Camel's original. But the record's B-side, the Mason Williams composition "Wanderlove," is among her most intriguing offerings. Here, her voice suggests the sound of purified air wafting through the violins and sitar strings. With eyes closed and ears centered on her intonation of Williams's lyrics, listeners cannot help but surrender to the lost yet hopeful landscape of "the lonely sea," "snowy mountains," and aspirations to alight on a place "where the cold winds never blow."

Though she would release a few more singles for radio play, Longet distinguished herself as an album artist. Her repertoire leaned toward a sweet-to-melancholy disposition. It worked to optimum effect when the songs transpired in a time-bending netherworld that was oblivious to any AM DJ's faltering attention span. Claudine Longet could make lyrics seem as atmospheric as the melodies, with seemingly minimal effort.

One of the best examples of this is "The Man in the Raincoat." In 1955, fourteen-year-old Canadian singer Priscilla Wright received international acclaim when she recorded it as a brassy torch tune. Longet slowed the tempo and was more convincing in the role of a naïf forced to cope with worldly rejection. The song boasts a strong narrative: Late one evening, a woman has a mysterious rendezvous with a man who possesses "laughing eyes and dark brown hair." She rides the streetcar with him on their first date; on their second, he takes her dancing. He turns out to be a heel who filches the money he borrowed from her to buy a ring and leaves town. But he continually haunts her whenever she passes "the place where we met."

With producer Tommy Li Puma as a guide and likely dictator, Longet expressed her material with the allure of an intimidated schoolgirl who felt she did not belong. "Claudine is human," the notes to an Australian edition of her album *Run Wild, Run Free* state, "and therefore vulnerable in an age that is finally recognizing vulnerability as an art form." No track better captures that frail charisma than "Sleep Safe and Warm (Theme from *Rosemary's Baby*)." With Mia Farrow supplying its wordless "la-las" on the opening credits to Roman Polanski's film, Christopher Komeda's melody seemed terrifying enough. Then, Eddie Snyder and Larry Kusik added English lyrics that turned the song into a menacing lullaby, the children's choir behind Longet sounding suspiciously similar to the one that accompanied her on a recording of "Happy Talk."

Li Puma and arranger Nick De Caro take most of the credit for perfecting Longet's ghostly glow. Their choices may not have been easy ones, particularly since Li Puma's predilections veered more toward jazz; the saxophone was his prized instrument. When he became A&M's A&R producer in 1966, Li Puma focused on sweeter pop. He also led Chris Montez from his "Let's Dance" days to softer, bossa nova–inspired versions of old and new standards.

Composer and performer Roger Nichols also thrived under Li Puma's watch. Around this time, Nichols assembled his sister Melinda and Murray Mac Leod for several sweetly textured tracks as the Small Circle of Friends. Alpert liked Nichols's work enough to secure him a place as one of the label's key songwriters. Around two years into his A&M tenure, Nichols came upon Paul Williams, a onetime young character actor who had set his sights on being a lyricist. Longet recorded the first song they wrote together, a sad little piece called "It's Hard to Say Good-Bye," which stands out as among Longet's most affecting tracks. Nichols and Williams continued a four-year working relationship, composing songs that included "The Drifter," which fit the airy and whimsical voices of both the Sandpipers and Harpers Bizarre.

On her 1969 album *Colours*, Longet embraced a new cadre of songwriters that included Donovan, Gordon Lightfoot, and Randy Newman. Former Beau Brummel Ron Elliott arranged the songs and played the guitars, Lincoln Mayorga manned the keyboard, and De Caro offered more smartly honed string arrangements. On this album, Longet explored quaint and willful anachronisms including "Am I Blue?" as well as scarier tracks, such as Gordon Lightfoot's "Pussywillows, Cat-Tails"—entries that make the album a bit more esoteric than her previous offerings. One tune, in particular, had a profound effect on her:

> John Denver, when he took over for Johnny Carson and *The Tonight Show* one night, asked me to be on it. We sang one of his songs, 'For Bobbie (for Baby).' It was the first time I sang live and in front of an audience. We were great friends at the time and stayed friends for many years. We learned to fly at the same time in Aspen, talked to each other on the radio as we made "touch and go" and got our pilot licenses at the same time. But that night on *The Tonight Show*, when I was so new and inexperienced, he was really keeping me up and flying free with his generous heart.

Longet also recalls:

> There was a day when we were to record Randy Newman's song 'I Think It's Gonna Rain Today,' which I thought was a bit out of my league—didn't quite know what to do with it. Then Randy walked in, smiled warmly at me, said hello, and sat at the piano. He played, I sang, Tommy said, 'Let's do it.' I believe it took only one take—that was a nice moment. Randy Newman is a prince.

And Longet did Newman's tune ultimate justice, capturing its emotional devastation like a dejected child, with just some somber violins and Newman's lonesome piano echoing in a big room.

Even after her marriage to him had dissolved, Claudine was still on genial enough terms with Andy Williams to sign onto his new record label, Barnaby. While Karen Carpenter made a wistful plea for intimacy on "(They Long to Be) Close to You," Claudine sang it like an audio apparition, mirroring Hal David's images of dreamy angels, falling stars, and moonlight-woven hair.

With *Let's Spend the Night Together*, Barnaby tried to squeeze her into a more "contemporary" mode, and the album featured compositions by Leonard Cohen, Brian Wilson, and Kris Kristofferson. The instrumental accompaniment was more minimal with some synthesizer. Dean Torrence (of Jan & Dean) designed a psychedelic drawing in the Peter Max fashion. Among the album's most creatively arranged pieces is "God Only Knows," with Longet's delicate and hesitant manner accenting Brian Wilson's otherworldly sentiments. Despite all the trendy finagling, the final product still came out

Claudine—as ethereal as ever, with the percussion plodding in vain to tug at her vocal flotation.

The Sandpipers

Sometimes recording artists reveal their ultimate artistic aspirations in a single song. For the Sandpipers, such a revelation appeared at the close of their 1968 album, *Softly*, in a song entitled "Gloria Patri (Gregorian Psalm Tone III)." In just twenty-one seconds, the track encapsulates the emotional and psychological effect their music had on avid listeners, as the trio incorporated shades of the unison chant that originated in the early days of the Roman Catholic Church. This spiritual connection comes as no surprise, considering that Jim Brady, Michael Piano, and Richard Shoff met while in the Mitchell Boys Choir.

All three Sandpipers were born in 1944, and they shared similar backgrounds. They also experienced growing pains together when they decided to graduate from choirs and form a pop group. Initially called the Four Seasons, they were blithely unaware that a quartet from New Jersey with that exact moniker was about to make a conquest. They soon became the Grads, tried some recordings for Valiant, and made occasional live performances at Lake Tahoe. Once they impressed Herb Alpert, the Grads made some A&M releases, including the 1966 single "Everything in the Garden." But when Tommy Li Puma suggested they record a recently penned folk song called "Guantanamera," they drifted right into the diaphanous "land of the palm trees."

"We really didn't become the Sandpipers until twenty minutes before we cut that record," Michael Piano recalls, "and we didn't even name ourselves— a secretary at A&M did those honors." Though A&M may have been unaware that Mitch Miller once used the "Sandpipers" sobriquet for his vocal harmonists on a number of late 1950s and early 1960s children's records, the name fit a sound that, from their recording of "Guantanamera" on, would connote summer romance and seaside contemplation.

Even by eccentric mid-1960s standards, "Guantanamera" was a curious offering that combined the ethnic associations of an exotic land with a relatively rootless singing style. The title got repeated over and again in a mix of masculine and feminine textures, the acoustic strums merged with the echoes, and the monologue was delivered in a schoolbook English that belied the song's Cuban origins. All of these idiosyncrasies made "Guantanamera" a welcomed aberration. Dick Clark was supportive when introducing them on *American Bandstand*, alerting the audience that this was "an unusual song."

The *Guantanamera* album contained a daring mixture of contemporary 1960s standards such as "Strangers in the Night" and "Cast Your Fate to the Wind," the French chanson "La Mer (Beyond the Sea)," a nod to the Italian canto with "Stasera Gli Angeli Non Volano (For the Last Time)," and slow, almost hypnotic adaptations of both "La Bamba" and the main melody from Bizet's *Carmen*. The Sandpipers were admirable for being able to present this international plate while sounding American enough to connote starry-eyed harmonizers at California campfires.

There was an additional feature: one (possibly another) wraithlike female vocalist, who materialized in their live shows as Pamela Ramcier. Ramcier billowed in and out of the main harmonies and, often clad in go-go boots, miniskirts, and sundry mod vestments, acted as an eye-catching human backdrop. Sounding like a supernatural siren, she was an enigma whose absence on any of the album credits made her all the more mystifying.

While they remained faithful to the simple melodies and were resistant to vocal pyrotechnics, the Sandpipers also took dares, stretching out the tempos in ways the songs' composers and original performers had never imagined. Their version of that otherwise nasty garage rocker, "Louie, Louie," follows a slow, sleepwalking cadence. At times it resembles a Spanish folk song, but more often it takes on the magnificence of an outer-space monody, with a dirge-like guitar and piano casting shadows over the radiant voices.

Nick De Caro and Mort Garson, who supplied the arrangements on this and additional Sandpipers efforts, gave a bright, reflective contrast to the voices by combining strings, guitars, and a harpsichord. Another album highlight is a Garson creation called "What Makes You Dream, Pretty Girl?" that edges toward psychedelia but never treads beyond the safe, diurnal world.

Among their most alluring tracks is a reinterpretation of the Lennon-McCartney song "Things We Said Today." The Beatles' recording came across as another mid-tempo number about romantic regret, but the Sandpipers dramatized its theme of inner trepidation. They bounced the lyrics around the echoplex and let them wander in a twilight world, the effect bolstered with a taunting guitar and harpsichord that plays against a meandering flute and wood-block percussion.

By the end of 1966, the Sandpipers had become synonymous with all matters soft and phantasmal. On their second album, *The Sandpipers*, cover designer Peter Whorf captured them in a moody pose, drifting along a shore-line as a blonde's enigmatic face looms before them. Their Gregorian pop is at its moodiest on their interpretation of Jimmie Rodgers's "It's Over," their voices coalescing into a low, sonorous near-hum that is vaguely reassuring, even as the lyrics "walk the silent street" of an ebbing romance. Another stand-out is the uncanny "Glass," a Curt Boettcher-esque production full of helium vocal rushes (similar to those of the Association) that induce images of cathedral windows while "the chandelier weeps crystal tears." The album also salutes the late Hawaiian singer-songwriter Kui Lee with his compositions, "I'll Remember You" and "Rain, Rain Go Away," the latter track sounding similar to Harpers Bizarre, with sugardusted vocals one would often hear on television jingles of the period.

With the exceptions of De Caro's work on the title track and the "Guantanamera" knockoff "Cuando Sali De Cuba," Perry Botkin Jr. made another stately contribution to vanilla pop with the arrangements found on *Misty Roses*. The album proceeds to contrast extremely tender pieces such as "The Honeywind Blows" and the Lennon-McCartney song "And I Love Her" with slightly uptempo stimulants such as Chip Taylor's "Strange Song" and Bert Kaempfert's "Wooden Heart." These examples demonstrate once again the Sandpipers' obliviousness to the codes of "cool" that were already lurking in many record executives' minds.

The intricate work that Li Puma had accomplished with Longet's early albums rebounded on the Sandpipers' *Softly*. This time, except for De Caro's input on the title song and "Quando M'Innamoro," Bob Thompson (who simultaneously worked on some tracks for Harpers Bizarre) handled the arrangements. The selection goes from the softhearted "Love Is Blue" to Donovan's skip-happy "Jennifer Juniper" and the mood setter "To Put Up with You" (which the American Breed also recorded at roughly the same time). Among the album's highlights is a rendition of Mason Williams's "Wanderlove" (here called "Cancion De Amor") that traipses the fragile borders between transcendent beauty and despair.

At the decade's transition, the Sandpipers commanded a presence in two movies that were thematically worlds apart. Many cult movies from the late 1960s and early 1970s would deploy a wash of lush strings or a volley of pretty pop songs to offset steamy sex. *Beyond the Valley of the Dolls*, a Twentieth Century Fox extravaganza full of Russ Meyer's predictable camp and hyper-mammarian mischief, included the Sandpipers singing the title song

the
sandpipers

softly as i leave you
for baby
i'll remember you
yesterday (ayer)
try to remember
michelle
rain, rain go away
bon soir dame
the french song
it's over
inch worm
glass

(alternately called "Beyond the Days of Now and Then") as two of the film's beautiful women make love to one another. In contrast, Alan J. Pakula's *The Sterile Cuckoo*, about a college-age girl (played by Liza Minnelli) coming to terms with her emotional tumults, included the Sandpipers' second most popular Top 40 entry, "Come Saturday Morning." The Fred Karlin–Dory Previn ballad is a bittersweet American classic that was also among the last of the great "honeywind" ballads.

The Sandpipers' actual *Come Saturday Morning* album, a Bones Howe and Bob Alcivar production, included Alcivar as arranger, Bill Holman handling the strings and horns, and Wrecking Crew stalwarts such as drummer Hal Blaine, rhythm guitarist Tommy Tedesco, bassist Joe Osborne, and, on both organ and piano, keyboardist Larry Knechtel. But *Come Saturday Morn-*

ing, like the Sandpipers' *The Wonder of You* LP that preceded it, lacked the mood consistency of the group's other albums—an unsettling indication that the label was making efforts to tamper with the Sandpipers' formula. This is exactly what happened with the trio's final A&M offering, *A Gift of Song*, on which the struggle to diversify led only to artistic indecision and halfhearted measures to sound more "current."

A Gift of Song's emphasis on solo performances over unison harmonies signaled the kind of blood sugar meltdown that would characterize other 1970s acts. The sentiments were still there, but the songs—stripped of the ultra-processing—did not stimulate the same physiological response. Remakes of Carole King's "It's Too Late," the Association's "Never My Love," and Bread's "If" showed their affinity for post–Brill Building MOR, but the Sandpipers' treatment of Clifton Davis's "Never Can Say Goodbye" and Jim Brady's vocal on Paul Williams's "An Old Fashioned Love Song" reveal how country and soul influences dimmed the group's vanilla rays. The album would also be the trio's swan song.

The Sandpipers reunited in the late 1970s, albeit in an altered form, with Gary Duckworth replacing erstwhile leader Michael Piano, on the 1977 RCA album *Overdue*. In this new incarnation, the Sandpipers also satisfied their fan base in the Philippines with *Ay, Ay, Ay, Manila!*—which was billed as "the first Tagalog album from an international group."

Those lulled by the harmonic sounds of these three former Mitchell Choirboys would have gladly listened to more and more variations on "Come Saturday Morning." Derek Taylor's poem for the first Sandpipers album, in which he rhapsodizes about "Earning/Yearning/Seeking a corner/Of the Cave/Somewhere away/From the battle/And the fire of Popwar" reflects a faraway time when someone still had the guts to blow his "cool" by singing to a seal.

12

The Cake Out in the Rain

The Carpenters and the Sugar-Depression 1970s

L ocking eyes with Richard Nixon was no easy task for Karen Carpenter. Even as she stood at her career's pinnacle, sold out packed houses, and glazed AM radio with song after song, this eternally self-conscious, semi-withdrawn, and sensitive woman was extremely intimidated before the man who, in May 1973, was still the face of world power.

The grandeur of this occasion—a White House reception for West German chancellor Willy Brandt—did not prevent Carpenter from having that empty sensation she often felt when the show was over and it was time to leave the stage. Here, two bastions of 1970s Americana stood in one room, both figures keeping the best possible poise while tottering at their respective precipices. What's more, by playing at the Nixon White House and incurring a "silent majority" distinction when Nixon referred to them as "young America at its best," the Carpenters lived up to the counterculture's criterion for evil.

A strict disciplinarian when it came to live concerts, Richard Carpenter was especially rigid toward musicians who wanted to meander on the melody. Improvisation was, for the most part, forbidden. Richard believed that audiences wanted to hear a duplication of the record—a specification that further alienated the Carpenters from the mounting hordes of "progressive" rock advocates who saw the traditional pop melody as a white picket fence in need of graffiti. These rock and soul ideologues had infiltrated the very halls of A&M Records. Individuals in A&M's publicity machine showed contempt for the duo, while Herb Alpert and Jerry Moss had to monitor all the information that leaked to assure that the Carpenters' "squeaky-clean" image remained projected intact.

In the early 1990s the *New York Times'* Rob Hoerburger captured the mood of the early 1970s with his musical assessment of why the Carpenters were so loved by many and so reviled by others: "Richard Carpenter, the duo's keyboardist and arranger, pitted his gentle sounds against loudmouths like Led Zeppelin and the psychedelic soul of Sly and the Family Stone. In comparison, the Carpenters sounded just plain weird, sort of like the Mamas and the Papas crossed with Lawrence Welk, with Mr. Carpenter emphasizing frothy melodies and overdubbing his and his sister's voices into a chorale-like swell."

The first incarnation began around 1967, when Richard Carpenter, dismayed by his jazzy Richard Carpenter Trio's lack of success, decided to assemble a pop group that offered a harmonic combination of the Association and the Beach Boys. Spectrum included Karen, Richard, Leslie Johnston (one of Richard's school chums, who complemented Karen on the vocals), guitarist Gary Sims, Danny Woodhams on bass, and Richard's continuing musical partner, John Bettis.

From the start, Richard wanted the accent on tight harmonies, overdubbed voices, relatively simple arrangements, and melodic lightness. As biographer Ray Coleman states, "Richard had always sought the 'goosebump reaction' that came, somewhat indefinably, from a certain blend of touching lyrics and haunting instrumental work."

For some reason, Spectrum did not gel with prospective record companies. Though the Association and the Lettermen put out clean choral Top 40 pop through the 1960s, Spectrum's "squareness" lost favor. "They're wearing turtleneck sweaters," one label executive told the group's manager, Ed Sulzer, "*blue velvet* suits; they have *short* hair; and they're singing words that we *can understand*! It's sophisticated—but we don't want to take a chance on it."

As a sidebar, by 1968, two American groups that had originated with a harder rock edge reinvented themselves more into a Lettermen mode. The Vogues, who had had success with the folk rock–driven "Five O'Clock World," united with former Bobby Vee arranger Ernie Freeman and ushered bow-tie balladeering into a new era by reviving standards such as the Four Lads' "Moments to Remember" and "No, Not Much." Most intriguing was the New Colony Six, which started as an avatar of Chicago rock. Its members, who named the band in honor of the British colonies, expressed a desire to bring rock 'n' roll back from England to its birthplace in the States. They wore outfits similar to those of Paul Revere & the Raiders and recorded songs with styles ranging from garage to bubblegum. But in 1967, after signing with the Mercury label, the group released a demo that featured sharply contrasting sides. One was the bubblegummy "Treat Her Groovy"; the other was a soft, creamy, string-filled ballad called "I Will Always Think About You." Liking the former and despising the latter, the Mercury executives awarded "Treat Her Groovy" with the most promotion. Despite this, the song did not win over the target market. "I Will Always Think About You" became the sleeper—its subtle, sweet harmonies featured a gentle tenor and offered an irresistible lure. The song catapulted the group into mainstream arenas such as *The Mike Douglas Show* and even helped the members get a date to pose for Montgomery Ward catalog photos.

While Richard Carpenter and John Bettis could not avoid being tagged "square," they still felt ill at ease treading on actual "squaresville" firmament. They took a vacation job as a duo in the summer of 1967, serenading a section of Disneyland's Main Street USA called Coke Corner. Clad in brocade vests and straw hats, Richard pounded at a piano, Bettis played a six-string banjo, and the team wooed park patrons with renditions of "A Bicycle Built for Two" and "In the Good Old Summertime." Such unblemished tributes to Americana made neither gentleman a likely spokesperson for flower-power fashions. Yet Richard and Bettis had momentary delusions of rebellion, upon which they acted by sneaking in tunes such as the Beatles' "A Day in the Life," much to the bewilderment of guests and the irritation of Disneyland's talent supervisor, Vic Guder (who would later surface as the subject of the satirical "Mr. Guder" on the Carpenters' *Close to You* album).

At the time, however, the 1960s rock "counterculture" was less consistent than some retrospectives care to remember. In 1968 the Lettermen occupied the pop charts simultaneously with the Doors, while television variety shows such as *The Smothers Brothers Comedy Hour* included Jefferson Airplane and Kate Smith in the same song-and-dance finale—with no irony intended. Such a tolerated contrast of musical sensibilities (which is totally unheard-of today) may explain why Karen and Richard Carpenter, along with their fellow Spectrum members, could appear together in matching velveteen outfits, sport a cheery demeanor, sing soft harmonies, refuse to exude any kind of sex appeal whatsoever, and still be the opening act for the "heavy metal thunder" of Steppenwolf.

Karen and Richard intensified their lustrous harmony approach following Spectrum's breakup, using multitrack tapes to blend and expand their two voices. They also got a break when Love Generation brothers John and Tom Bahler lent a sympathetic ear to their music. The Bahlers were still working for the Ford Motor Company with the promotional pop group the Going Thing. They auditioned Karen and Richard while assembling new talent to promote Ford's upcoming Maverick. The Bahlers recommended them, while Ford offered them a contract (plus a free Mustang), but Herb Alpert entered the picture after hearing an audition tape and lured the Carpenters to A&M instead.

The moment he heard Karen Carpenter's voice, Alpert had an instant epiphany. His mind rambled to when he was a high school teenager on a trip to Lake Arrowhead. Staring up at speakers installed in the trees, he was spellbound by the lilting voice of Patti Page singing "You Belong to Me." "This voice was buzzing into my body," he later recalled. By a fortuitous coincidence, Page was among Karen's biggest influences. And like Page, Karen commanded a soft touch that may seem self-effacing by jazz and blues standards, but that was quietly self-affirming to others.

Karen's voice sprinkled moondust all over him, but Alpert took a big risk by letting Karen and Richard join the A&M roster. By the late 1960s, the label that had brought the world the Sandpipers and Claudine Longet was adding Joe Cocker, Spooky Tooth, and Humble Pie to its storehouse of talent. Some of the A&M staff, hostile to the Carpenters' middlebrow persona and sound, allegedly laughed behind Alpert's back and gave the duo a cold reception. Biographer Ray Coleman has suggested that the rather awkward photo of the siblings on the cover of their debut album, *Offering*, was the result of mean-spirited designers who were at odds with the brother-sister reincarnation of Pat Boone.

Offering included the duo's radio wave entry—the remarkable reinterpretation of the Lennon-McCartney song "Ticket to Ride." From the moment the somber, baroque-style piano intro leads to Karen intoning, "I think I'm gonna be sad," audiences that would get to know and love the Carpenters were already forewarned of the group's emotional pull. The song's melancholy mood, which Lennon's vocal swagger had pretty much smothered on the Beatles' relentlessly mid-tempo version, comes alive. Karen read the lyrics lucidly and evenly, and she was not afraid to sound ill at ease when drawing out the ludicrous "yeah" that the Beatles so casually dangled at the end of each opening line. The recording was so unaffected, the singing so sweet and unadulterated, that the lyrics were splayed out naked for the first time.

The single that got the world's attention was a less well-known Burt Bacharach–Hal David tune that Richard Chamberlain and Dionne Warwick had recorded years beforehand, to no fanfare. Alpert himself, particularly troubled by the "sprinkled moonlight" line, was not especially thrilled with "(They Long to Be) Close to You." The melody, a knockoff of the same melodic template as "Raindrops Keep Falling on My Head" and "This Guy's in Love with You," also posed a possible hindrance to grabbing the AM radio listeners' interest.

The final decision regarding the song's arrangement could have been a disaster. There was no attempt to rock it up or jazz it down. The Carpenters instead led the melody along on a short leash, keeping to the structure as Bacharach and David had intended. Though Karen was still the group's official drummer, the recording called for the Wrecking Crew finesse of Hal Blaine, who plied the mild percussive background. Richard, who was also initially ambivalent about the song, adjusted to the session by relaxing at the piano and tinkling along with those floral extras. Richard and the Carpenters' early recording engineer, Ray Gerhardt, were savvy enough to process the trumpet's sound into a multitrack player.

As a vocalist, Karen exuded undeniable sweetness and clarity, yet she also betrayed a drooping effect that was characteristic of Anne Murray, Melissa Manchester, and other MOR stars who were emerging at the time. Despite her wilting warble, Karen gave the tunes staying power, making every word and phrase mesmerizing with her distinct pronunciation. Her generically American accent invoked an even more refined version of Patti Page, but the beatific background harmonies remain the record's most intriguing feature. Richard went from being skeptical about the tune to ecstatic, especially when a string section flowed in at the song's closing—a feature that made him a true believer in the song's power to gain favor with younger listeners precisely by breaking all of the "progressive rock" rules.

Roger Nichols and Paul Williams, meanwhile, continued to be A&M's resident songwriters. Their partnership came to a new plateau in the name of pure commercialism when the advertising executive of a major West Coast banking firm requested a theme to draw in more customers. One of California's major lending institutions, the Crocker Citizens Bank, was looking for a song to reinforce the bank's image as a cozy nest in which young, married, and upwardly mobile couples could invest their funds. With Nichols composing at the piano and Williams scribing the lyrics, "We've Only Just Begun" was born in approximately ten minutes. The actual commercial, which featured Nichols tinkling out the evocative melody and Williams singing the reassuring words, caught Richard Carpenter's ear. The song was the ideal vehicle for Karen, and she sang it with a mixture of maternal reassurance and insecurity. She sounded yearning, uncertain, and passive-aggressive—a searcher needing to be nurtured.

"American popular music has always reflected the aspirations and intended identities of its listeners," Tom Nolan wrote in a 1975 edition of the *A&M Compendium* newsletter. "The mothers and fathers of rock criticism in the sixties 'discovered' that fans were buying more than music—they were purchasing lifestyles. . . . So here are these neatly dressed kids, a polite-seeming brother and sister team, materializing like a weird hallucination in the midst of acid rock and offering their alternative to 'In-a-Gadda-Da-Vida,' singing, of all things, a *bank commercial*."

Karen was a martinet when it came to their concert material, but neither she nor Richard exerted any overbearing star magnetism in live shows. For the most part, however, that unaffected demeanor added to their charisma. Most did not mind witnessing the Carpenters getting (what *Candid Camera*'s Allen Funt used to call) "caught in the act of being themselves." Karen and Richard behaved as might be expected of a brother and sister who'd moved from the suburbs of New Haven, Connecticut, to the suburbs of Downey, California.

In the summer of 1970, "We've Only Just Begun" enthused newlyweds and became a favorite theme of high school yearbooks, college-bound dreamers, and, of course, incurable romantics of every age. Teenagers sent fan let-

ters extolling the Carpenters for providing music that they and their parents could enjoy together. Their follow-up album, *Close to You*, attracted more positive attention as the Carpenters earned Grammy Awards for both Best New Artist and Best Contemporary Vocal Group. But Karen's sad tone, as well as the soft and plaintive manner of many of the song arrangements, suggested that uncertainty loomed behind "so much of life ahead."

Nichols and Williams were Karen's ideal songwriters. She was just twenty-one when she recorded "Rainy Days and Mondays," but, sounding as if she had experienced life from the inside out, she still managed to charm and comfort every fan who commiserated with her in her "lonely clown" sensations. She was equally convincing on the amorously desperate "I Won't Last a Day Without You." Oddly, the Carpenters gained prominence at this juncture just as easy-listening vocalists like Andy Williams and instrumentalists like Ferrante & Teicher started dropping off America's *Billboard* charts. The audiences for these older stars were still there, but for some reason the numbers never again reflected the demand for their music.

The Carpenters' ascent into the pop charts also corresponds, in an almost supernatural manner, to the low-sugar mood that overtook America. Even those who are repelled by facile sociology might not be able to resist the temptation to conjure parallels between Karen's sad songs, bouts with low self-esteem, eating disorder, search for love, and other nagging uncertainties to a larger social malaise. Karen Carpenter's melancholy music provided a humanistic backdrop to the OPEC-induced energy crisis, stagflation, and other early 1970s issues that sullied America's dreams.

One need only correlate the advent of the Carpenters to another Top 40 song during the summer of 1971. When the Lizard King perished and *Godspell* resurrected Christ as a clown, Top 40 listeners found some consolation in an unassuming yet intoxicating number called "Love Means (You Never Have to Say You're Sorry)." The title, appropriated from a famous closing line in the movie *Love Story*, has sad connotations, but the record's dreamy textures evoke the beauty of a secular love ballad aspiring to the weightlessness of a heavenly hymn. Even the name of the group that performed it—Sounds of Sunshine—said it all.

Sounds of Sunshine's "Love Means" was extra special. Notwithstanding "that rainy day feeling" of a Carpenters-era lament, it had healthy amounts of echo-laden effervescence. The wistful voices, cushioned on a bed of violins, served as a bittersweet reminder of pop's former greatness. As was befitting a

country enthralled by a cinematic love story that featured a fatally ill protagonist, however, American pop became increasingly dour as it sulked toward
the countrified "Me and You and a Dog Named Boo." Even teen idol David
Cassidy, getting nervous about his sweet image, endeavored to impress inter-
viewers with his fondness for Jimi Hendrix.

The sugar was as diluted as that cake left out in the rain in Jim Webb's
"Mac Arthur Park." Strangely enough, all those sweetly coated "summer-
chimes" of groups like the Association succumbed to a bitter flavor at about

the same time that William Duffy came out with *Sugar Blues*, a bestselling book that wagged a self-righteous finger at one of life's few cheaper pleasures. Duffy attempted to single out refined white sugar as an addictive substance synonymous with heroin. His pontifications were served up as a complement to Top 40 weepies like the Fortunes' "Here Comes That Rainy Day Feeling Again." Perhaps Karen Carpenter, as well, was reacting to the hysteria. In 1973 she freaked out upon seeing a photo of herself exhibiting some paunch, and, on the advice of a diet guru, immediately tried to eliminate fattening foods, including her favorite snack, ice cream.

Karen and Richard were both consumed by chart logistics, scowling desperately each day over the trades while their hearts palpitated over sales reports. The nation and the world requested repeated doses of their white sugar charm, even if Richard sometimes got defensive and bragged about his vast Mothers of Invention record collection. All in all, the Carpenters usually showed little reaction when the press snarled out appellations that Karen summarized as, "Vitamin-swallowing, Colgate-smiling, bland Middle America!"

Richard intuited that the era needed more life, and he layered on the brother-sister background harmonies more and more, overdubbing Karen's voice with a vibrant touch that helped to fight the droop. No better example distinguishes Karen's voice than a comparison of her version of "Superstar" with Rita Coolidge's original recording. Coolidge, like Bette Midler, was another of those MOR earth mothers who affected a country-soul delivery— the female answer to Boz Scaggs. Richard happened onto the song, about a groupie's longing for the rock star of her dreams, after watching Midler perform it on *The Tonight Show*. Neither Midler nor Coolidge had inhibitions about the line, "I can hardly wait to sleep with you again," but big brother Richard assumed the Pat Boone role by cleaning it up for his sister, substituting "*be* with you again."

The act of airbrushing away the song's blatant eroticism was less a prudish move than a smart artistic decision on Richard's part. The substituted line changes the meaning and mood of the song, stressing the theme of romantic, even spiritual, longing. Once Richard liberated "Superstar" from its fixed sexual meaning, Karen needed only one take to capture an utterly vulnerable state of mind—a clear, linear delivery connoting the dilemma of a full-hearted woman exposed to the world's emotional vacuum.

The exactitude behind the Carpenters' sessions and live performances conformed to a musical science. "The original Carpenters are highly skilled choral singers," Frank Pooler wrote in a 1973 issue of *Choral Journal*, "and were selected by Richard Carpenter for that reason. Their vocal ensemble sound is based on an absolute uniformity and a frontally focused brilliant 'ē' vowel. . . . All of the other vowels and voiced consonants seek to maintain that knife-edged 'ē,' which is often produced while wearing what the group calls a 'Disneyland smile.'"

The smooth vanilla consistency induced *Rolling Stone's* Lester Bangs to call the Carpenters "ice cream music," but Pooler was more thoughtful in identifying the formula as "the voice control that can move an absolutely unified sound through all registers of the voice and from a soft to loud dynamic with unyielding equality of color."

Letting down his guard, Richard gave full approval of that notorious fuzz guitar solo that grates against the otherwise fluffy texture of "Goodbye to Love." This stylistic departure prompted a few previously loyal fans to send the group hate mail, while others politely scoffed at the prospect that the Carpenters were selling out to stadium rock's vanilla-hostile ethos. Even Tony Peluso, the actual guitarist on the session, whose long hair and hippy attire contrasted with the sweater-friendly image maintained by Karen and Richard, expressed reservations about this not-altogether-welcomed heavy metal moment.

"Goodbye to Love," which Richard wrote with Bettis, was another Carpenters tune that would become more transparently autobiographical over time. Its sour declaration of romantic independence reflected the way Karen was known to have turned inward whenever the prospects of finding someone fitting her stern specifications appeared remote. Though fellow band members had to cajole her to finally emerge from behind the drums, Karen matched her brother's sonic precision when she got to center stage. Her admiring road manager, Paul White, once observed that she "hit the notes like radar. Some singers hit them a little under and slide up or down. Karen was pure." In August 1972 a presumably complimentary critic from the *Hollywood Reporter* credited her voice with having a "crystalline, saccharine, lyrical presentation."

By 1973 the Carpenters had replaced their recalcitrant drummer, Jim Squeglia, with Cubby O'Brien, the erstwhile Mouseketeer from the original

1950s version of *The Mickey Mouse Club*. In February of that year, the Carpenters comforted all those hoping the group would stay sweet by releasing "Sing," a tyke-tailored sing-along from *Sesame Street* that included a kids' chorus conducted by former Ray Conniff Singer Jimmy Joyce.

Before long, the Carpenters succumbed to those ever-receding mirrors of nostalgic thought. Richard and Bettis knocked heads for a ballad that induced backward glances at an earlier "innocence" and those "oldies but goodies" that make "today seem rather sad." By 1973 the film *American Graffiti* was celebrating the early 1960s, a time that probably did not seem so innocent in 1960, when nuclear warheads took sharper aim and the Brothers Four looked even further back on "Greenfields." The Carpenters managed to put together an entire concept album titled *Now and Then*, the highlight being the Carpenter-Bettis masterpiece "Yesterday Once More," which looked back on halcyon radio days. The eclectic set went from the sublime—a lush and pastoral easy-listening instrumental called "Heather," which Richard arranged from a Johnny Pearson composition—to an oldies medley, complete with smarmy, continuous DJ interruptions.

Karen Carpenter had become a vocalist's vocalist. Jane Morgan, a mid- to late 1950s recording star with her own manicured interpretations of songs such as "Fascination," "The Day the Rains Came" and the Victor Young theme "Around the World," expressed her admiration for the singer. Morgan's husband happened to be Jerry Weintraub, whom the Carpenters wooed to be their new manager in 1976. That year, the Carpenters' moods went from a breezy revival of Herman's Hermits' "There's a Kind of Hush (All Over the World)" to personal themes of romantic longing and insomnia on "I Need to Be in Love," in which Karen laments about asking "perfection of a quite imperfect world."

In 1977, with the release of their *Passage* album, the Carpenters tried for a few more brassy and percussive effects, even some congas. Songs on the album ranged from an elaborate rendition of "Don't Cry for Me Argentina" (from the musical *Evita*), with backing by the Greg Smith Singers and the Los Angeles Philharmonic Orchestra, to a cover of Klaatu's "Calling Occupants of Interplanetary Craft." The latter, which made a stellar impression in Japan as well, includes electronically elevated voices and an entreaty for cosmic peace that is reminiscent of the early 1960s Joe Meek–Geoff Goddard production, "Sky Men." The Carpenters also broke into country's radio waves with "Sweet, Sweet Smile."

But by 1978, Karen's biological transformation complemented her ethereal singing more than ever. "I was struck by Karen's fragility," Nancy Naglin wrote in the August 1978 issue of *Country Music Magazine*, "the impossible and alluring slenderness of her body and, most especially, the translucent quality of her skin." As the group began to face faltering Top 40 successes, Karen was sometimes defensive, as she was during an interview with *Radio Report*, in which she declared, "I'm getting sick of this image thing. What is the matter with a brother and sister team who happen to be the first ones who just record and enjoy life?"

As her appearance grew more ethereal, Karen occasionally tainted her delivery with a few earthy pretensions. She tried edging out of the "goody-two-shoes" image on her 1979 solo album, a Phil Ramone production that incorporated some disco in an attempt to present her as a more worldly woman. She chose, however, to shelve the album, in deference to the Carpenters' need to stay a twosome. (It would be sixteen years before the album was released.) About three years elapsed before the Carpenters released their next album, *Made in America*. Its 1981 single, "Touch Me When We're Dancing," summarizes much of the spirit—an amalgam of post-disco rhythms and *de rigueur* saxophone—that pervaded 1980s adult contemporary music. By then, pop music had pretty much forfeited its childhood.

Richard, who had always admired Perry Como, felt gratified when Jerry Weintraub saluted the Carpenters by proclaiming, "You are the Perry Comos of today!" Como projected an outward calm that, as far as most can assume, was a reflection of the performer's inner peace. Karen, in contrast, exuded a loner's resolve. Even when slinking down to eighty pounds, she could sing under grueling circumstances and become immersed in needlepoint when the surroundings racked her nerves. On February 4, 1983, a month before she was to celebrate her thirty-third birthday, Karen collapsed and died from a heart attack. From that point on, many who had previously ignored Karen's and Richard's songbook suddenly took the time to listen. Those who had enjoyed the Carpenters' mellow manifesto all along felt closer to the sad songs that, suddenly, seemed even sadder.

"Humans loved what we did," John Bettis reflects, "but the self-appointed arbiters of what humans *should* like hated it. Why, because I'm a white, middle-class kid who speaks about life and struggles with it, is that negative? Those who denigrated Richard and Karen sprang from the same background but were in major denial. They didn't want to be that person anymore. We committed the arch sin of being ourselves."

In the early 1990s, as music critics began to reassess what had previously been perceived as "treacle," Rob Hoerburger accessorized his belated appreciation of the Carpenters with a sartorial summary: "They always dressed as if they were going to church, and they sang sticky songs about love (but never sex). Worst of all, parents loved their music." Realizing, of course, that the hipster arguments against "syrupy" music seem progressively desperate with the passing years, Hoerburger conceded by dubbing Karen and Richard Carpenter "America's most defiant squares."

The Carpenters may have clung to their "squareness" with grit, but they never pretended to be saints. Karen could snap back at anyone who did not meet her standards of perfection, including fellow band members, the crew, Richard's prospective girlfriends, and, of course, obnoxious reporters. Back in 1974, when America was reeling in political scandal and President Nixon abdicated in disgrace, even "young America at its best" got fed up with the patronizing remarks about their wholesome image. The tawdry British press was the target of their ire. Concluding their British tour, Karen and Richard sent a gift to six of the United Kingdom's major record label executives. As Carpenters biographer Ray Coleman explains: "Inside a velvet box was a gold ring, inscribed on one side with the word *love*, and on the other, *fuck*."

13

ABBA's
Vanilla Ice

"They say we have no soul, but in Europe,
and especially in Sweden, it's a different kind of soul."

—Björn Ulvaeus

O n a frigid Scandinavian Christmas Day in 1964, fourteen-year-old
Agnetha Fältskog leapt out of a sulk when her parents presented her
with a yellow plastic record player and a copy of Neil Sedaka's *The
Dreamer.* She listened to the record over and again that day, singing along
while looking out from her icy bedroom window. Sedaka's high-pitched, double-tracked tenor was not unlike the sound she would emit with ABBA a
decade later.

For Fältskog, singing was a solitary occupation. She was especially fond
of piping out love songs tailored for brittle hearts. Connie Francis, who conveyed the depths of romantic rejection like few others, was among her
favorites. Francis was a guiding spirit, the girl balladeer who sang about the
fear of loneliness and the allure of unreachable boys. Anguished cries on old
standards like "Who's Sorry Now?" and early 1960s teen themes like "Where

the Boys Are" (which Sedaka cowrote) also vibrated out of Fältskog's tinny speaker to warm the frost.

Tucked away in the provincial Swedish town of Jönköping, Fältskog relied on music as one of her few emotional comforts. If Joe Meek was an "indoor boy," Fältskog was the ultimate indoor girl. Quick to nurture her own musical inclinations, she was already playing piano, writing songs, and performing with an all-girl vocal trio by the time she was thirteen. She, like many light pop dignitaries, also had experience in a church choir. On a romantically challenged night a few years later, she sat alone and commiserated with her piano over a problem boyfriend. Within half an hour, she composed her first official song—the slow and pensive "I Was So in Love."

Fältskog, the eternal little girl looking for emotional completion, had at times an almost breathless, out-of-body voice. She was capable of tempering Connie Francis's dramatic yearnings with cool Scandinavian reserve—a contrast to Anni-Frid "Frida" Lyngstad, who was five years older and who projected a deeper, worldlier sound. Lyngstad started her career as more of a cabaret jazz singer and sported auburn hair before she became ABBA's resident Norwegian. She was also among the "Norwegian Lebensborn," children conceived in romantic liaisons between Norwegian women and German soldiers during World War II. Like Fältskog, she had self-esteem issues, but the more she took to the stage, the freer she felt.

By the early 1960s, more and more of Sweden's middle-class youngsters were embracing the pop folk of American acts like the Brothers Four and the Kingston Trio, even preferring it to beatnik jazz. Björn Ulvaeus was both an arranger and guitarist in a Swedish band called the Hootenanny Singers, a group whose polite and refined style made them a safe alternative to such self-consciously primitive "beat" groups as the Hep Stars, to which Benny Andersson contributed keyboards. While Ulvaeus recalls being impressed by Swedish versions of Mitch Miller–era treasures such as Patti Page's "Mockin' Bird Hill," Lyngstad remembers liking a Swedish cover of Doris Day's "*Que Sera, Sera.*"

Andersson and his Hep Stars tinkered away at faux R&B numbers such as "Cadillac," but he, like the other future ABBA members, swooned over songs that were full of sentiment, lush string ornamentations, and huggable melodies. The Hep Stars' style underwent remarkable changes as the band mixed the innocence of Brian Hyland, on "Save Your Heart for Me," with the more mysterious, yet sweetly textured sunshine pop of Curt Boettcher's

"Musty Dusty," which they recorded while working with Boettcher's former Our Productions partner Steve Clark.

Andersson and Ulvaeus used Fältskog's and Lyngstad's voices for the first time in 1970, on a recording entitled "Hey Old Man!" In June 1972 the four released their first single under the name Björn & Benny, Agnetha & Anni-Frid. "People Need Love," a song full of timely brotherhood themes, with a beat similar to Joe South's "Games People Play," had rambunctious vocals that even the cute bit of yodeling at the end could not assuage. This Swedish answer to America's post-Woodstock Coca-Cola jingle about teaching the world to sing "in perfect harmony" sounded relatively harsh.

The rough edges became smoother, however, when Andersson and Ulvaeus heightened Fältskog's and Lyngstad's voices. Andersson, especially, had a yen for the physical, psychological, and spiritual boost inherent in soprano-enriched choirs. "The highest note was as high as they could manage," he would reflect, "and then the rest was adapted to wherever that note was. It gave everything some kind of extra energy." He further enhanced their higher register by altering the tape speeds, all in the spirit of angelic audio, and possibly nostalgia for a Scandinavian girl's choir called Postflickorna (the Post Girls), which he'd enjoyed as a kid.

These overlapping, high-pitched feminine sounds—layered and processed through overdubbing—created a luminous "third voice." Once he began working with ABBA in 1972, engineer Michael B. Tretow tweaked them higher and higher. A fanatic for electrical gadgetry, he experimented constantly with reel-to-reel tape. He, like Joe Meek before him, tinkered with effects that were already perfected to varying capacities in the United States. Through trial and error, he arrived at his own method of converting Sweden's Metronome studio into a self-contained universe, where piano chords played backward against layers of reverberated strings, and multilayered vocals merged with tape-induced time fugues. Oddly, Tretow once cited the Eagles and James Taylor as models for good acoustics, but his confectionary choral approach made ABBA all the more novel amid drowsy early 1970s fare from bands such as America and Fleetwood Mac, as well as the macramé melodies of singer-songwriters Jim Croce and Carole King.

Around March 1972, Tretow achieved one of his ABBA milestones while recording "Ring Ring." He distorted the instruments, recorded an electric guitar, and overdubbed the same guitar part at an altered recording speed to make it sound bigger and more encompassing. Applying the same technique to the entire band, Tretow imbued ABBA with sonic ventilation. While Phil Spector would layer his sessions with R&B fealty, ABBA and Tretow arranged for "Ring Ring" to play more like a circus calliope. Fältskog and Lyngstad took on the properties of instruments, their voices bending and expanding according to Tretow's push-button ingenuity. When an English-language version of the song was required, Fältskog was delighted that the group enlisted Neil Sedaka to collaborate with Phil Cody on a new set of words.

A year after they entered "Ring Ring" in the 1973 Eurovision Song Contest and received third place, the contest's rules changed. Now the public could override the "official jury" on final song selections. The next Eurovision spectacle took place at England's Brighton Beach on April 6, 1974. Five hundred million viewers tuned in to watch what looked like four glam rockers primping away to a driving beat and an ethereal harmony. Perhaps the Anglo locale helped, but "Waterloo," essentially the story of a woman's amorous capitulation likened to Napoleon's 1815 surrender to the Prussians and Brits, won first prize.

Compared to Eurovision's usual conservative fare, ABBA—the kings and queens of rock-era cabaret—were considered revolutionary. "Waterloo" conquered America by June of that year. ABBA biographer Carl Magnus Palm cites one particular stateside critic who declared that the song "slices through the morass of soul ballads and country cornflakes on the airwaves with laser beam ease." Despite its hard guitar edge, Fältskog and Lyngstad softened it with helium-hewn tones that operated less as conventionally human voices and more as vocal ionizers warding off the rhythmic impurities.

By 1975, ABBA flaunted its "third voice" all the more. Fältskog, triumphant as a more candied Connie Francis, was the true star. This was particularly true on "SOS," the tune that became the group's most remembered single and that showcased what Tretow called that multi-layered "cry in her voice." After "SOS," ABBA wooed the Americans with "I Do, I Do, I Do, I Do, I Do." Andersson and Ulvaeus wrote it in homage to the easy-listening instrumentalist and Pat Boone arranger Billy Vaughn, whom they had admired since boyhood. From its opening, the song incorporates Vaughn's trademark twin-saxophone approach, the phrases sounding a bit like his famous 1954 recording, "Melody of Love."

ABBA also had the advantage of using film clips even before the art of the music video became a cable television staple. A then-unknown Lasse Hallström (who would gain prominence with the film *My Life as a Dog*) directed ABBA's most renowned promos. Challenged by a limited budget, Hallström made them as direct and as simple as possible. There were no chiaroscuro narratives, no intricate cinematic statements; just the group in flashy apparel, often looking into the camera and smiling with a beguiling lack of smarm. Often, as was the case with the songs "SOS" and "Knowing Me, Knowing You," Fältskog stood before the lens with either a lovelorn frown or a meditative look worthy of a scene from director and fellow Swede Ingmar Bergman.

As ABBA's star ascended, listeners as well as detractors were amazed at the group's independence from its contemporaries. Glam rock, country rock, heavy metal, Philly soul, and even the softer MOR sounds of the Carpenters had a subordinate impact on the band—if they exerted any influence at all. Only disco, with its mechanized beat and instrumental lushness, enabled ABBA to gain more cachet with novelty-starved Americans. Seeking to acclimate to the glare of Giorgio Moroder's cotillion ball, the members found the funk rhythm too foreign and had to concentrate on George McCrae's record "Rock Your Baby" to get the right tempo for "Dancing Queen." The reverberant vocals on ABBA's smirk-free lament about a disco bunny lost in the glitter were a contrast to another record that swallowed the airwaves around that time. Britain's art-rockers 10cc sprayed the studio walls with harmonies that have similar vanilla enhancements on the 1975 single "I'm Not in Love." The song achieved international success but emitted sardonic fallout.

By 1977, "Knowing Me, Knowing You" should have decimated any presumptions that ABBA's songs were bereft of emotional content. Ulvaeus's lyrics, a paean to failed marriage, are fraught with images involving "old familiar rooms" where children once played and where barrenness waits. Its divorce theme commanded the pathos of the best plaintive country ballads from the 1960s. Even its sound, with the mournful voices pitted against the sparkly acoustic guitar and rippling keyboards, has an understated sincerity. The bass and the drum intensify Lyngstad's suspense as she laments "no more carefree laughter." But as Fältskog joins in to chime about "only emptiness, nothing to say," the band boasts a toothpaste-commercial clarity that is reminiscent of the Ray Conniff Singers. The countervailing guitar solo that terminates each chorus functions more as a demonic device—heavy metal calliope music suggesting that life, despite its woebegone romances, is a circus that goes "on and on and on."

Hallström's clips also dramatized the group's personal intrigues. Ecstatic Lyngstad was a stunning contrast to real-life partner Andersson, whose eyes

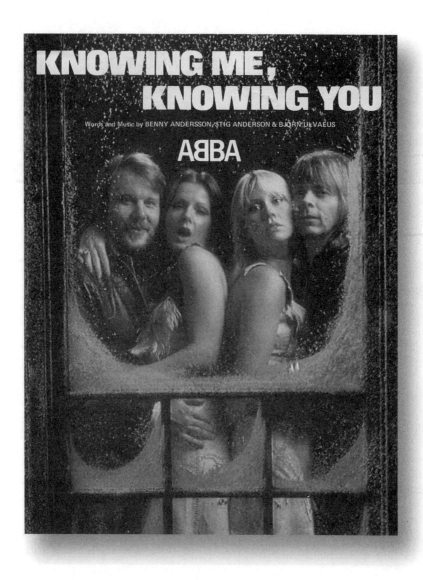

danced even when he wasn't smiling. Ulvaeus seemed affably aloof, while Fält-skog continued to function as ABBA's emotional lightning rod: her large, dole-ful orbs atoned for the rest of the group's unflappable expressions. Video poses, such as Lyngstad's opening shot in "Knowing Me, Knowing You," or Fältskog's soft-focus flirtation to the camera on "Take a Chance on Me," have the glossy, ultra-lit dimensions typical of many Ray Conniff Singers and Andre Koste-lanetz album covers of the era.

Next to "Knowing Me, Knowing You," "Eagle" was the definitive ABBA video. The recording is full of hard guitar flourishes and a rather darkly plod-ding beat, but the words and sentiment reflect a summery, soft-shell disposi-tion. Ulvaeus claims he was inspired to write it after reading Richard Bach's bestselling novel, *Jonathan Livingston Seagull,* a post-hippie salutation to the freedom of being airborne. Here, Fältskog and Lyngstad sing in unison throughout, their voices soaring like the feathered friend in reduced gravity.

When Hallström directed *ABBA: The Movie,* he gave "Eagle" an espe-cially surrealistic touch. The film depicts the group's 1977 Australian tour, from the viewpoint of a DJ who is intent on getting an interview. Just at the point when he is about to relinquish hope of meeting the elusive Swedes, he encounters them in an elevator. The initial moment is tense, quiet, and awk-ward, but when ABBA agrees to answer his questions, the elevator doors close to the camera, and the film digresses into an elaborate dream sequence. As ABBA sings about flocks of eagles flying "over mountains, and forests and seas," the elevator becomes a beatific means of transport, taking on the visual grandeur of a metallic starship wafting into the stratosphere. Hallström achieved this with a then-novel visual effect called a "flutter box," invented for the 1978 film *Superman* but used here to give the illusion of traversing outer space.

ABBA reinforced Bobby Vee's maxim about performing sad songs in a happy manner. Their voices sparkled even when the lyrics were gloomy. In many ways, they recaptured, with newer technologies and more electric gui-tars, the sheen of Germany's Gunter Kallmann Chorus. Just as Kallmann's singers invited receptive listeners to let the cheery and eerie images unwind, ABBA liberated an inner child, albeit one that tended to brood. And like Kall-mann's chorus, the ABBA members, especially Fältskog and Lyngstad, did not have an absolute command of English. They pronounced their lyrics more clearly and crisply than many American-born pop stars; ABBA's phonetics made them seem accessible, yet alien. *Time* magazine critic Richard Lacayo wrote, "They have a way of making English sound like Esperanto."

While astute at wooing younger audiences, ABBA nonetheless special-ized in what the Germans call *schlager*—a term that means "pop song" but that has often been synonymous with "easy listening." "Bereft of any inflections whatsoever from American jazz or rhythm & blues," Carl Palm declares, "typical *schlager* music has its roots in genres as diverse as German military marches, Austrian operettas, Italian and Eastern European folk music, and the French *chanson.*" Years later, ABBA members Ulvaeus and Andersson, as well as their flamboyant manager, Stikkan "Stig" Anderson, referred to *schlager* as "country with a German beat."

Being perceived as what one Swedish critic called "*schlager* broilers of the computer age," ABBA received its hardest knocks in its home country. ABBA's middle-class *schlager* roots contrasted with Sweden's Music Movement, a left-ist faction that advocated "Progg" (progressive rock). While their distaste for a pop music business driven by the moronic lingo of chart numbers is under-standable, the Music Movement cognoscenti also harbored a reverse Puri-tanism in its taboo against ear candy. Its comrades were likely to have few to no problems with sex and drugs, but became self-righteously indignant toward any work deemed sweet or "syrupy." They were the schoolmarms of musical politics. Lyrics meant simply to entertain or to induce nostalgia—without any direct political import—were deemed unworthy. Album-only radio stations, agog over "progressive" rock, would ignore ABBA, assuming they were a throwaway pop singles act.

ABBA's mid-1970s success also shed some light on international tastes. *Creem* magazine declared 1976 "the Year of ABBA." The pressing plants at CBS's European wing toiled overtime, pulling out copies of "Money, Money, Money" as if they were strings of vinyl taffy. Even before the band toured there, Australia led the pack of ABBA-philes. The group's vast appeal Down Under remains a semi-mystery. With its affinity for sweets, Australia—the land where one can buy musk-flavored Lifesavers—might also have more appreciative taste buds for music as well. The forty-five-minute television show *The Best of ABBA*, telecast in March 1975, exceeded the telecast of the 1969 Apollo lunar landing as Australia's most watched event. The group's 1977 Australian tour allowed them to vie with, perhaps even upstage, the arrival of Queen Elizabeth II on her simultaneous visit to the country. Years later, Australia would be the home of ABBA's premiere imitators: the group Björn Again, which took advantage of both the early 1990s ABBA renaissance and the film *Muriel's Wedding.*

On Christmas Eve 1978, Fältskog and Ulvaeus separated. Andersson and Lyngstad would also terminate their long-term relationship. The music like-wise took on more of a melancholy tint, with songs about changing lives and amorous second thoughts. In the fracas, ABBA never attempted to look more innocent than they were. A sheet-music cover for "Knowing Me, Knowing You" has the gals flanking the guys in provocative poses while gazing through frosty panes. "The Winner Takes It All" video (which Hallström made ten days before Fältskog's and Ulvaeus's formal divorce) even paired the four members in a manner that suggested they had swapped partners.

Still, ABBA miraculously maintained vanilla propriety while adjusting to worldly times. The clip that accompanied the 1979 single "Chiquitita" was so unflinching in its optimism that more jaundiced viewers may have registered their amazement with a knee-jerk smirk. Here, ABBA returned to its European predilections for tight melody and folk textures. As they sit by a hoary mountainside, dwarfed by an enormous, smiling snowman, Ulvaeus strums away at his guitar while the rest sing along. To reinforce the song's goodwill, ABBA donated its publishing royalties to UNICEF after "Chiquitita" was selected as the official theme of that year's United Nations' International Year of the Child.

The divorces and separations were a fact of life by 1980. ABBA released the album *Super Trouper*—a collection that was highlighted by "Happy New Year," in which yesterday's dreams are likened to "confetti on the floor." In November 1981 ABBA released *The Visitors*, with the title track supposedly about the tenuous lives of Soviet dissidents, but with lyrics that are ambiguous enough to narrate a solitary mental breakdown.

The Visitors concentrated more on solo ventures, but Fältskog and Lyngstad still delivered their harmonies with sparkly precision. The vocal chimes surface through the intricate arrangements of "One of Us," another emotional tapestry about failed relationships, as well as "When All Is Said and Done" and "Like an Angel Passing Through My Room." In the ABBA chronology, this was the work that brought them to a final "maturity." It's a darker, headier concept album that encourages listeners to sit beside the speakers and contemplate the lyrics. Still, relative to the times, *The Visitors'* Euro-pop mannerisms sound vanilla compared to those of Joy Division.

Soon, Fältskog had the honor of performing the group's official final single, "The Day Before You Came." This, like many ABBA songs, existed concurrently with moving images. In the video, Fältskog looks as crestfallen as ever, waiting for a train while an attractive man ogles her. Ulvaeus, who tended to reserve his best lyrical glum for his now ex-wife's voice, tells an affecting story, as Fältskog sings with a backwash of angelic vocal overdubs that contrast with the menacing throb of Andersson's synthesizer. Perhaps knowing this would essentially be the group's final record, Ulvaeus asked Fältskog to sound as artless as possible, conveying to the listener that she is just an everyday woman trying to claw out of her emotional stasis. She recites her banal activities like some character in a Harold Pinter play, but sees them in a new light when the man she assumes to be her human savior arrives.

Fältskog was singing by herself in the 1980s on several CDs that more or less thrust the little girl lost into adult rock—Euro-pop interlarded with the "power ballad." Producers included 10cc's Eric Stewart, on *Eyes of a Woman* in 1987, and Chicago's Peter Cetera, who even offered his non-vanilla voice on a duet for the judiciously titled 1988 album *I Stand Alone*. By the 1990s, however, Fältskog had become a Garboesque recluse. She made scant effort to promote these solo ventures, was averse to interviews, and insisted on being left alone with her children.

Tentatively retired and perhaps starting on her autobiography, Fältskog endured the calm before a new storm. In 1991, the Munich Philharmonic Orchestra released an easy-listening instrumental collection of ABBA songs, a feat not matched since French pop-orchestral artist Franck Pourcel did the same, with the band's full cooperation, back in 1979. With the 1992 release of the *Abba-esque* EP and the accompanying video, which featured the two male singers in Fältskog and Lyngstad drag, Britain's Erasure presented a gay-friendly revamp of ABBA's already androgynous image. The traveling musical *Mamma Mia!* would also reinforce ABBA's enduring place in popular mythology.

Even in mercenary America, where commercial calculation is not bridled by Scandinavian guilt, ABBA had detractors. "For most European kids," *Creem* magazine would write with fashionable condescension in 1977, "the rock 'n' roll revolution happened not in the fifties but, via the Beatles, in 1963–4. The consequence is that European music remains remarkably un-black. On the one hand, this has meant the development of kraut rock—arty and complex and improvised and technical. On the other hand, it's meant ABBA."

"We have met the enemy and they are them," *Rolling Stone*'s Robert Christgau also preached in the 1970s when reviewing ABBA's *Greatest Hits Vol. 2*. In the 1990s, however, when ABBA lovers came out of the closet, *The Rolling Stone Encyclopedia of Rock and Roll* shared the revelation that ABBA was Nelson Mandela's favorite pop act.

In this regard, ABBA offers today's R&B-bred listeners a kind of exoticism in reverse. Just as they gave 1970s audiences a few extra moments of luminescence before the earth tones devoured the scenery, ABBA stirs new fans to taste the passion that inspired someone to proclaim on the Internet that ABBA's music "is like vanilla ice cream for your ears."

14

A Zillion Chocolate Kisses

Like a reincarnation of Stephen Foster, Tommy Page stood mortified by a late-twentieth-century version of the marauding minstrel. The incubi took the shape of the New Kids on the Block—five scrubbed-up white boys from the Boston area. Their assimilation of R&B was so slavish that they, like many subsequent "boy bands," did not need the insulting application of burnt cork to convey what they imagined was a "street cred" demeanor.

As pranksters, the New Kids were at times unrelenting in their tiny attacks. During one show, as Page sang his self-penned ballad "A Shoulder to Cry On," Joey McIntyre and Donnie Wahlberg hopped onstage to taunt him with water pistols. During another performance, the Kids threw stuffed animals at him, and on another occasion they covered their heads with plastic garbage bags and ran across the stage in their undershorts. As their behavior worsened,the Boston brats offered Page the hooligan advice to "loosen up!"

The most dramatic and frightfully symbolic Kids assault occurred while Page performed one of his more dance-friendly compositions, "A Zillion Kisses." After being showered with a water hose and bags full of Hershey's Kisses, Page was soon stepping in a mire of water and chocolate that melted under the stage lights. Trying not to slip and fall, he could easily have been reduced to a chocolate-glazed Al Jolson, clambering on his knees in an ingratiating minstrel posture that might have pleased the Kids to no end.

And what did Page do to elicit such provocation? He dared to be a sweet ballad singer during relatively sour times. Through the 1980s, pop music splintered into many categories as it survived the acidic peel of punk, was coiffed into "new wave," and mellowed into more power-ballad variations. The vocally untrained and generally monotonic sounds coming out of England, in the form of a style called "new romantic," relied heavily on the post-disco synth-pop backbeat. Then, from the manicured environs of Melbourne, Australia, two vocalists named Russell Hitchcock and Graham Russell formed Air Supply. Chart successes like "Lost in Love" and "All Out of Love" survived as MOR hallmarks, but Air Supply's vocal milieu got bogged down in the rustic, Engelbert Humperdinck–inspired inflections of such 1970s predecessors as Morris Albert ("Feelings"). The chorus to "All Out of Love" may have ascended to sweet vanilla, but the main verses were spiked with the musical equivalent of bong water.

Page, born in West Caldwell, New Jersey, grew up aware of these musical trends when he formed, with his brother, a group called Broken Promises. Though the band did not go far, Page continued writing songs and pursuing his dream while managing odd jobs. As a coat-check boy in a dance club, he befriended the resident DJ, who, in turn, was happy to play a song that Page had recorded on his own called "Turning Me On." Coincidentally, Mark Kamins—the same talent mogul who is purported to have discovered Madonna—happened to be there, and he liked the tune. That night, Tommy Page launched his solo career.

In 1989 Page had his first success with "A Shoulder to Cry On." Lyrically, it was a variation on the romantic friendship themes of Paul Anka's "Put Your Head on My Shoulder," Simon & Garfunkel's "Bridge over Troubled Water," and Carole King's "You've Got a Friend." Propelled by his pensive piano and a string orchestra, Page celebrates a sensitive mood of despair while reminding the listener to count on him as an absentee guide. "Unlike most songs on the radio about love," Page explained in 1990, "this was a song about true friendship. And the idea that when the whole world's gone, there's always that one person that's by your side when everybody else deserts you."

Page did strike up a creative friendship with New Kid Jordan Knight, with whom he wrote the tenderhearted, though slightly more R&B inflected,

"I'll Be Your Everything" (which went to *Billboard*'s #1 spot in early 1990). Three of those wily New Kids even supplied background vocals. But touring with the New Kids got Page lumped into the 1980s dance-pop milieu. He made a modest impact with his first album, simply titled *Tommy Page*. Its final track, one of the best on the album, is a sad, romantic excursion called "Minetta Lane." Here, Page asks, through the tones of an echoing piano, "Whatever happened to love, sweet love, did it fade away and die?" The track ends with the sound of departing footsteps, a gesture that makes any Page fan quake whenever walking along the song's namesake—a small Greenwich Village street that is almost invisible to the unwary tourist.

By the time he released his second album, *Paintings in My Mind*, that same year, Page had perfected his invocations of "faded memories of another place and time." He was evolving further from dance pop to straight-ahead ballads, though he often retained the saxophone, synth-pop textures, and reverberating drum percussion that was typical of slightly harder-edged British acts like Duran Duran and the Thompson Twins. But his reliance on "old-fashioned" melody styles and his fearless desire to project a delicate voice were disarming. "When someone changes," he told *Teen Beat* magazine in 1991, "a lot of people expect you to all of a sudden go into R&B music or become really danceable, but I went the other way around. I made music a little more sweet than it used to be."

On a video he made in 1990 to demonstrate his songwriting process, Page was forthright about his inner world: "A lot of people ask me, 'Tommy there are so many songs about love, like how could you be in love this many times?' And the truth is I don't think I've really ever been truly in deep love with somebody. But a lot of the songs about love are songs I think of, well, if I was in love, this is how I'd like it to be. . . . It's more like a fantasy. That's the concept, and the reason why I named the album *Paintings in My Mind*. . . . It's a theory that a picture is a frozen captured moment in true life, which means that if you see a picture, that means that that has really happened. But a painting is anything that you can dream up or imagine in your mind. And that's a lot to do with the songs that I write. They're paintings; they're not pictures. They're not real things that have necessarily happened, but the things that I want to happen."

In 1991, Page released *From the Heart*, which opens with his version of the Michael Bolton–Diane Warren ballad, "Whenever You Close Your Eyes." Bolton may have blustered with "blue-eyed soul," but Page eases into a slow, dreamy mode as he calls out, "I need to know that I am in your world." Along with engineer and keyboardist Guy Roche, Page handled this and some of the album's other lush arrangements. The collection does veer into dance territory on some tracks, but the most notable songs are Page compositions such as "Madly in Love," "I Still Believe in You and Me," and "I'll Never Forget You," as well as his intimate version of the 1970s Eric Carmen–Rachmaninoff chestnut, "Never Gonna Fall in Love Again."

Page once said that one of his favorite movies is *Somewhere in Time*, the story of a man who wills himself back to a turn-of-the-century resort hotel to reunite with the ideal love of a past existence. Based on Richard Matheson's novel *Bid Time Return*, the 1980 film, starring Christopher Reeve and Jane Seymour, incurred the scorn of dubious critics. But it has ignited romantic passion (and even a Web site) among many since its theatrical debut. Page was particularly impressed by John Barry's soundtrack, which pairs snippets from "Rhapsody on a Theme of Paganini" with the composer's own time-bending, melancholic strings—an effect that culminates in Roger Williams's enchanting piano rendition in the bittersweet finale.

From the Heart appears to have adapted some of Barry's wistful style. In the liner notes, Page makes a point of dedicating the album "to all the beautiful people in Asia who welcome me with open arms." His Eastern appeal revealed a sensibility shift that started in the early 1990s, when MTV began to favor brasher fare, and more and more Japanese listeners embraced a golden era of American pop that Americans were forgetting.

Page, though likely not consciously aware of it, became a Stephen Foster for his times—the purveyor of the "dulcem melodie" in an era when driving rhythms increasingly dominated the marketplace. In his most tender moments, Page's voice echoes a history of vanilla vocalizers. He harbors the happy sentiments of Frankie Avalon, the melodic savvy of Bobby Vee, the vulnerable sighs of Shelley Fabares, the sentimentality of Brian Hyland, the contours of the Lettermen, the tortured dreams of Joe Meek, the layered chiffon of Curt Boettcher, the healing harmonics of the Sandpipers, the day-bright dexterity of ABBA, and, last but not least, the plaintive echoes of the Cascades' "Rhythm of the Rain," which opened this adventure and inspired the fictional Wayne Willoughby to rethink his sonic judgments. Tommy Page joins these forbears, who occasionally chime through the discord with melodies piping through ceiling speakers at drugstores and malls. His is another disembodied and lone voice calling out in the wilderness from a parallel time and place—"a friend to rely on" as night encroaches.

Source Notes

AI: Author interviews. Other sources are in order of appearance.

Introduction: I Hear the Great White Milkshake

Benning, Lee Edwards. *Make Mine Vanilla*. New York: A Fireside Book, 1992.

Clarke, Donald. *The Rise and Fall of Popular Music*. New York: St. Martin's Press, 1995.

Chapter 1: White-Bread Rhapsodies

AI: Frankie Avalon, Bob Marcucci.

Fox, Ted. *In The Groove: The People Behind the Music*. New York: St. Martin's Press, 1986.

Austin, William W. *Susannah, Jeanie and the Old Folks at Home: The Songs of Stephen Foster from His Time to Ours*. New York: Macmillan Publishing Co., 1975.

Hitchcock, H. Wiley. Notes to album *Songs by Stephen Foster*. Elektra/Nonesuch, 1987.

Douglas, Ann. *The Feminization of American Culture*. New York: The Noonday Press, 1977, 1998.

Tawa, Nicholas. *Sweet Songs for Gentle Americans: The Parlor Song in America, 1790–1860*. Bowling Green, Ohio: Bowling Green University Popular Press, 1980.

Howard, John Tasker. *Stephen Foster: America's Troubadour*. New York, Thomas Y. Crowell Company, 1934.

Mark Twain cited in Ken Emerson's *Doo-Dah!: Stephen Foster and the Rise of American Popular Culture*. New York: Simon & Schuster, 1997.

Hamm, Charles. *Yesterdays: Popular Song in America*. New York: W.W. Norton & Company, 1983.

Dannen, Frederic. *Hit Men*. New York: Vintage Books, 1991.

Kerouac, Jack. *On the Road: Fortieth Anniversary Edition*. New York: Viking, 1997.

Mailer, Norman. "The White Negro," *Dissent*, vol. IV, Summer 1957.

Ferlinghetti, Lawrence. "Junkman's Obbligato," from *A Coney Island of the Mind*. New York: New Directions, 1958.

Tamarkin, Jeff. "Vanilla Nice," *Goldmine*, 22 February 1991.

Smith, Joe. *Off The Record: An Oral History of Popular Music*. New York: Warner Books, 1988.

John Perkins quoted in the Joseph F. Laredo notes to *The Best of The Crew Cuts: The Mercury Years*, Polygram Records, Inc./Karussell International, 1997.

Pat Boone, from a personal letter to the author, dated June 15, 1999.

Burke, Ken. "Pat Boone: A Founding Father Denied!" *Roctober*, Summer 2000.

Cohn, Nik. *Rock from the Beginning*. New York: Pocket Books, 1970.

Chapter 2: Twinkle and Shine! The Mitch Miller Years

AI: Mitch Miller.

Clooney, Rosemary (with Joan Barthel). *Girl Singer: An Autobiography*. New York: Doubleday, 1999.

Sony Music 100 Years: Soundtrack of a Century. New York: Sony Music Entertainment Inc., 1999.

Tamarkin, Jeff. "Vanilla Nice: Boone in the U.S.A." *Goldmine*, February 22, 1991.

Fox, Ted. *In the Groove: The People Behind the Music*. New York: St. Martin's Press, 1986.

Hotchner, A. E. *Doris Day: Her Own Story*. New York: Bantam, 1976.

Chapter 3: Bobby Tomorrow

AI: Bobby Vee, John Beecher, Snuff Garrett.

Goldrosen, John, and John Beecher. *Remembering Buddy: The Definitive Biography of Buddy Holly*. New York: Da Capo Press, 1996.

Amburn, Ellis. *Buddy Holly: A Biography*. New York: St. Martin's Griffin, 1995.

Bobby Vee, quoted in Steve Kolanjian's notes to *Bobby Vee: Legendary Masters Series*. EMI, 1990.

Burns, Gordon. "Such Nice Boys," *Guardian*, 12 April 1997.

Chapter 4: Johnny Angelfood

AI: Stu Phillips.

Shelley Fabares, quoted in notes to the CD reissue of *Shelley! / The Things We Did Last Summer*. Collectables, 2000.

Gould, Glenn (Tim Page, ed.). *The Glenn Gould Reader*. New York: Vintage Books, 1984, 1990.

Callahan, Mike. Notes to *The Chordettes: 25 All-Time Greatest Recordings*. Varese Sarabande, 2000.

Parr, A. H. *The Lennon Sisters: Sweethearts of Song*. Garden City, New York: Doubleday & Company, 1960.

Chapter 5: Vanilla Expressionism: Joe Meek's "Paradise Garden"

AI: Charles Blackwell, John Repsch.

Humphrey Littleton, quoted in the Arena documentary *The Very Strange Story of the Legendary Joe Meek*. BBC Television, 1992.

Adams, Dave, "The First Meeting," *Thunderbolt*, No. 6, 1992.

Cleveland, Barry. *Creative Production Music: Joe Meek's Bold Techniques*. Vallejo, California: Mix Books, 2001.

Boone, Pat. *Between You, Me and the Gatepost*. Englewood Cliffs, New Jersey: Prentice-Hall, Inc., 1960.

"All the Stars in Heaven," recorded by Davy Kaye, released February 1965 (Decca F12703).

Repsch, John. *The Legendary Joe Meek: The Telstar Man*. London: Cherry Red Books, 2000, Appendix.

Young, Frank M. "Everybody's Got to Face It One Day . . .": Joe Meek's Songwriting Legacy," *TelstarWeb*, 1997.

No author. "Going Places: Don Charles: No Music-Bound Tonsils for Him," from an article reprinted in *Thunderbolt*, No. 11, 1994.

Joe Meek, quoted in an interview for "The Flip Side," a *World in Action* documentary for Granada Television, 1964.

Notes to the CD compilation *Joe Meek's Girls*. RPM Records, 1996.

Newson, Mark. "The Kenny Hollywood Interview." *Thunderbolt*, No. 21, 1997.

Chapter 6: "Sealed with a Kiss": America's Shadow Anthem

AI: Brian Hyland, Peter Udell, Snuff Garrett.

Chapter 7: Summerchime: Sunshine Pop's Precursors

AI: John Gummoe, Bob Morgan.

Smith, Joe (Mitchell Fink, ed.). *Off the Record: An Oral History of Popular Music*. New York: Warner Books, 1988.

Warner, Jay. *The Da Capo Book of American Singing Groups*. New York: Da Capo Press, 2000.

Chad Stuart, quoted by Dawn Eden in the notes to *Painted Dayglow Smile: A Collection*. Sony Legacy, 1992.

Chad Stuart, quoted on *The Official Chad & Jeremy Website*. An Electric Paintbox Production. www.chadandjeremy.net.

Chad Stuart, quoted in the notes to the CD reissue of *Before and After*. Sundazed, 2002.

Jonathan King, in his notes to the CD collection *King of Hits*. Jonathan King Enterprises, 2001.

Burr, Dan. Notes to the CD reissue of *Jonathan King / Hedgehoppers Anonymous*. Wounded Bird Records, 2001.

Chapter 8: Vanilla Psychedelia: Curt Boettcher's "Upholstered Folk"

AI: Bob Morgan, Bobb Goldsteinn.

Randy Sparks, quoted in *Encyclopedia of Popular Music*, Muze UK Ltd., 1989–2002.

Bobb Goldsteinn and Dotti Holmberg, quoted in the notes to *Dotti Holmberg: Sometimes Happy Times*. Sundazed, 2002.

McCarthy, Ray. "Curt Boettcher Interview." *ZigZag*, No. 48, December 1974.

David Bash's notes to the CD *The Millennium: Magic Time . . . The Millennium/Ballroom Recordings*. Sundazed, 2001.

No author. *The Urantia Book*, paperback edition. Chicago: Urantia Foundation, 1999.

Chapter 9: A Name That's Lighter than Air

Natchez, Marty. "The Association: Collectively Collectible." *Goldmine*, October 12, 1984.

Jules Alexander, interviewed in 1983 on *Inside the Association*. Broadcast in the summer of 1983 on WFBE in Flint, Michigan.

Phillips, John (with Jim Jerome). *Papa John: An Autobiography by John Phillips*. Garden City, New York: Dolphin Books, 1986.

Ryan, Tim. "Fame by Association." *Honolulu Star-Bulletin*, March 10, 2000.

Ted Bluechel, to interviewer John Harper in 1982 on a North Carolina radio show called *Sixties Pack at Six*.

Chapter 10: The Doodletown Dimension

AI: Ethel Gabriel, Johnny Mann.

Notes to *Sunshine Days: Volume One*. Varese Sarabande, 1997.

Notes to *Nuggets Vol. 7: Early San Francisco*. Rhino Records, 1985.

Dick, Philip K. *Flow My Tears, the Policeman Said*. New York: Vintage Books, 1974, 1993.

Sutin, Lawrence, ed. *The Shifting Relities of Philip K. Dick: Selected Literary and Philosophical Writings*. New York: Vintage Books, 1995.

Chapter 11: "Come Saturday Morning": The Rarefied Worlds of Claudine Longet and the Sandpipers

AI: Claudine Longet, conducted by fax in March 2001 and initially used for the notes to *The Very Best of Claudine Longet*. Varese Sarabande, 2000.

Michael Piano, quoted on the back cover notes to a Pickwick reissue of the
Come Saturday Morning album. Pickwick International, 1979.

Chapter 12: The Cake Out in the Rain

Hoerburger, Rob. "Revisionist Thinking on the Carpenters." *New York Times,*
November 3, 1991.

Coleman, Ray. *The Carpenters: The Untold Story.* New York: HarperCollins,
1994.

Schmidt, Randy, ed. *Yesterday Once More: Memories of the Carpenters and
Their Music.* Cranberry Township, Pennsylvania: Tiny Ripple Books, 2000.

Nolan, Tom. "The Grumbling Began: The Carpenters as the Enemy?" (From
"The Carpenters: An Appraisal"). *A&M Compendium,* July 1975.

Pooler, Frank. "The Choral Sound of the Carpenters." *Choral Journal,* April
1973.

Bangs, Lester. "The Carpenters and the Creeps." *Rolling Stone,* March 4, 1971.

Naglin, Nancy. "The Carpenters Go Country?" *Country Music Magazine,*
August 1978.

Moran, Bill. "If Somebody Would Just Let Us Know What the Problem
Is . . ." *Radio Report,* May 29, 1978.

Hoerburger, Rob. "Revisionist Thinking on the Carpenters." *New York Times,*
November 3, 1991.

Chapter 13: ABBA's Vanilla Ice

Palm, Carl Magnus. *Bright Lights, Dark Shadows: The Real Story of ABBA.*
New York: Omnibus Press, 2002.

Lacayo, Richard. "What's That Chirping?" *Time,* October 11, 1993.

Frith, Simon, and Peter Langley. "Money Money Money: How ABBA Won
Their Waterloo." *Creem,* Vol. 8, No. 10, March 1997.

Chapter 14: A Zillion Chocolate Kisses

Tommy Page, quoted in the video *I'll Be Your Everything.* Warner Reprise
Video, 1990.

Tommy Page, quoted in an interview with editor Avi Mandava. *Teen Beat,*
June 1991.

Vanilla Pop Discography

The following Discography is a selective listing for those seeking vanilla titles. The entries include artists, singles with *Billboard* chart positions, album titles with label numbers and years of release, as well as some outstanding album tracks when applicable. The lists include only those singles and albums possessing reasonably vanilla-flavored sounds. The albums with the most vanilla moods (those likely to include more vanilla tracks), as well as the most vanilla singles, are in **bold**. Some artists, like the Lettermen, the Ray Conniff Singers, and the Sandpipers do not require their singles in bold because they are more flavor-consistent than others. And to broaden the discussion, I've also included a list of songs "At Flavor's Edge," which I feel do not fit squarely into the category but have enough vanilla tendencies to merit mention. Some singles (when warranted) have both their A and B sides, each title separated by a "/". The outstanding non-single album titles are also included, with their respective albums named in parentheses at the end of each sub-list. A bracketed number shall occasionally indicate whether or not an album includes [2] or more discs. In some instances, Adult Contemporary chart listings appear with the initials AC. Since the investigation into Vanilla Pop can often be subjective, I present this Discography as a starting guide for readers intrepid enough to embark on their own tasty explorations.

ABBA

Singles (all on Atlantic):
"SOS" (3265) #15 1975
"Fernando" (3346) #13 1976
"Dancing Queen" (3372) #1 1976
"Knowing Me, Knowing You" (3387) #14
    1977
"Chiquitita" (3629) #29 1979
"The Winner Takes It All" (3776) #8 1980

Albums (on Atlantic unless otherwise noted):
Ring Ring (Polar 242) 1973
Waterloo (18101) 1974
ABBA (18146) 1975
Greatest Hits (18189) 1976
Arrival (18207) 1977
The Album (19164) 1978
Voulez-Vous (16000) 1979
Super Trouper (16023) 1980
The Visitors (19332) 1981
The Singles (The First Ten Years) (80036)
    1982 [2]

Album cuts of note:
"I Am Just a Girl" (from *Ring Ring*)
"Eagle"
"Thank You for the Music" (from *The
    Album*)
"Happy New Year" (from *Super Trouper*)
"The Day Before You Came" (from *The
    Singles* [*The First Ten Years*])

The Arbors

Singles (all on Date)
"A Symphony for Susan" (1529) #51 1966
"Just Let It Happen" / "Dreamer Girl"
    (1546) #113 1967
"Graduation Day" / "I Win the Whole
    Wide World" (1561) #59 1967
"With You Girl" / "A Love for All Seasons"
    (1570) 1967
"Valley of the Dolls" (1581) 1967
"The Letter" (1638) #20 1969
"I Can't Quit Her" / "For Emily, Whenever
    I May Find Her" (1645) #67 1969

"Touch Me" (1651) 1969
"Julie, I Tried" (1672) 1970

Albums (on Date unless otherwise noted):
A Symphony for Susan (TES 4003) 1966
The Arbors Sing "Valley of the Dolls" (TES
    4011) 1967
*The Arbors: Featuring "I Can't Quit Her" /
    "The Letter"* (TES 4017) 1969
The Very Best of the Arbors (CD Taragon
    TARCD-1049) 1998

Album cuts of note:
"Open a New Window" (from *A Symphony
    for Susan*)
"Endless Summer" (from *The Arbors Sing
    "Valley of the Dolls"*)

The Association

Singles:
"Cherish" (Valiant 747) #1 1966
"Pandora's Golden Heebie Jeebies" /
    "Standing Still" (Valiant 755) #35
    1966
"No Fair at All" / "Looking Glass" (Valiant
    758) #51 1967
"Windy" / "Sometime" (Warner 7041) #1
    1967
"Never My Love" (Warner 7074) #2 1967
"Everything That Touches You" / "We Love
    Us" (7163) #10 1968
"Time for Livin'" / "Birthday Morning"
    (7195) #39 1968
"Goodbye Columbus" / "The Time It Is
    Today" (7267) #80 1969
"Across the Persian Gulf" (Elektra E-47146)
    1981

Albums (on Warner Brothers unless otherwise noted):
And Then . . . Along Comes the Association
    (Valiant 5002 / Warner Bros. 1702)
    1966
Renaissance (Valiant 5004 / Warner Bros.
    1704) 1967
Insight Out (1696) 1967

Birthday (1733) 1968

Greatest Hits (1867) 1968

Goodbye Columbus [Original Soundtrack] [including Charles Fox instrumentals)] (1786) 1969

The Association: French EP & SP Collection (Magic Records PM 806 5230142) 1999

Just the Right Sound: The Association Anthology (Rhino/Warner R2 78303) 2002 [2]

Album cuts of note:

"Message of Our Love"

"Remember"

"Changes" (from *And Then . . . Along Comes the Association*)

"Memories of You"

"Songs in the Wind" (from *Renaissance*)

"Happiness Is" (from *Insight Out*)

"Rose Petals, Incense and a Kitten"

"Barefoot Gentleman" (from *Birthday*)

Frankie Avalon

Singles (all on Chancellor):

"I'll Wait for You" (1026) #15 1958

"Venus" (1031) #1 1959

"Bobby Sox to Stockings" (1036) #8 1959

"Why" (1045) #1 1959

"Where Are You" (1052) #32 1960

"Togetherness" (1056) #26 1960

"A Perfect Love" (1065) #47 1960

"Who Else but You" (1077) 1961

"Voyage to the Bottom of the Sea" (1081) #101 1961

Albums (on Chancellor unless otherwise noted):

Frankie Avalon (CHL-5001) 1958

The Young Frankie Avalon (CHLS-5002) 1959

Summer Scene (CHLS-5011) 1960

A Whole Lotta Frankie (CHL-5018) 1961

And Now About Mr. Avalon (CHLS-5022) 1961

You Are Mine (CHLS-5027) 1962

Christmas Album (CHLS-5031) 1962

Frankie Avalon Sings Cleopatra (CHLS-5032) 1963

Young and in Love (CHL-69801) 1960

Frankie Avalon's 15 Greatest Hits (United Artists UAS-6382) 1964

Frankie Avalon: 25 All-Time Greatest Hits (CD Varese Sarabande 302 066 304 2) 2002

Album cuts of note:

"Too Young to Love" (from *The Young Frankie Avalon*)

"Love Letters in the Sand"

"The Things We Did Last Summer" (from *Summer Scene*)

"I'll Never Stop Loving You" (from *You Are Mine*)

Blades Of Grass

Singles (all on Jubilee):

"Happy" (5582) #87 1967

"Just Another Face" (5590) 1967

"Help!" (5605) 1967

"I Love You Alice B. Toklas" (5635) 1968

Albums:

The Blades of Grass Are Not for Smoking (Jubilee 8007) 1967

The Blades of Grass Are Not for Smoking + bonus tracks (CD Revola CR REV8) 2002

Album cuts of note:

"Satin Slipper"

"Walk Away Renee"

Curt Boettcher (see also Sagittarius)

Eternity's Children:

"Mrs. Bluebird" (Tower 416) #69 1968

"Sunshine Among Us" (Tower 439) #117 1968

"From You Unto Us" (Liberty 56162) 1970

Eternity's Children (Tower ST-5123) 1968

The GoldeBriars:

"Pretty Girls and Rolling Stones" (Epic 9673) 1964

"Castle on the Corner" / "I've Got to Love Somebody" (Epic 9719) 1964"June Bride Baby" / "I'm Gonna Marry You" (Epic 9806) 1965
The GoldeBriars (Epic BN 26087) 1964
Straight Ahead (Epic BN 26114) 1964

Dotti Holmberg:
Sometimes Happy Times (CD Sundazed SC 11114) 2002

The Millennium:
Begin (Columbia 9663) 1968
Begin + bonus tracks (CD Columbia Special Products 75030) 1995
Again (CD Poptones 5012) 2000 [Japanese import]
The Millennium Continues (CD Trattoria Family Club PSCR-5878) 2000
The Second Millennium (CD Archives 906) 2000
Magic Time: The Millennium / Ballroom Sessions (CD Sundazed 11102) 2001 [3]
Voices of the Millennium (CD Rev-Ola 16) 2003
Pieces (CD Sonic Past Music 9002) 2003

Sandy Salisbury:
"Come Softly" (Together 125) 1970

Summer's Children:
"Milk and Honey" / "Too Young to Marry" (Date 2-1508) 1966 (This can be found on *Magic Time: The Millennium / Ballroom Sessions* (CD Sundazed 11102) [3] 2001)

Curt Boettcher rereleases:
"Share With Me" / "Sometimes" (Together 117) 1969
(This can be found on *Misty Mirage* (CD Poptones 5007) 2000)
Another Time (CD Sound City Music 9006) 2003

Pat Boone
Singles (all on Dot Records):

"Friendly Persuasion (Thee I Love)" (15490) #5 1956
"Love Letters in the Sand" (15570) #1 1957
"April Love" (15660) #1 1957
"If Dreams Came True" (15785) #7 1958
"Gee, But It's Lonely" (15825) #21 1958
"I'll See You in My Dreams" (16312) #32 1962
"As Tears Go By" (16825) 1966

Albums (on Dot Records unless otherwise noted):
Pat Boone (DLP 3012) (Boone's first album but released in 1957)
Howdy! (DLP 3030) 1956
"Pat" (DLP 3050) 1957
Pat's Great Hits (DLP 3071) 1957
Pat Boone Sings Irving Berlin (DLP 3077) 1958
Star Dust (DLP 25118) 1958
Pat Boone Sings (DLP 25158) 1959
***Tenderly* (DLP 25180) 1959**
Moonglow (DLP 25270) 1960
Great! Great! Great! (DLP 25346) 1960
Moody River (DLP 25384) 1961
I'll See You in My Dreams (DLP 25399) 1962
Pat Boone Sings "Days of Wine and Roses" and Other Great Movie Themes (DLP 25504) 1963
***The Touch of Your Lips* (with Gordon Jenkins)** (DLP 25546) 1964
Near You (with Pete King) (DLP 25606) 1965
Pat Boone Sings Winners of the "Reader's Digest" Poll (DLP 25667) 1966
Great Hits of 1965 (DLP 25685) 1966
Memories (DLP 25748) 1966
The Gold Collection (14 new recordings of his old songs) (CD Gold Label GLD CD 8000) 1999
Pat's Big Ones (CD Connoisseur Collection SDVSOP CD 328) 2000 [2]

Album cuts of note:
"All Alone"

"Always"
"Soft Lights and Sweet Music"
"What'll I Do?" (from *Pat Boone Sings Irving Berlin*)
"Tenderly"
"True Love"
"Secret Love"
"The Nearness of You" (from *Tenderly*)
"Meet Me Tonight in Dreamland" (from *Memories*)
"Love Is a Many-Splendored Thing"
"Moon River" (from *Pat Boone Sings "Days of Wine and Roses" and Other Great Movie Themes*)
"Long Ago and Far Away"
"My Romance" (from *The Touch of Your Lips*)

The Brothers Four

Singles (all on Columbia):
"Greenfields" (41571) #2 1960
"My Tani" (41692) #50 1960
"The Green Leaves of Summer" (41808) #65 1960
"Four Strong Winds" (42888) #114 1963
"Somewhere" / "Turn Around" (43211) #131 1965
"Try to Remember" / "Sakura" (43404) #91 1965
"I'll Be Home for Christmas" (43919) 1966

Albums (on Columbia unless otherwise noted):
The Brothers Four (CL 1402/CS 8197) 1960
BMOC (Best Music On/Off Campus) (CL 1578/CS 8378) 1961
Rally 'Round (CL 1479/CS 8270) 1961
Roamin' with the Brothers IV (CL 1625/CS 8425) 1961
The Brothers Four Songbook (CL 1697/CS 8497) 1961
Greatest Hits (CS 8603) 1962
The Big Folk Hits (CS 8833) 1963
Sing of Our Times (CS 8928)
More Big Folk Hits (CS 9013) 1964
The Honey Wind Blows (CS 9105) 1965
Try to Remember (CS 9179) 1965

A Beatles Songbook: The Brothers Four Sing Lennon/McCartney (CS 9302) 1966
A New World's Record (CS 9502) 1967
Four Strong Winds (CS 9812) 1969
Let's Get Together (CS 9818) 1969
The Honey Wind Blows / Sing of Our Times (CD Collectors' Choice Music 397) 2004

Album cuts of note:
"Song from *Moulin Rouge*"
"When Everything Was Green" (from *Try to Remember*)
"The Honey Wind Blows"
"Feed the Birds"(from *The Honey Wind Blows*)
"Umbrellas in the Rain"
"Here Today and Gone Tomorrow" (from *A New World's Record*)

The Caravelles

Singles:
"You Don't Have to Be a Baby to Cry" / "The Last One to Know" (Smash 1852) #3 1963
"Have You Ever Been Lonely?" / "Don't Blow Your Cool" (Smash 1869) #94 1964
"Have You Ever Been Lonely / "Gonna Get Along Without You Now" (Decca F 11816) 1964
"You Are Here" / "How Can I Be Sure?" (Fontana TF 466) 1964

Albums:
You Don't Have to Be a Baby to Cry (Smash SRS-67044) 1963
The Story of The Caravelles (CD Marginal MAR 108) 1998

Album cuts of note:
"Tonight You Belong to Me"
"Don't Sing Love Songs"
"Forever" (from *You Don't Have to Be a Baby to Cry*)

The Carpenters

Singles (all on A&M):
"Ticket to Ride" (1142) #54 1970

"(They Long to Be) Close to You" (1183) #1 1970
"We've Only Just Begun" (1217) #2 1970
"For All We Know" (1243) #3 1971
"Rainy Days and Mondays" (1260) #2 1971
"Superstar" (1289) #2 1971
"Bless the Beasts and the Children" (1289) #67 1971
"Goodbye to Love" (1367) #7 1972
"Yesterday Once More" (1446) #2 1973
"Only Yesterday" (1677) #4 1975
"Solitaire" (1721) #17 1975
"There's a Kind of Hush (All Over the World)" (1800) #12 1976
"I Need to Be in Love" (1828) #25 1976

Albums (on A&M unless otherwise noted):
Offering (1969)
Close to You (4271) 1970
Ticket to Ride (4205) 1971
Carpenters (3502) 1971
A Song for You (3511) 1972
Now & Then (3519) 1973
The Singles: 1969–1973 (3601) 1973
Horizon (4530) 1975
A Kind of Hush (4581) 1976
Passage (4703) 1977
Christmas Portrait (A&M 4726) 1978
Made in America (3723) 1981
Voice of the Heart (4854) 1983
An Old-Fashioned Christmas (320) 1985
Yesterday Once More (6601) 1985 [2]
From the Top (A&M 75021-6875-2) 1991 [4]
Carpenters Collection (Time Life Music SUD-1) 1993

The Cascades
Singles:
"There's a Reason" / "Second Chance" (Valiant 6021) 1962
"Rhythm of the Rain" (Valiant 6026) #3 [#1 Adult Contemporary] 1962
"The Last Leaf" / "Shy Girl" (Valiant 6028) #60 / #91 1963

"My First Day Alone" / "I Want to Be Your Lover" (Valiant 6032) 1963
"A Little Like Lovin'" / "Cinderella" (RCA 47-8206) #116 1963
"For Your Sweet Love" / "Jeannie" (RCA 47-8268) #86 1963
"Little Betty Fallin' Star" / "Those Were the Good Old Days" (RCA 47-8321) 1964
"Awake" (RCA 47-8402) 1964

Albums:
Rhythm of the Rain (Valiant 405) 1963
Rhythm of the Rain (WEA International WPCP-3532) [Japan Import] 1990
The Very Best of the Cascades (Taragon TARCD-1046) 1998

Chad & Jeremy
Singles:
"Yesterday's Gone" / "Lemon Tree" (UK Ember EMBS 180) 1963
"Like I Love You Today" / "Early in the Morning" (UK Ember EMBS 186) 1963
"If I Loved You" / "No Tears for Johnny" (UK Ember EMBS 205) 1964
"Yesterday's Gone" / "Lemon Tree" (World Artists 1021) #21 1964
"A Summer Song" / "No Tears for Johnny" (World Artists 1027) #7 1964
"Willow Weep for Me" / "If She Was Mine" (World Artists 1034) #15 1964
"If I Loved You" / "Donna Donna" (World Artists 1041) #23 1965
"What Do You Want with Me?" / "A Very Good Year" (World Artists 1052) #51 1965
"Before and After" / "Fare Thee Well (I Must Be Gone)" (Columbia 43277) #17 1965
"If She Was Mine" / "Willow Weep for Me" (UK United Artists UP 1070) 1965
"From a Window" / "My Coloring Book" (World Artists 1056) #97 1965
"I Have Dreamed" / "Should I?" (Columbia 43414) #91 1965
"Distant Shores" / "Last Night" (Columbia 43682) #30 1966

"You Are She" / "I Won't Cry" (Columbia 43807) #87 1966

Albums:

Yesterday's Gone (World Artists WAM-2002 / WAS-3002) 1964

Chad & Jeremy Sing for You (World Artists WAM-2005 / WAS-3005) 1965

Chad & Jeremy Sing for You (UK Ember NR 5021) 1965

Second Album (UK Ember NR 5031) 1965

Before and After (Columbia CS 9174) 1965

I Don't Want to Lose You Baby (Columbia CS 9198) 1965

John Barry Meets Chad & Jeremy (UK Ember NR 5032) 1966

The Best of Chad & Jeremy (UK Ember NR 5036) 1966

Distant Shores (Columbia CS 9364) 1966

Of Cabbages and Kings (Columbia CS 9471) 1967

The Ark (Columbia CS 9699) 1968

Sing for You / Second Album (+ bonus tracks) (CD Repertoire REP 4286-WY) [German Import] 1992

Painted Dayglow Smile: A Collection (CD Sony Legacy 47719) 1992

The Ark (CD Sony SRCS 9269) [Japan Import] 1997

Distant Shores (+ bonus tracks) (CD Sundazed SC 11068) 2000

Before and After (+ bonus tracks) (CD Sundazed SC 11117) 2002

Of Cabbages and Kings (+ bonus tracks) (CD Sundazed SC11118) 2002

Album cuts of note:

"Sleep Little Boy" (from *Chad & Jeremy Sing for You*)

"Can't Get Used to Losing You" (from *Before and After*)

"Everyone's Gone to the Moon"

"The Way You Look Tonight" (from *Distant Shores*)

"Painted Dayglow Smile" (from *The Ark*)

The Ray Charles Singers

Singles:

"Autumn Leaves" (MGM 12068) #55 1955

"Love Me with All Your Heart (*Cuando Callenta El Sol*)" (Command 4046) #3 1964

"Al-Di-La" (Command 4049) #29 1964

"One More Time" (Command 4057) #32 1964

Albums:

Something Special for Young Lovers (Command 866) 1964

Songs for Lonesome Lovers (Command 874) 1964

Songs for Latin Lovers (Command 886) 1965

One of Those Songs (Command 898) 1966

At the Movies (Command 923) 1968

Love Me with All Your Heart: The Command Performances (CD Varese Sarabande VSD-5626) 1995

The Chordettes

Singles (all on Cadence):

"True Love Goes On and On" (1239) 1954

"Mr. Sandman" (1247) #1 1954

"Hummingbird" (1267) 1956

"Born to Be with You" (1291) #5 1956

"Lay Down Your Arms" / **"Teen Age Goodnight"** (1299) #16 / #45 1956

"Echo of Love" (1319) 1957

"Come Home to My Arms" (1307) 1956

"Just Between You and Me" / **"Soft Sands"** (1330) #8 / #73 1957

"Zorro" (1349) #17 1958

"A Broken Vow" (1382) #102 1960

"Never on Sunday" / **"Faraway Star"** (1402) #13 / #90 1961

"White Rose of Athens" (1417) 1961

Albums (on Columbia unless otherwise noted):

Harmony Time, Volume 1 (CL-6111) 1950

Harmony Time, Volume 2 (CL-6170) 1951

Harmony Encores (CL 6218) 1952

Sing Your Requests (CL 6285) 1954

Close Harmony (Cadence CP-1002) 1955

Never on Sunday (Cadence CP-25062) 1962

Listen (CBS CI-956)

The Best of the Chordettes (CD Rhino R2-70849) 1985

Greatest Hits (CD Curb 77781) 1995

They're Riding High, Says Archie (CD Collectables 5250) 1997

25 All-Time Greatest Recordings (CD Varese Sarabande 302 066 097 2) 2000

The Story (CD-ROM EMI Plus 724357616003) 2000

Born to Be with You (CD Disky 64584) 2001

Harmony Time 1 & 2 (CD Collectables COL-CD-7403) 2002

Harmony Encores / Sing Your Requests (CD Collectables COL-CD-7430) 2002

The Ray Conniff Singers

Singles (all on Columbia):

"Invisible Tears" (43061) #57 1964

"Happiness Is" (43352) #26 AC 1965

"Somewhere My Love" (43626) #9 1966

"Wednesday's Child" (43939) #29 AC 1967

"Winds of Change" (44492) #7 AC 1968

"I've Got My Eyes on You" (44724) AC #23 1969

Albums (on Columbia unless otherwise noted):

It's the Talk of the Town (CS-8143) (First album using Singers as foreground) 1960

Young at Heart (CS-8281) 1960

Somebody Loves Me (CS-8442) 1961

Speak to Me of Love (CS-8950) 1964

Invisible Tears (CS-9064) 1964

Happiness Is (CS-9261) 1966

Somewhere My Love (CS-9319) 1966

This is My Song (CS-9476) 1967

Hawaiian Album (CS-9547) 1967

It Must Be Him (CS-9595) 1968

Honey (CS-9661) 1968

Turn Around, Look at Me (CS-9712) 1968

I Love How You Love Me (CS-9777) 1969

Jean (CS-9920) 1969

Bridge Over Troubled Water (CS-1022) 1970

We've Only Just Begun (CS-30410) 1970

Love Story (CS-30498) 1971

I'd Like to Teach the World to Sing (KC-31220) 1972

Alone Again (Naturally) (31629) 1972

The Way We Were (KC-32802) 1973

Plays the Carpenters (CBS/Sony SOPM-129) 1974

Laughter in the Rain (KC-33332) 1974

Love Will Keep Us Together (KC-33884) 1975

Instrumental Favorites (Time Life Music R986-03) 1994

Album cuts of note:

"It's Dark on Observatory Hill" (from *Young at Heart*)

"I Only Have Eyes for You" (from *Somebody Loves Me*)

"Kisses Sweeter than Wine" (from *Invisible Tears*)

"You Stepped Out of a Dream" (from *Happiness Is*)

"Wichita Lineman" (from *I Love How You Love Me*)

"If You Could Read My Mind" (from *Love Story*)

The Cowsills

Singles (all on MGM):

The Rain, the Park, & Other Things (13810) #2 1967

"We Can Fly" / "A Time for Remembrance" (13886) #21 1968

"In Need of a Friend" / "Mister Flynn" (13909) #54 1968

Albums (on MGM unless otherwise noted):

The Cowsills (SE-4498) 1967

We Can Fly (SE-4534) 1968

Captain Sad and His Ship of Fools (SE-4554) 1968

The Best of the Cowsills (SE-4597) 1969
II x II (SE-4639) 1970
The Best of the Cowsills (CD Rebound
Records 314 520 204-2) 1998
*20th Century Masters: The Millennium
Collection* (CD Polydor 549947) 2001

Album cuts of note:
"Dreams of Linda" (from *The Cowsills*)
"Meet Me at the Wishing Well"
"Newspaper Blanket" (from *Captain Sad
and His Ship of Fools*)

The Crew-Cuts
Singles (all on Mercury):
"Crazy 'Bout Ya Baby" (70341) #8 1954
"Sh-Boom" (70404) #1 1954
**"Twinkle Toes" / "Dance Mr. Snowman
Dance"** (70491) 1954
"Earth Angel" (70529) #3 1955
"Mostly Martha" (70741) #31 1955
"Young Love" (71022) #17 1957

Albums:
On the Campus (Mercury MG-20140) 1954
Crew-Cut Capers (Mercury MG-20143)
1954
Music à la Carte (Mercury MG-20199)
1955
The Crew-Cuts on Parade (Mercury MPT
7501) 1956
Surprise Package (RCA Victor SP-1933)
1958
You Must Have Been a Beautiful Baby (RCA
LSP-2067) 1960
The Crew-Cuts Sing Out! (IRCA Victor PR-
102) 1960
High School Favorites (Wing MGW-12180)
1962
The Crew-Cuts: The Great New Sound
(Camay CA-3002) 1963
The Best of the Crew-Cuts: The Mercury Years
(CD Polygram/Karussell 552 762-2)
1997

The Mike Curb Congregation
Singles (all on MGM):

"Burning Bridges" / "We'll Sing in the
Sunshine" (14151) #34 1970
"Sweet Gingerbread Man" / "Fly Me a Place
for the Summer" (14265) #115 1971
"See You in September" / "The Very Same
Time Next Year" (14391) #108 1972
"It's a Small World" (14494) #108 1973

Albums:
Come Together (CoBurt 1002) 1970
Sweet Gingerbread Man (CoBurt 1003)
1970
*"Burning Bridges" & Other Great Motion
Picture Themes* (MGM SE-4761) 1971
Put Your Hand in the Hand (MGM SE-
4785) 1971
Song for a Young Love (MGM SE-4844)
1972
Sing Their Hits from The Glen Campbell
Show (MGM SE-4804) 1972
The Mike Curb Congregation (Curb Records
3129)
Greatest Hits (CD Curb Records D2-
77443) 1991
Walt Disney's Greatest Hits (CD Curb
Records D2-77686) 1995

Vic Dana
Singles (all on Dolton):
"Little Altar Boy" (48) #45 1961
"I Will" (51) #47 1962
"More" (81) #42 1963
"Shangri-La" (92) #27 1964
"Love Is All We Need" (95) #53 1964
"Garden in the Rain" (99) #97 1964
"Red Roses for a Blue Lady" (304) #10
1965
"Bring a Little Sunshine (to My Heart)"
(305) #66 1965
**"Moonlight and Roses (Bring Mem'ries of
You)"** (309) #51 1965
"Crystal Chandelier" (313) #51 1965
"I Love You Drops" (319) #30 1966

Albums:
More (Dolton 8026) 1963
Shangri-La (Dolton 8028) 1964

Red Roses for a Blue Lady (Dolton 8034)
1965
Golden Greats (CD EMI CDP 7 91678 2)
1989
The Complete Hits of Vic Dana (CD Eric
Records 11510-2) 2000

Doris Day (See Mitch Miller)
The Doodletown Pipers

Singles:
"Get a Horse" / "Magic Penny" (Reprise
0433) 1966
"A Summer Song" / "Summertime,
Summertime" (Epic 10200) #29
AC 1967
"Jessie" / "Image of You" (Epic 10254)
1967

Albums (all on Epic):
Here Come the Doodletown Pipers (BN
26222) 1966
Sing-Along '67 (BN 26307) 1967
Love Themes: Hit Songs for Those in Love
(BN 26340) 1967

Album cuts of note:
"Spanish Flea"
"Sweet Maria" (from *Sing-Along '67*)
"Cherish"
"There's a Kind of Hush" (from *Love
Themes: Hit Songs for Those
in Love*)

Craig Douglas

Singles (all U.K.):
"Pretty Blue Eyes" (Top Rank JAR 268)
1960
"The Girl Next Door" (Top Rank JAR 543)
1961
"Time" (Top Rank JAR 569) 1962
"Rainbows" (Columbia DB 4854)
1962

Albums:
Only Sixteen [compilation] (CD See for
Miles Records SEE CD 34) [French
Import] 1989

Shelley Fabares

Singles (all on Colpix):
"Johnny Angel" (621) #1 1962
"Johnny Loves Me" (636) #21 1962
"The Things We Did Last Summer" (654)
#46 1962

Albums:
Shelley! (Colpix 426) 1962
The Things We Did Last Summer Colpix
431) 1962
Shelley! / *The Things We Did Last Summer*
(CD Collectables COL-CD-6223)
2000

Album cuts of note:
"Picnic" (from *Shelley!*)
"Sealed with a Kiss" (from *The Things We
Did Last Summer*)

Percy Faith, His Orchestra,
& Chorus

Singles (all on Columbia)
"Yellow Days" (44166) AC #13 1967
"Can't Take My Eyes Off You" (44319)
AC #24 1967
"Theme from *A Summer Place*" (44932)
AC #26 1969

Albums:
Today's Themes for Young Lovers (Columbia
CS 9504) 1967
For Those in Love (Columbia CS 9610)
1968
*Angel of the Morning (Hit Themes for
Young Lovers)* (Columbia CS 9706)
1968
Those Were the Days (Columbia CS 9762)
1969
Love Theme from **Romeo and Juliet**
(Columbia CS 9906) 1969
Leaving on a Jet Plane (Columbia CS 9983)
1970
I Think I Love You (Columbia C 30502)
1971
Day by Day (Columbia KC 31627)
1972

Today's Themes for Young Lovers / For Those in Love (CD Collectables COL-CD-7429) 2002

Album cuts of note:
"The 59th Street Bridge Song (Feelin' Groovy)"
"Yellow Days"
"There's a Kind of Hush"
"A World of Whispers"
"Happy Together" (from *Today's Themes for Young Lovers*)
"Never My Love"
"For Those in Love"
"Live for Life" (from *For Those in Love*)
"Theme from 'A Summer Place'" (vocal version) (from *Love Theme from* Romeo and Juliet)

The Fleetwoods

Singles:
"Come Softly to Me" (Dolphin 1) #1 1959
"Graduation's Here" (Dolton 3) #39 1959
"Mr. Blue" (Dolton 5) #1 1959
"Outside My Window" (Dolton 15) #28 1960
"(He's) The Great Impostor" (Dolton 45) #30 1961
"Lovers by Night, Strangers by Day" (Dolton 62) #36 1962

Albums:
Mr. Blue (Dolton BLP-2001/BST-8001) 1959
The Fleetwoods—Gretchen, Gary, and Barbara (Dolton BLP-2002/BST-2002) 1960
The Fleetwoods' Greatest Hits (Dolton BLP-2018/BST-8018) 1962
Softly (Dolton BLP-2005/BST-8005) 1961
Deep in a Dream (Dolton BLP-2007/BST-8007) 1961
The Fleetwoods Sing the Best Goodies of the Oldies, Vol. 1 (Dolton BLP-2011/BST-8011) 1961
The Fleetwoods Sing for Lovers by Night (Dolton BLP-2020/BST-8020) 1963

Goodnight My Love (Dolton BLP-2025/BST-8025) 1963
Before and After (Dolton BLP-2030/BST-8025) 1965
Folk Rock (Dolton BLP-2039/BST-8039) 1965
In a Mellow Mood (Sunset SUM-1131/SUS-5131) 1966
Come Softly to Me: The Very Best of the Fleetwoods (CD EMI 0777 7 98830 2 8) 1993
Mr. Blue (CD Van Meter VM-3001) 1997 [reissued in original mono, with extra stereo tracks]

Album cuts of note:
"Serenade of the Bells" (from *Mr. Blue*)
"Lavender Blue (Dilly Dilly)"
"One Little Star" (from *Deep in a Dream*)
"My Special Lover" (from *The Fleetwoods Sing for Lovers by Night*)
"Goodnight My Love"
"The End of the World" (from *Goodnight My Love*)
"Softly, as I Leave You" (from *Before and After*)

The Four King Cousins

Albums:
Introducing the Four King Cousins (Capitol ST-2990) 1968

The Four Preps

Singles (all on Capitol):
"Dreamy Eyes" (3576) #56 1956
"26 Miles (Santa Catalina)" (3845) #2 1958
"Lazy Summer Night" / "Summertime Lies" (4023) #21 1958
"Cinderella"/"Gidget" (4078) #69 1958
"Charmaine" (4974) #116 1963
"I'll Set My Love to Music" (5351) 1965
"The Girl in the Shade of the Striped Umbrella" (5687) 1966

Albums (on Capitol unless otherwise noted):
The Things We Did Last Summer (T 1090) 1958

Dancing and Dreaming (ST 1216) 1959
Early in the Morning (DT 1291) 1960
The Four Preps on Campus (ST 1566) 1961
Campus Encore (Live) (1647) 1962
Campus Confidential (ST 1814) 1963
Songs for a Campus Party (ST 1976) 1963
How to Succeed in Love (If You're Really Trying) (ST 2169) 1964
Collectors Series (CD CDP 7 91626 2) 1989
Best of the Four Preps (CD Curb Records D2-77590) 1993
Four Preps on Campus / Campus Encore (CD Collectors' Choice 167) 2001

Album cuts of note:
"The Things We Did Last Summer"
"A Tree in the Meadow"
"Graduation Day"
"Love Letters in the Sand" (from *The Things We Did Last Summer*)
"Sukiyaki"
"Theme from *Dr. Kildare* (from *Songs for a Campus Party*)
"Lollipops and Roses"
"My Special Angel" (from *How to Succeed in Love (If You're Really Trying)*)

The GoldeBriars (See Curt Boettcher)

Harpers Bizarre
Singles (all on Warner Brothers):
"The 59th Street Bridge Song (Feelin' Groovy)" (5890) #13 1967
"Come to the Sunshine" (7028) #37 1967
"Anything Goes" / "Malibu U." (7063) #43 1967
"Chattanooga Choo Choo" / "Hey, You in the Crowd" (7090) #45 1967
"Both Sides Now" / "Small Talk" (7200) #123 1968
"Battle of New Orleans" (7223) #95 1968

Albums (on Warner Brothers unless otherwise noted):
Feelin' Groovy (WS 1693) 1967
Anything Goes (WS 1716) 1967

The Secret Life of Harpers Bizarre (WS 1739) 1968
Harpers Bizarre 4 (WS 1784) 1969
Feelin' Groovy: The Best of Harpers Bizarre (CD Warner Archives 2-46261) 1997
Feelin' Groovy (+bonus tracks) (CD Sundazed SC 6176) 2001
Anything Goes (+bonus tracks) (CD Sundazed SC 6177) 2001
The Secret Life of Harpers Bizarre (+ bonus tracks) (CD Sundazed SC 6178) 2001
Harpers Bizarre 4 (+ bonus tracks) (CD Sundazed SC 6179) 2001

Album cuts of note:
"Happyland"
"Raspberry Rug" (from *Feelin' Groovy*)
"Pocketful of Miracles"
"Snow"
"High Coin" (from *Anything Goes*)
"Me, Japanese Boy"
"The Drifter" (from *The Secret Life of Harpers Bizarre*)
"Witchi Tai To"
"I Love You, Alice B. Toklas" (from *Harpers Bizarre 4*)

Brian Hyland
Singles:
"Itsy Bitsy Teenie Weenie Yellow Polka Dot Bikini" / "Don't Dilly Dally Sally" (Leader 805) #1 1960
"(The Clickity Clack Song) Four Little Heels" (Kapp 352) #73 1960
"Let Me Belong to You" (ABC-Paramount 10236) #20 1961
"I'll Never Stop Wanting You" / "The Night I Cried" (ABC-Paramount 10262) #83 1961
"Ginny Come Lately" (ABC-Paramount 10294) #21 1962
"Sealed with a Kiss" (ABC-Paramount 10336) #3 1962
"Warmed Over Kisses (Left Over Love)" (ABC-Paramount 10359) #25 1962
"I May Not Live to See Tomorrow" (ABC-Paramount 10374) #69 1962

"If Mary's There" (ABC-Paramount 10400)
#88 1963
"Save Your Heart for Me" (ABC-
Paramount 10452) #63 1963
"The Joker Went Wild" (Philips 40377)
#20 1966
"Run, Run, Look, and See" (Philips
40405) #25 1966
"Holiday for Clowns" (Philips 40444) #94
1967
"Tragedy" (Dot 17176) #56 1969
"Stay and Love Me All Summer" (Dot
17258) #83 1969

Albums:

The Bashful Blond (Kapp KS-3202) 1961
Let Me Belong to You (ABC-Paramount
ABC-400) 1961
The Joker Went Wild (Philips PHS 600-217)
1966
Tragedy / A Million to One (Dot DLP
25926) 1969
Stay and Let Me Love You All Summer Long
(Dot DLP-25954) 1969
Greatest Hits (CD MCA MCAD-11034)
1994
Hits & Rarities (CD Birchmount Music
7054) 2001

The Gunter Kallmann Chorus

Singles:

"Wish Me a Rainbow" / "The Day the
Rains Came" (4 Corners 138) #63
1966

Albums (on 4 Corners of the World,
unless otherwise indicated):

Serenade for Elisabeth (FCS-4209) 1962
Serenade for a Lady in Love (FCS-4218)
1964
Songs for My Love (FCS-4226) 1966
Wish Me a Rainbow (FCS-4235) 1967
Chanson D'Amour: With All My Heart
(FCS-4237) 1967
Call It Love (FCS-4242) 1967
Live for Love (FCS-4248) 1967
In Hollywood (FCS-4254) 1968

Love Is Blue (FCS-4256) 1968
Lounge Legends: Gunter Kallmann Choir
(CD Polydor 589 792-2) 2002

Album cuts of note:

"Portrait of My Love"
"Two for the Road" (from *Call It Love*)
"When I Look in Your Eyes" (from *In
Hollywood*)
"Happy Heart" (from *Lounge Legends:
Gunter Kallmann Choir*)

Jonathan King

Singles:

"Everyone's Gone to the Moon" /
"Summer's Coming" (Parrot 9774)
#17 1965
"Where the Sun Has Never Shone" / "Green
Is the Grass" (Parrot 9804) #97 1966
"The Land of the Golden Tree" (U.K.
Decca F12457) 1966
"Icicles" / "In a Hundred Years from Now"
(U.K. Decca F12517) 1966
"Seagulls" (U.K. Decca F12540) 1967
"Round, Round" (Parrot 3011) #122 1967

Albums:

Or Then Again . . . (Parrot PAS 71013)
1967
Pandora's Box (U.K. Records/ United Artists
53104) 1973
The Butterfly That Stamped (CD Castle
[U.K. Import] 1989 [2]
Jonathan King / Hedgehoppers Anonymous
(CD Wounded Bird Records WOU
1013) 2001
King of Hits (CD U.K. Records UKBOX-
CD001) 2001 [8]

The Lennon Sisters

Singles:

"Tonight You Belong to Me" / "When the
Lilacs Bloom Again" (Coral 61701)
#15 1956
"Sad Movies (Make Me Cry)" / "I Don't
Know Why" (Dot 16255) #56
1961

Albums:

Let's Get Acquainted (Brunswick BL54031) 1957

Lawrence Welk Presents the Lennon Sisters (Brunswick BL54039) 1958

The Lennon Sisters Sing Twelve Great Hits (Dot DLP 3292 / DLP 25292) 1960

Sad Movies Make Me Cry (Dot DLP 3398 / DLP 25398) 1960

Christmas with the Lennon Sisters (Dot DLP 25343) 1961

#1 Hits of the 1960s (Dot DLP 3589 DLP 25589) 1964

Solos by the Lennon Sisters (Dot DLP 25659)

Somethin' Stupid (Dot 25797) 1967

On the Groovy Side (Dot DLP 25829) 1967

The Lennon Sisters Today!! (Mercury SR 61164) 1968

Among Our Souvenirs (CD Ranwood 1912) 1994 [2]

Yesterday and Today (CD (Ranwood 7039) 1994

Album cuts of note:
"Everything That Touches You"
"Green Tambourine" (from *The Lennon Sisters Today!!*)

The Lettermen

Singles (all on Capitol):
"The Way You Look Tonight" (4586) #13 1961

"When I Fall in Love" / "Smile" (4658) #7 1961

"Come Back Silly Girl" / "A Song for Young Love" (4699) #17 1962

"How Is Julie?" / "Turn Around, Look at Me" (4746) #42 1962

"Silly Boy (She Doesn't Love You)" (4810) #81 1962

"Again" / "A Tree in the Meadow" (4851) #120 1962

"Theme from 'A Summer Place'" / "Sealed with a Kiss" (5437) #16 1965

"Secretly" / "The Things We Did Last Summer" (5499) #64 1965

"I Only Have Eyes for You" (5649) #72 1966

"Our Winter Love" / "Warm" (5813) #72 1967

"Goin' Out of My Head" / "Can't Take My Eyes Off You" (2054) #7 1967

"Put Your Head on My Shoulder" (2324) #44 1968

"I Have Dreamed" (2414) #129 1969

"Hurt So Bad" (2482) #12 1969

"Shangri-La" / "When Summer Ends" (2643) #64 1969

"Traces/Memories Medley" (2697) #47 1969

"Everything Is Good About You" (3020) #74 1971

"Love" (3192) #42 1971

Albums (on Capitol unless otherwise noted):
A Song for Young Love (ST-1669) 1962

Once Upon a Time (ST-1711) 1962

Jim, Tony, and Bob (ST-1761) 1962

College Standards (ST-1829) 1963

The Lettermen in Concert (Live) (ST-1936) 1963

A Lettermen Kind of Love (ST-2013) 1964

The Lettermen Look at Love (ST-2083) 1964

She Cried (ST-2142) 1964

Portrait of My Love (ST-2270) 1965

The Hits of the Lettermen (ST-2359) 1965

You'll Never Walk Alone (ST-2213) 1965

More Hit Sounds of the Lettermen! (ST-2428) 1966

A New Song for Young Love (ST-2496) 1966

The Best of the Lettermen (ST-2554) 1966

Warm (ST-2633) 1967

Spring! (ST-2711) 1967

The Lettermen!!! . . . and "Live!" (ST-2758) 1967

Goin' Out of My Head (ST-2865) 1968

Put Your Head on My Shoulder (ST-147) 1968

The Best of the Lettermen, Vol. 2 (ST-138) 1969

I Have Dreamed (ST-202) 1969

Hurt So Bad (St-269) 1969

Traces/Memories (ST-390) 1970
Reflections (ST-496) 1970
Everything's Good About You (ST-634) 1971
Feelings (ST-781) 1971
Love Book (ST-836) 1971
When I Fall in Love (CD CDL-57249) 1989
Collectors Series (CD CDP 7 98537 2) 1992
A Song for Young Love / Once Upon a Time (CD Collectors' Choice Music 72435-42813-2-7) 2002

Album cuts of note:
"Evening Rain"
"Remembering Last Summer"
"Summer's Gone" (from *Once Upon a Time*)
"Summer's Come and Gone"
"I Will Love You"
"When You Wish Upon a Star" (from *Jim, Tony, and Bob*)
"Listen People"
"Try to Remember" (from *A New Song for Young Love*)
"Willow Weep for Me"
"Venus"
"Portrait of My Love" (from *Portrait of My Love*)
"Don't Let the Sun Catch You Crying"
"Softly, As I Leave You" (from *She Cried*)
"Never My Love"
"I Wanna Be Free"
"Medley: Love Is Blue / Greensleeves" (from *Goin' Out of My Head*)
"Hello, I Love You" (from *Put Your Head on My Shoulder*)

Gary Lewis and the Playboys

Singles (all on Liberty):
"Save Your Heart for Me" (55809) #2 1965
"Everybody Loves a Clown" (55818) #2 1965
"My Heart's Symphony" / "Tina (I Held You in My Arms)" (55898) #13 1966
"Where Will the Words Come From" (55933) #21 1966
"Jill" (55985) #52 1967

"Sealed with a Kiss" (56037) #19 1968
"Rhythm of the Rain" (56093) #63 1969

Albums:
This Diamond Ring (Liberty 7408) 1965
Everybody Loves a Clown (Liberty 7428) 1965
Golden Greats (Liberty 7468) 1966
(You Don't Have To) Paint Me a Picture (Liberty 7487) 1967
Gary Lewis Now! (Liberty 7568) 1968
Gary Lewis and the Playboys: Legendary Masters Series (CD EMI CDP-7-93449-2) 1990

Album cuts of note:
"The Night Has a Thousand Eyes" (from *This Diamond Ring*)
"Mr. Blue"
"My Special Angel" (from *Everybody Loves a Clown*)

Claudine Longet

Singles (all on A&M):
"Meditation (*Meditacao*)" / "Sunrise, Sunset" (817) #98 1966
"Here, There, and Everywhere" / "A Man and a Woman" (832) #126 1967
"Hello, Hello" / "Wanderlove" (846) #91 1967
"Good Day Sunshine" / "The Look of Love" (864) #100 1967
"Think of Rain" (875) 1967
"Small Talk" / "The Man in the Raincoat" (877) 1967
"Snow" / "I Don't Intend to Spend Christmas Without You" (895) 1967
"I Love How You Love Me" (897) 1967
"Love Is Blue (*L'Amour Est Bleu*)" (909) #71 1968
"It's Hard to Say Goodbye" / "Sleep Safe and Warm" (954) 1968
"Who Needs You" / "Walk in the Park" (967) 1968
"Hurry on Down" / "I Think It's Gonna Rain Today" (1024) 1969
"Love Can Never Die" / "Colours" (1059) 1969
"Lazy Summer Night" (1098) 1969

Albums (on A&M unless otherwise noted):

Claudine (ASP 4121) 1967
The Look of Love (SP 4129) 1967
Love Is Blue (SP 4142) 1968
Colours (SP 4163) 1969
Run Wild, Run Free (SP 4232) 1970
We've Only Just Begun (Barnaby CBS Z 30377) 1971
Let's Spend the Night Together (Barnaby MGM BR-15001) 1972
Best of Claudine Longet (Century Records CECC-00681) 1994
Claudine Longet: Digitally Remastered Best (CD A&M / Polydor POCM-1573) [Japan Import] 1998
We've Only Just Begun (CD Vivid Sound VSCD-059) [Japan Import] 1999
Sugar Me (CD Vivid Sound VSCD-061) [Japan Import] 1999
The Very Best of Claudine Longet (CD Varese Sarabande 302 066 118 2) 2000
Cuddle Up with Claudine Longet (CD Munster—Vampi Soul) [Spain Import; includes complete Barnaby sessions from 1970 to 1974] 2003

Album cuts of note:

"Until It's Time for You to Go"
"Sunrise, Sunset" (from *Claudine*)
"Creators of Rain"
"End of the World" (from *The Look of Love*)
"Holiday"
"When I Look in Your Eyes" (from *Love Is Blue*)
"Pussywillows, Cat-Tails"
"Let It Be Me" (from *Colours*)
"Everybody's Talkin'"
"Lazy Summer Night" (from *Run Wild, Run Free*)

The Love Generation

Singles (all on Imperial):

"Groovy Summertime" / "Playin' on the Strings of the Wind" (66243) #74 1967

"Montage from How Sweet It Is (I Know That You Know)" / "Consciousness Expansion" (66310) #86 1968

Albums (on Imperial unless otherwise noted):

The Love Generation (LP-12351) 1967
A Generation of Love (LP-12364) 1967
Montage (LP-12408) 1968
Love and Sunshine: The Best of the Love Generation (CD Sundazed SC 11120) 2002

The Johnny Mann Singers

Single:

"Up-Up and Away" / "Joey Is the Name" (Liberty 55972) #91 1967

Albums (on Liberty unless otherwise noted):

Golden Folk Song Hits 1 (LST-7353) 1962
Invisible Tears (LST-7387) 1964
The Ballad Sound of the Johnny Mann Singers (LST-7391) 1964
If I Loved You (LST-7411) 1965
Roses & Rainbows (LST 7422) 1965
I'll Remember You (LST-7436) 1965
Daydream (LST-7447) 1966
Countryside (LST-7476) 1966
Flowing Voices of the Johnny Mann Singers (Sunset SUS-5115) 1966
At Our Best (Sunset SUS 5288)
Don't Look Back (LST-7535) 1967
We Can Fly! Up-Up and Away (LST-7476) 1967
Heart Full of Song (Sunset SUS-5196) 1967
A Man and a Woman (LST-7490) 1967
Love Is Blue (LST-7553) 1968
This Guy's in Love with You—The Look of Love (LST 7587) 1968
Goodnight My Love (LST 7620) 1969
Golden Mann (LST 7629) 1969

Album cuts of note:

"Softly, As I Leave You"

"Ferry 'Cross the Mersey" (from *If I Loved You*)
"Rainbows"
"Land of Love"
"Instant Happy" (from *Don't Look Back*)
"Neon Rainbow" "Yellow Days"
"White on White" (from *Love Is Blue*)
"Portrait of My Love"
"Yellow Balloon" (from *We Can Fly! Up-Up and Away*)
"Heart Full of Soul" (from *Heart Full of Song*)

Joe Meek

These singles, recorded under Joe Meek's auspices, are listed by song title, recording artist, label, and catalog number. Very few, if any, of these records ever crossed over the Atlantic for commercial success, hence the absence of *Billboard* chart listings. An * indicates songs credited to Meek, or his various pseudonyms, as the composer.

"Andy"* (Andy Cavell) Pye 7N15539 1963
"Angel Face" (Gerry Temple) HMV POP 1114 1963
"Angel of Love"* (Don Charles) Decca F11602 1963
"Angela Jones" (Michael Cox) Triumph RGM 1011 1960
"Because" / "Can't You Hear the Beat of a Broken Heart?"* (Iain Gregory) Pye 7N15397 1961
"Christmas Calling" (Valerie Masters) Columbia DB7426 1964
"Cry My Heart"* (Diana Dee)
"Don't Tell Me Not to Love Him" / "With This Kiss"* (Yolanda) (as Robert Duke) Triumph RGM 1007 1960
"Dreams Do Come True"* (Heinz) Decca F11652 1963
"Everybody's Talking" (The Puppets) Pye 7N15556 1963
"Hey There, Senorita"* (Andy Cavell) HMV POP1080 1962
"In April" (Michael Cox) HMV POP1065 1962

"It Matters Not" / "Upside Down"* (Mark Douglas) Ember EMB-S166 1962
"It's Goodbye Then" (John Leyton) (album cut from *The Two Sides of John Leyton* HMV CLP1497) 1961
"Look for a Star" (Heinz)(album cut from *A Tribute to Eddie* Decca LK4599) 1964
"Magic Star"* (Kenny Hollywood) Decca F11546 1962
"May Your Heart Stay Young Forever" (Pat Reader) Pye Piccadilly 7N35077 1962
"Mr. Lovebug"* / "Pocket Full of Dreams and Eyes Full of Tears"* (Iain Gregory) Pye 7N15435 1962
"Moonlight Rendezvous"* (Don Charles) Decca F11464 1962
"My Friend Bobby"* / "Hey There Stranger"* (Pamela Blue) Decca F11761 1962
"Paradise Garden"* (Peter Jay) Pye 7N15290 1960
"Please Let It Happen to Me"* (Jenny Moss)
"Seventeen Come Sunday" (Gerry Temple) HMV POP339 1961
"Sky Men" (Geoff Goddard) HMV POP1213 1963
"Summer Without Sun" (Charles Kingsley Creation) Columbia DB7758 1965
"Tell Laura I Love Her" (John Leyton) Top Rank JAR 426 1960
"Three Cups and a Saucerful of Tears" (Wes Sands) Columbia DB4996 1963
"Time Will Tell" (Iain Gregory) Pye 15295 1960
"Walk [with] Me, My Angel"* (Don Charles) Decca F11424 1962

Album Compilations:
The Joe Meek Story: The Pye Years (CD Sequel NEXCD 171) 1991
304 Holloway Road: Joe Meek, The Pye Years, Vol. 2 (CD Sequel NEX CD 216) 1993
Joe Meek Presents: 304 Holloway Road (CD Sequel 1038 2) 1996

RGM Rarities, Vol 1: The R 'n' R Era (CD
  RGM Sound Ltd. GEMCD 012)
  1997
Joe Meek: The Alchemist of Pop (CD
  RGM Sound, Ltd. CMEDD 496)
  2002 [2]
Let's Go: Joe Meek's Girls (RPM Records
  RPM 166) 1996
The Complete Heinz (CD Repertoire REP
  4718-WR) 1999
Remembering John Leyton: The Anthology
  (Castle Music CMDDD 405)
  2002 [2]

The Millennium (See Curt Boettcher)

Mitch Miller

The following list of Mitch Miller productions represents, admittedly, a trickle
of the work produced by the man and his
artists. Though it includes several vocalists at the vanilla flavor's edge, the list is
more mindful of the various innovations—echo, double-tracking, and manicured singing—that were hallmarks of
the Miller style and influenced the vanilla
pop artists who are this book's primary
focus. Let's just say that this is a modest
starting point. All singles listed are on
Columbia unless otherwise noted.

The Brothers Four
"Greenfields" (41571) #2 1960

Doris Day
"I'll Never Stop Loving You" (40505) #13
  1955
"Whatever Will Be, Will Be (*Que Sera,
  Sera*)" (40704) #2 1956
"Everybody Loves a Lover" (41195) #6
  1958
"Please Don't Eat the Daisies" (41630)
  #102 1960

Percy Faith and His Orchestra
"The Song from *Moulin Rouge* (Where Is

Your Heart?)" (with Felicia Sanders)
  (39944) #1 1953
"Till" (with chorus) (40826) #63 1957

The Four Lads
"Moments to Remember" (40539)
  #2 1955
"No, Not Much" (40629) #2 1956
"My Little Angel" (40674) #22 1956
"A House with Love in It" (40736) #16
  1956
"Who Needs You" (40811) #9 1957
"Put a Light in the Window" / "The Things
  We Did Last Summer" (41058) #8
  1957
"There's Only One of You" (41136) #10
  1958
"Enchanted Island" (41194) #12 1958

The Four Voices
"Sealed with a Kiss" (41699) 1960

Johnny Mathis
"Wonderful! Wonderful!" (40784) #14
  1957
"It's Not for Me to Say" (40851) #5 1957
"Chances Are" / "The Twelfth of Never"
  (40993) #1 / #9 1957
"Misty" (41483) #12 1959

Mitch Miller & His Orchestra and Chorus
"The Yellow Rose of Texas" (40540) #1 1955
"Under Paris Skies" (40100) #26 1953

Mitch Miller & The Gang
Sing Along with Mitch (1160) 1058
Christmas Sing Along with Mitch (1205)
  1958
More Sing Along with Mitch (1243) 1958
Still More! Sing Along with Mitch (1283)
  1959
Folk Songs Sing Along with Mitch (1316) 1959
Party Sing Along with Mitch (1331) 1959
Fireside Sing Along with Mitch (1389) 1959
Saturday Night Sing Along with Mitch (1414)
  1960

Sentimental Sing Along with Mitch (1457) 1960

Memories Sing Along with Mitch (8342) 1960

Happy Times! Sing Along with Mitch (8368) 1961

TV Sing Along with Mitch (8428) 1961

Your Request Sing Along with Mitch (8471) 1961

Patti Page

"The Tennessee Waltz" (Mercury 5534) #1 1950

"Mockin' Bird Hill" (Mercury 5595) #2 1951

"And So to Sleep Again" (Mercury 5706) #4 1951

"Allegheny Moon" (Mercury 70878) #2 1956

Marty Robbins

"A White Sport Coat (And a Pink Carnation)" (40864) #2 1957

The New Christy Minstrels

Singles (all on Columbia):
"Green Green" (42805) #14 1963
"Saturday Night" (42887) #29 1963
"Today" (43000) #17 1964
"Silly Old Summertime" (43092) #92 1964
"Chim Chim Cheree" (43215) #81 1965
"Chitty Chitty Bang Bang" (44631) #114 1969

Albums (all on Columbia unless otherwise noted):
Merry Christmas (CS-8696) 1963
Today (Columbia CS-8959) 1964
The Quiet Sides (CS-9080) 1965
Chim Chim Cher-ee (CS-9169) 1965
Christmas with the Christies (CS-9356) 1966
On Tour Through Motortown (CS-9616) 1968
The Definitive New Christy Minstrels (CD Collectors' Choice 42) 1998 [2]

The New Christy Minstrels Coat Your Minds with Honey (Raven RVCD-86) [Australian import] 1999

Album cuts of note:
"We Need a Little Christmas" (from *Christmas with the Christies*)
"Where Did Our Love Go?" (from *On Tour Through Motortown*)
"I'll Coat Your Mind with Honey" (from *The New Christy Minstrels Coat Your Minds with Honey*)

The New Classic Singers

Albums (all on Capitol):
The New Classic Singers (ST-2440) 1966
Big Hit Sounds of the New Classic Singers (ST 2599) 1967

Album cuts of note:
"Cherish"
"See You in September" (from *Big Hit Sounds of the New Classic Singers*)

The New Colony Six

Singles:
"I Will Always Think About You" (Mercury 72775) #22 1968
"Can't You See Me Cry" (Mercury 72817) #52 1968
"Things I'd Like to Say" (Mercury 72858) #16 1968
"I Could Never Lie to You" (Mercury 72920) #50 1969
"I Want You to Know" (Mercury 72961) #65 1969
"Barbara, I Love You" (Mercury 73004) #78 1970
"Roll On" (Sunlight 1001) #56 1971
"Long Time to Be Alone" (Sunlight 1004) #93 1971

Albums:
Revelations (Mercury 61165) 1968
Attacking a Straw Man (Mercury 61228) 1969
Colonized! Best of the New Colony Six (CD Rhino R2 71188) 1993

Roger Nichols Trio / Roger Nichols and the Small Circle of Friends

Singles (all on A&M):
"Don't Go Breaking My Heart" (as Roger Nichols Trio) (801) 1966
"Love Song, Love Song" / "Snow Queen" (as Roger Nichols Trio) (830) 1967
"I Can See Only You" (as Roger Nichols and the Small Circle of Friends (926) 1968

Albums:
Roger Nichols and the Small Circle of Friends (A&M 4139) 1968
The Complete Roger Nichols and the Small Circle of Friends (CD A&M POCM-2065) [Japan] 1997

Album cuts of note:
"With a Little Help From My Friends"
"I'll Be Back" (from *Roger Nichols and the Small Circle of Friends*)

Tommy Page

Singles (all on Sire):
"A Shoulder to Cry On" / "Christmas Without You" (27645) #29 1989
"I'll Be Your Everything" (19959) #1 1990
"When I Dream of You" / "You're the Best Thing (That Ever Happened to Me)" (19839) #42 1990

Albums (on Sire unless otherwise noted):
Tommy Page (25740) 1989
Paintings in My Mind (CD 9 26148-2) 1990
From the Heart (CD 9 26583-2) 1991
A Friend to Rely On (CD 2-45035) (Warner Japan 4964) 1992
Time (CD Golden Pony 00632) 1994
Loving You (CD Canyon International 01007) 1996

Album cuts of note:
"I Think I'm in Love"
"Minetta Lane" (from *Tommy Page*)
"Paintings in My Mind" (from *Paintings in My Mind*)

"I Still Believe in You and Me"
"Madly in Love"
"Never Gonna Fall in Love Again" (from *From the Heart*)

Sagittarius (see also Curt Boettcher)

Singles:
"My World Fell Down" (Columbia 44163) #70 1967
"The Keeper of the Games" (Columbia 44613) 1967
"Hotel Indiscreet" (Columbia 44289) 1967
"In My Room" (Together Records 105) #86 1969

Albums:
Present Tense (Columbia 9644) 1967
The Blue Marble (Together Records 1002) 1969
Present Tense + bonus tracks (CD Sundazed 10053) 1997
The Blue Marble + bonus tracks (CD Poptones MC 5036) 2001

Album cuts of note:
"Another Time"
"Glass"
"Musty Dusty" (from *Present Tense*)
"I Sing My Song"
"Lend Me a Smile"
"I See in You" (from *The Blue Marble*)

The Sandpipers

Singles (all on A&M):
"Guantanamera" / "What Makes You Dream, Pretty Girl?" (806) #9 1966
"Louie, Louie" / "Things We Said Today" (819) #30 1966
"Glass" / "It's Over" (851) #112 1967
"*Quando M'Innamoro*" / "Wooden Heart" (939) #124 1968
"The Wonder of You" / "That Night" (1044) 1969
"Wave" / "Temptation" (1085) 1969

"Come Saturday Morning" / "Pretty
Flamingo" (1185) #17 1969/70
"Santo Domingo" / "Beyond the Valley of
the Dolls" (1208) AC #17 1970
"Free to Carry On" (1227) #94 1970

Albums (on A&M unless otherwise noted):

Guantanamera (SP 4117) 1966
The Sandpipers (SP 4125) 1967
Misty Roses (SP 4135) 1968
Softly (SP 4147) 1968
Spanish Album (SP 4159) 1968
The Wonder of You (SP 4180) 1969
The Sterile Cuckoo [Original Soundtrack]
(Paramount PAS 5009) 1969
Greatest Hits (SP 4246) 1970
Come Saturday Morning (SP 4262) 1970
A Gift of Song (SP 4328) 1971
Foursider (SP 3525) 1971
Overdue (RCA VPL 1 4048) 1977
Ay, Ay, Ay, Manila! (RCA XFPLI-021)
[Pressed in the Philippines]
Guantanamera / The Sandpipers (CD
Collectors' Choice Music CCM-180-
2) 2000

Album cuts of note:

"*La Mer* (Beyond the Sea)"
"Angelica" (from *Guantanamera*)
"Try to Remember"
"I'll Remember You"
"Rain Rain Go Away"
"Softly, As I Leave You" (from *The Sandpipers*)
"And I Love Her"
"Strange Song"
"The Honeywind Blows"
"Misty Roses"
"Wooden Heart" (from *Misty Roses*)
"Softly"
"Love Is Blue (*L'Amour Est Bleu*)"
"Cancion de Amor (Wanderlove)"
"To Put Up with You"
"Gloria Patri (Gregorian Psalm Tone III)"
(from *Softly*)
"Where There's a Heartache"
"Beyond the Valley of the Dolls" (from
Come Saturday Morning)

Sounds Of Sunshine

Singles:

"Love Means (You Never Have to Say You're
Sorry)" (Ranwood R 896) #39 1971
"I Do All My Crying in the Rain" / "It's
Hard to Say Good-Bye Forever"
(Ranwood R 912) #39 1971

Albums:

*Love Means You Never Have to Say You're
Sorry* (Ranwood R-8089) 1971
Nadia's Theme (Pickwick 6823) 1972

The Sunshine Company

Singles (all on Imperial):

"Happy" (66247) #50 1967
"Back on the Street Again" (66260) #36
1967
"Look, Here Comes the Sun" / "It's
Sunday" (66280) #56 1968
"On a Beautiful Day" (66308) #106 1968

Albums:

Happy Is the Sunshine Company (Imperial
P-12359) 1967
Sunshine Company (Imperial P-12368) 1968
Sunshine & Shadows (Imperial P-12399)
1968
The Sunshine Company (CD Rev-Ola CR
REV 13) 2002

Album cuts of note:

"I Just Want to Be Your Friend"
"Up-Up and Away" (from *Happy Is the
Sunshine Company*)

Bobby Vee

Singles (all on Liberty):

"One Last Kiss" (55251) #112 1960
"Devil or Angel?" (55270) #6 1960
"Rubber Ball" / **"Everyday"** (55287) #6
1960
"Stayin' In" / "More than I Can Say"
(55296) #33/61 1961
"How Many Tears" (55325) #63
1961

"Take Good Care of My Baby" (55254) #1
1961
"Run to Him" / "Walkin' with My Angel"
(55388) #2 / #53 1961
"Please Don't Ask About Barbara" (55419)
#15 1962
"Sharing You" (55451) #15 1962
"Punish Her" (55479) #20 1962
"The Night Has a Thousand Eyes" /
"Anonymous Phone Call" (55521) #3
/ #110 1962
"Charms" / "Bobby Tomorrow" (55530)
#13 1963
"Be True to Yourself" / "A Letter from
Betty" (55581) #34 / #85 1963
"Come Back When You Grow Up" (55964)
#3 1967
"Beautiful People" (56009) #37 1967
"Let's Call It a Day Girl" (56124) #92 1969

Albums (on Liberty unless otherwise
noted):
Bobby Vee Sings Your Favorites (ST-7165) 1960
Bobby Vee (ST-7181) 1961
With Strings & Things (ST-7186) 1961
Bobby Vee Sings Hits of the Rockin' Fifties
(ST-7205) 1961
Take Good Care of My Baby (ST-7211)
1962
A Bobby Vee Recording Session (ST-7232)
1962
Bobby Vee's Golden Greats (ST-7245) 1962
Merry Christmas from Bobby Vee (ST-7267)
1962
The Night Has a Thousand Eyes (ST-7285)
1963
Bobby Vee Sings the New Sound from
England! (ST-7352) 1964
Come Back When You Grow Up (ST-7534)
1967
Just Today (ST-7554) 1968
Do What You Gotta Do (ST-7592) 1968
Legendary Masters (CD EMI CDP-7-
92774-2) 1990
The Essential & Collectable Bobby Vee (EMI
7243 4 97788 2 5 1998 [2]

Album cuts of note:
"Will You Love Me Tomorrow"
"Raining in My Heart"
"Little Flame" (from *Take Good Care of My*
Baby)
"My Golden Chance"
"Teardrops Fall Like Rain" (from *A Bobby*
Vee Recording Session)
"Theme for a Dream"
"Silent Partner"
"Lovers Goodbye" (from *The Night Has a*
Thousand Eyes)
"Sealed with a Kiss" (from *Just Today*)
"Now There's Only Me"
"One Boy Too Late"
"This Is Your Day" (previously unreleased
from *The Essential & Collectable Bobby*
Vee)

Bobby Vinton

Singles (all on Epic unless otherwise
noted):
"Roses Are Red (My Love)" (9509) #1
1962
"Rain Rain Go Away" (9532) #12 1962
"Blue on Blue" (9593) #3 1963
"Blue Velvet" (9614) #1 1963
"There! I've Said It Again" (9638) #1 1963
"My Heart Belongs to Only You" (9662) #9
1964
"Mr. Lonely" (9730) #1 1964
"Long Lonely Nights" (9768) #17 1965
"L-O-N-E-L-Y" (9791) #22 1965
"Theme from "*Harlow*" (Lonely Girl)"
(9814) #61 1965
"Satin Pillows" (9869) #23 1965
"Coming Home Soldier" (10090) #11 1966
"Please Love Me Forever" (10228) #6 1967
"Halfway to Paradise" (10350) #23 1968
"I Love How You Love Me" (10397) #9
1968
"To Know You Is to Love You" (10461) #34
1969
"The Days of Sand and Shovels" / "So
Many Lonely Girls" (10485) #34 1969
"Sealed with a Kiss" (10861) #19 1972

"My Melody of Love" (ABC 12022) #3 1974

Albums (on Epic unless otherwise noted):
Roses Are Red (26020) 1962
Bobby Vinton Sings the Big Ones (26035) 1963
Blue Velvet (26068) 1963
There! I've Said It Again (26081) 1964
Tell Me Why (26113) 1964
Mr. Lonely (26136) 1965
Bobby Vinton Sings for Lonely Nights (26154) 1965
Drive-In Movie Time (26170) 1965
Satin Pillows and Careless (26182) 1966
Please Love Me Forever (26341) 1967
Take Good Care of My Baby (26382) 1968
I Love How You Love Me (26437) 1969
Vinton (26471) 1969
My Elusive Dreams (26540) 1970
Ev'ry Day of My Life (31286) 1972
Sealed with a Kiss (31642) 1972
Melodies of Love (ABC 851) 1974

Album cuts of note:
"Oh, How I Miss You Tonight"
"Hello Loneliness"
"So Many Lonely Girls" (from *Bobby Vinton Sings for Lonely Nights*)
"Theme from *A Summer Place*"
"The Song from *Moulin Rouge*" (from *Drive-In Movie Time*)
"Careless"
"Everyone's Gone to the Moon" (from *Bobby Vinton Sings Careless & Satin Pillows*)
"Serenade of the Bells" (from *Take Good Care of My Baby*)
"Come Softly to Me"
"The End of the World"
"Greenfields" (from *Sealed with a Kiss*)

The Vogues

Singles (all on Reprise):
"Just What I've Been Looking For" (0663) 1968

"Turn Around, Look at Me" (0686) #7 1968
"My Special Angel" (0766) #7 1968
"Till" (0788) #27 1968
"No, Not Much" (0803) #34 1969
"Earth Angel (Will You Be Mine)" (0820) #42 1969
"Moments to Remember" (0831) #47 1969
"Greenfields" (0844) #92 1969
"God Only Knows (0887) #101 1970

Albums (on Reprise unless otherwise noted):
Turn Around, Look at Me (6314) 1968
Till (6326) 1969
Memories (6347) 1969
The Vogues' Greatest Hits (6371) 1970
Greatest Hits (CD Rhino R2 70245) 1988
Turn Around, Look at Me / Till (CD Taragon TARCD-1089) 2001

Album cuts of note:
"The Impossible Dream"
"Come into My Arms Again"
"No Sun Today" (from *Turn Around, Look At Me*)
"I've Got My Eyes on You"
"I'll Know My Love (By the Way She Talks)"
"Love Is a Many-Splendored Thing" (from *Memories*)

Robin Ward

Singles (all on Dot Records):
"Wonderful Summer" / "Dream Boy" (16530) #14 1963
"Winter's Here" / "Bobby" (16578) #123 1964

Albums:
Wonderful Summer (Dot DLP 3555) 1963
Wonderful Summer (CD WEA International WMC5-90) [Japan Import] 1985
The Story of Robin Ward (CD Missing Records MISS 002) 1998

Mark Wynter

Singles (all on Pye U.K.)
"Venus in Blue Jeans" (7N 15466) 1962
"Go Away Little Girl" (7N 15492) 1962
"Shy Girl" (7N 15525) 1963
"And I Love Her" (7N 15716) 1964
"Babe I'm Gonna Leave You" (7N 15994) 1965

Albums (all U.K. releases):
Just for Fun (EP Pye NEP 24167) 1963
It's Mark Time (EP Pye NEP 24176) 1963
Wynter Time (EP Pye NEP 24185) 1964
Mark Wynter (Marble Arch MAL 647) 1967
Go Away Little Girl: The Pye Anthology (CD Sequel Records CMAR696) [2] 2000

Some Vanilla Singles from Other Artists

The Beach Boys: "In My Room" (Capitol 5069) #23 1963
Marcie Blane: "Bobby's Girl" (Seville 120) #3 1962
Bread: "If" (Elektra 45720) #4 1971
David & Jonathan: "Michelle" (Capitol 5563) #18 1966
Skeeter Davis: "The End of the World" (RCA 8098) #2 1963
Jason Donovan: "Sealed with a Kiss" (PWL 39) [U.K. single] 1989
Shelby Flint: "Angel on My Shoulder" (Valiant 6001) #22 1960
Shelby Flint: "Little Dancing Doll" (Valiant 6031) #103 1963
The Four Voices: "Sealed with a Kiss" (Columbia 41699) 1960

The Hillside Singers: "I'd Like to Teach the World to Sing (In Perfect Harmony)" (Metromedia 231) #13 1971
The Left Banke: "Pretty Ballerina" (Smash 2074) #15 1967
The Lemon Pipers: "Rice Is Nice" (Buddah 31) #46 1968
Bob Lind: "Elusive Butterfly" (World Pacific 77808) #5 1966
Henry Mancini, with Orchestra and Chorus: "Moon River" (RCA Victor 7916) #11 1961
The Murmaids: "Popsicles and Icicles" (Chattahoochee 628) #3 1963
Patience & Prudence "Tonight You Belong to Me" (55022) #4 1956
Patience & Prudence "Gonna Get Along Without Ya Now" (55040) # 11 1956
Paul Petersen: "My Dad" (Colpix 663) #6 1962
The Peppermint Trolley Company: "Baby You Come Rollin' Across My Mind" (Acta 815) #59 1968
Debbie Reynolds: "Tammy" (Coral 61851) #1 1957
The Smoke Ring: "No, Not Much" (Buddah 77) #85 1969
The Strawberry Alarm Clock: "Good Morning Starshine" (Uni 55125) #87 1969
Spanky & Our Gang: "Like to Get to Know You" (Mercury 72796) #17 1968
Roger Williams, with the Ralph Carmichael Chorus: "Born Free" (Kapp 767) #7 1966
The Yellow Balloon: "Yellow Balloon" (Canterbury 508) #25 1967

At Flavor's Edge

In putting this book together and consulting with others, I received initial reactions of bewilderment. Once I'd explained the entire concept, however, friends flooded me with song suggestions that are, in my estimation, not as vanilla as they could be. If every song with pretty voices or pretty strings had vanilla credentials, this book would be oversized and underfocused. So, to placate those who made these suggestions and perhaps challenge readers to discern their own dividing lines, I've provided what I hope is a provocative sampling of songs that, to varying degrees, come close to being vanilla but—for reasons of sounding either a bit too folksy (even bluesy at times) or overwrought with virtuosity—slightly miss the mark.

The Critters: "Younger Girl" (Kapp 752) #42 1966

The Critters: "Mr. Dieingly Sad" (Kapp 769) #17 1966

The Cyrkle: "Red Rubber Ball" (Columbia 43589) #2 1966

The Cyrkle: "Turn-Down Day" (Columbia 43729) #16 1966

Liz Damon's Orient Express: "1900 Yesterday" (White Whale 368) #33 1970

The Fifth Dimension: "Up-Up and Away" (Soul City 756) #7 1967

The Free Design: "Kites Are Fun" (Project 3 1324) #114 1967

Lesley Gore: "Sunshine, Lollipops, and Rainbows" (Mercury 72433) #13 1965

Terry Jacks: "Seasons in the Sun" (Bell 45,432) #1 1974

The Jamies: "Summertime, Summertime" (Epic 9281) #26 1958

Just Us: "I Can't Grow Peaches on a Cherry Tree" (Colpix 803) #34 1966

The Left Banke: "Walk Away Renee" (Smash 2041) #5 1966

The Mamas and the Papas: "Dedicated to the One I Love" (Dunhill 4077) #2 1967

Mercy: "Love (Can Make You Happy)" (Sundi 6811) #2 1969

Ricky Nelson: "Lonesome Town" (Imperial 5545) #7 1958

Olivia Newton-John: "I Honestly Love You" (MCA 40280) #1 1974

Peter and Gordon: "A World Without Love" (Capitol 5175) #1 1964

The Poni-Tails: "Born Too Late" (ABC-Paramount 9934) #7 1958

Tommy Roe: "It's Now Winter's Day" (ABC 10888) #23 1967

Linda Scott: "I've Told Ev'ry Little Star" (Canadian American 123) #3 1961

Spanky & Our Gang: "Lazy Day" (Mercury 72732) #14 1967

The Strawberry Alarm Clock: "Tomorrow" (Uni 55046) #23 1967

The Sundowners: "Always You" (Decca 32171) 1967

Johnny Tillotson: "Poetry in Motion" (Cadence 1384) #2 1960

The Turtles: "You Showed Me" (White Whale 292) #6 1969

Index

Joe Maphis and His
    Orchestra, 90
Joel, Billy, 1–2, 5, 16
Joey Bishop Show, The, 155
John Barry Seven, the, 102
John, Dr., 80
John, Elton, 124
Johnny & the Hurricanes, 44
"Johnny Angel," xv, 50–55,
    138
"Johnny Loves Me," 52
Johnny Mann Singers, the, xv,
    36–38, 154–155, 158
"Johnny Remember Me," 67
Johnston, Bruce, 119
Johnston, Leslie, 174. *See also*
    Spectrum
"Joker Went Wild, The," 80
Jolson, Al, 200
Jonathan Livingston Seagull, 193
Jones, Gloria, 93
Jones, Tom, 95
Joplin, Janis, 133
Jordanaires, the, 12
Joy Division, 195
Joyce, Jimmy, 184
Jubilee, 127
Jukebox Jury, 103
Jung, C. G., 134
Jungle Book, The, 95
Just for Fun, 46
"Just Let It Happen," 142
"Just the Way You Are," 7

Kaempfert, Bert, 56, 170
Kallmann, Gunter. *See* the
    Gunter Kallmann
    Chorus
Kamins, Mark, 200
Kapp Records, 78, 157
Karlin, Fred, 171
Kaye, Carol, 86
Kaye, Danny, 100

Kaylan, Howard, 134
"Keeper of the Games,
    The," 120
Keller, Jack, 41
Keller, Jerry, 41
Kelly's Heroes, 158
Kenny, Nick, 15
Kenton, Stan, 133
Kern, Jerome, 105, 107, 109
Kerouac, Jack, 7
King and I, The, 105
King, Carole, 38–41, 172, 189,
    200
King, Jonathan, 105–106
Kingston, Bob, 69
Kingston Trio, the, 92–94,
    112, 188
Kinks, the, 97
Kirkman, Terry, 126–128, 130.
    See also the Association
Kirkland, Mike, 93. *See also* the
    Brothers Four
Klaatu, 184
Knechtel, Larry, 171
Knight, Jordan, 200. *See also*
    New Kids on the Block
"Knowing Me, Knowing You,"
    xv, 191–193, 195
Koda, Cub, x
Komeda, Christopher, 166
Kornfeld, Artie, 146
Kostelanetz, Andre, 97, 193
Kristofferson, Kris, 167
Kusik, Larry, 166

"La Bamba," 169
"La Mer (Beyond the Sea),"
    169
Labelle, Patti, 79
Lacayo, Richard, 193
Laine, Frankie, 22, 25
"Land of Make Believe," 67
Lansdowne Studios, 66

Lanham, Roy, 99
Lanson, Snooky, 6
Lapano, Gabe, 86
Larson, Glen, 88, 90–91, 93.
    See also the Four Preps
Last, James, 157
"Last Leaf, The," 86
Laugh-In, 138
"Lavender Blue (Dilly Dilly),"
    100
Lawrence, Steve, 100, 158
Lazo, Mike, 100. *See also* the
    Tempos
"Lazy Summer Night," 90
Le Ruban Bleu nightclub, 30
Leander, Mike, 71
"Leaves Grow Grey," 148
Led Zeppelin, 127, 174
Lee, Kui, 170
Left Banke, the, 112
Legrand, Michel, 155, 158
Leiber, Jerry, 2
"Lemon Tree," 102
Lennon, Janet, 150. *See also* the
    Lennon Sisters
Lennon, John, 112, 142,
    169–170, 177
Lennon Sisters, the, 53–55, 61,
    114, 150–152
Lennon Sisters Today!!, The, 151
Les Brown and His Band of
    Renown, 27
"Let Me Belong to You," 76
Let the Games Begin, 155
"Let the Good Times In," 148,
    150
"Let's Dance," 166
Let's Get Acquainted, 53
"Let's Kiss and Make Up," 45
Let's Spend the Night Together,
    167
"Letter, The," 142
"Letter from Betty, A" 41